BARCELONA AND CATALONIA

BARCELONA AND CATALONIA

CONTENTS

DISCOVER 6

EXPERIENCE 64

NEED TO KNOW 202

Left: Effervescent colour in Palau de la Música Catalana
Previous page: Catedral de Barcelona lit against the dusky sky
Cover: Striking façade of Gaudí's Casa Batlló

DISCOVER

Plaça de Catalunya at sunset

WELCOME TO BARCELONA AND CATALONIA

Rugged Catalonia and its avant-garde capital are tantalizingly different from the rest of Spain. Here Gaudí's buildings inspire modern-day fairy tales, beaches bite the coast and giant papier-mâché figures are paraded through the streets during festivals. Whatever your dream trip to Barcelona and Catalonia includes, this DK travel guide is the perfect companion.

1

2

3

1 Ricardo Bofill's Walden 7 housing project in Sant Just Desvern.

2 Sunny Costa Brava beach.

3 Street food at Barcelona's La Boqueria market.

4 Buzzy, café-lined Plaça Reial, Barcelona.

4

Tucked in an untamed crook between Pyrenean peaks and the Mediterranean Sea, Catalonia's landscapes brim with natural splendour. Endless sandy beaches and turquoise coves stretch from the wild Costa Brava down into the long, pale strands of the sun-baked Costa Daurada. The snowcapped Pyrenees, ideal for Alpine sports, tower to the north, while across the heartland, vineyards drop in corduroyed terraces. These glorious landscapes, immortalized in the works of Joan Miró and Salvador Dalí, gaze back at us from Catalonia's myriad museums and galleries.

Just as enticing are the region's bustling cities and dreamy medieval villages. Barcelona, the Catalan capital, has inspired artists for centuries. Its spirit is embodied in Picasso's paint, Gaudí's bricks and, more recently, in the innovative culinary scene. Barcelona has a stellar foodie reputation, with experimental chefs reinventing classic cuisine and fantastic street food. Other cultural centres are no less alluring. Girona enchants with its beautifully preserved medieval core, while Tarragona has some of the finest Roman monuments in Spain. Skimming the coast, fishing villages offer unrivalled spots to sample freshly grilled sardines with a chilled glass of cava and gorgeous sea views.

So, where to start? We've broken Catalonia down into easily navigable chapters, with detailed itineraries, expert local knowledge and colourful, comprehensive maps to help you plan the perfect visit. However long you stay, this DK travel guide will ensure that you see the very best that Barcelona and Catalonia have to offer. *Benvingut!* Enjoy the book, and enjoy Barcelona and Catalonia.

REASONS TO LOVE BARCELONA AND CATALONIA

Blending Gothic churches with Modernist landmarks, traditional parades with a dynamic arts scene, centuries-old taverns with ritzy cocktail bars, Catalonia is a constant contradiction that keeps us coming back for more.

1 GAUDÍ'S BARCELONA

Spain's most famous architect has left his mark across Catalonia's capital, with colourful, scaly rooftops, confection-like façades, intriguing chimneypots and the dazzling spires of the truly iconic Sagrada Família *(p106)*.

WORLD-CLASS ART 2

Catalonia lives and breathes creativity, from its celebrated museums and galleries to the enchanting Dalí Triangle *(p187)* and the canvases of Catalonia's revered masters.

3 FESTIVALS

From cutting-edge electronica to honey and herbs, just about everything is celebrated in style with its own festival. *Festes* break out across the region all year long, but don't miss Barcelona's big one – La Mercè – in September *(p56)*.

MEANDERING AROUND MARKETS 4

Barcelona's La Boqueria tantalizes with its colourful produce and the scent of fresh pastries. Lively markets, great for people-watching, are found in every village.

THE COSTA BRAVA 5

Peppered with stunning little coves chipped out of the shoreline and soaring, chalky cliffs, the Costa Brava offers 200 km (125 miles) of rugged beauty and mellow living.

SITGES'S VIBRANT NIGHTLIFE 6

At night the terraces of Sitges's *(p197)* bars and restaurants fill up with revellers. Head to the Plaça de la Indústria, a bar-lined square at the heart of the town's LGBTQ+ scene.

GIRONA 7

This stunning medieval city, all cobbles and stone arches, was used as a backdrop in *Game of Thrones*. Climb the cathedral steps and then wend through the old Jewish Quarter, catching glimpses of the show's Braavos scenery.

8 INNOVATIVE CUISINE

Renowned Catalan chef Ferran Adrià changed the face of dining around the world with his adventures in molecular gastronomy. Across Catalonia, his protégés showcase his techniques at their own dazzling restaurants.

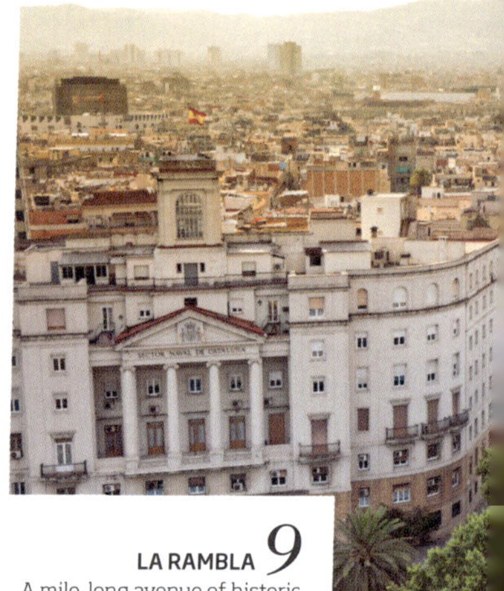

LA RAMBLA 9

A mile-long avenue of historic buildings cutting through the heart of old Barcelona, café-lined La Rambla bubbles with life. Tourists can take part in the Spanish ritual of the *passeig* (stroll) in the shade of the leafy plane trees.

10 PENEDÈS'S CAVA

Catalonia is the home of cava and tiny Penedès *(p194)* is a paradise for aficionados of fizz. Its vineyards are the perfect place to go for tastings and to meet master winemakers.

FC BARÇA 11

Barcelona's most famous football club is "more than a club" for its devoted following. Discover the team's epic sporting history at the FC Barcelona Museum in Camp Nou *(p146)*.

HUMAN TOWERS 12

A mainstay of Catalan folk culture, these extraordinary human pyramids are both nail-biting and heartwarming to witness, as small children scamper up to the top to add a final few feet and onlookers cheer their support.

EXPLORE BARCELONA AND CATALONIA

This guide divides Barcelona into three colour-coded sightseeing areas, as shown on this map. Find out more about each area on the following pages. For sights beyond the city centre see p142, and for Catalonia see p164.

TRAVESSERA DE GRACIA
GRÀCIA
AVINGUDA DE GAUDÍ
AVINGUDA DIAGONAL
PASSEIG DE SANT JOAN
PASSEIG DE GRÀCIA
RAMBLA DE CATALUNYA
Sagrada Família
EIXAMPLE
Casa Batlló
EIXAMPLE
p102
PLAÇA DE LES GLÒRIES CATALANES
GRAN VIA DE LES CORTS CATALANES
RONDA DE SANT PERE
PLAÇA DE CATALUNYA
AVINGUDA MERIDIANA
Museu d'Art Contemporani (MACBA)
LA RAMBLA
BARRI GÒTIC
Catedral de Barcelona
EL RAVAL
Museu Picasso
OLD TOWN
p66
EL POBLENOU
El Born Centre de Cultura i Memória
PLAÇA REIAL
Palau Güell
LA RIBERA
Parc de la Ciutadella
Museu Marítim and Drassanes
PLAÇA D'ANTONI LÓPEZ
Estació de França
PLAÇA DEL PORTAL DE LA PAU
PORT VELL
Dàrsena Nacional
Marina Port Vell
Parc de la Barceloneta
PORT OLÍMPIC
BARCELONETA
Platja Barceloneta
Platja Sant Sebastià
Mediterranean Sea
0 metres 500
0 yards 500
N

GETTING TO KNOW BARCELONA AND CATALONIA

Buzzing Barcelona and the sun-drenched Costa Brava are big draws, but Catalonia's dreamy Romanesque villages, vineyard-strewn hills, pristine wilderness and soaring mountain landscape are not to be missed. With everything within easy distance, this Spanish region is the perfect destination for city-goers and outdoor enthusiasts alike.

PAGE 66

OLD TOWN

Barcelona's medieval core is a maze of crooked streets and narrow lanes that open dramatically into splendid squares. It's the perfect place to saunter along hairpin alleys, hunt for vintage treasures or just savour a coffee on a street-side table. Crowned by an enormous Gothic cathedral, the Old Town is home to some of the city's best-loved sights, including the tree-shaded promenade of La Rambla. Lined with a host of enticing shops, charming cafés and tiny tapas bars, and thronging with a vibrant array of performance artists, this far-reaching street is the city's beating heart.

Best for
Medieval buildings and quirky museums

Home to
Catedral de Barcelona, La Rambla, Palau Güell, Palau de la Música Catalana, Museu Picasso

Experience
Sampling tapas in a hidden corner of Barri Gòtic

PAGE 102

EIXAMPLE

Laid out in the late 19th century, after the medieval walls were finally dismantled, Eixample is an elegant grid of broad avenues lined with graceful mansions that link the old city to the former villages of Gràcia and Sants. Prosperity and creativity created a perfect storm as the area became a canvas for Modernista architects, with Gaudí's masterpiece – the Sagrada Família – at the centre of it all. Towards the bottom of Carrer de Casanova is "Gaixample"– several blocks that make up the heart of Barcelona's lively LGBTQ+ scene, with specialist bookshops, hip boutiques and chic clubs.

Best for
Modernisme and LGBTQ+ life

Home to
Casa Batlló, La Pedrera, Sagrada Família

Experience
A summer jazz concert on the roof of La Pedrera

→

PAGE 124

MONTJUÏC

Rising above the city, Montjuïc has been Barcelona's vantage point for centuries. The journey to the top of the hill is a reward in itself, whether strolling through leafy parks, zipping up in the funicular or soaring high in the vertiginous cable car. This tranquil spot, crowned by Castell de Montjuïc, is perfect for a picnic or to take in the Magic Fountain, an extravaganza of colour and music – utterly kitsch and impossible not to love. Yet the museums steal the show. With Catalan treasures, contemporary art and a reproduced Spanish village, Montjuïc is a cultural treasure trove.

Best for

Strolling and picnicking

Home to

Fundació Joan Miró, Museu Nacional d'Art de Catalunya

Experience

Riding the swaying cable car up to the Castell de Montjuïc, admiring the city spread below

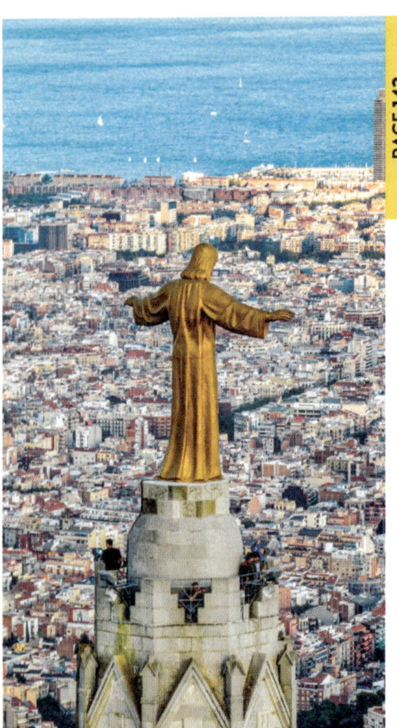

PAGE 142

BEYOND THE CENTRE

Before they were absorbed by Barcelona, the villages around the city had distinct identities and many retain a small-town atmosphere. Those who venture outside the city centre are rewarded with myriad sights, including the legendary Camp Nou (Europe's biggest football stadium), Gaudí's gingerbread-like Park Güell and the pretty little Gothic convent at Pedralbes. To escape the heat and crowds, nothing beats hitting the shaded hiking paths that wend up the Collserola hills to Tibidabo and its charming, old-fashioned funfair.

Best for

Football and funfairs

Home to

Camp Nou, Monestir de Pedralbes, Park Güell

Experience

Sneaking away from the crowds to the peace and quiet of the Monestir de Pedralbes

PAGE 164

CATALONIA

Sun-drenched, pine-fringed beaches nip at the flank of this rugged region, while inland ancient volcanic landscapes give way to the fragrant *matollar* (scrubland) and sloping vineyards. The dazzling costas Brava and Daurada lure travellers to Catalonia. Peppered with fishing villages and secret coves, this is *the* place for skewers of freshly grilled sardines and a chilled *cervesa* on the beach. To the north, the Alpine playground of the Pyrenees towers above lonely valleys punctuated with Romanesque hamlets. Stepping south, Catalonia is a patchwork of contradictions. Girona is a love letter to a medieval era, while LGBTQ+ friendly Sitges offers 17 beaches and a packed programme of festivals. In Tarragona a Roman past collides with seaside fun, and the Dalí Triangle keeps things sublimely surreal.

Best for
Unspoiled coastline and medieval towns

Home to
Monestir de Montserrat, Monestir de Poblet, Girona, Tarragona's Roman ruins, Romanesque architecture

Experience
Listening to the boys' choir at the Montserrat monastery

1

2

3

4

←

1 Majestic Santa Maria del Mar basilica in Barcelona.

2 Standing in the inner courtyard of La Pedrera.

3 Picasso's etchings at El Col·legi d'Arquitectes de Catalunya.

4 A freshly baked spread.

Catalonia is a treasure trove of must-see sights and unique experiences. Covering the length and breadth of the region and taking in vibrant cities and beautiful natural spaces, these itineraries will help you make the most of your trip.

5 HOURS
in Barcelona

Morning

Set out on foot to explore the ever-moody Barri Gòtic *(p98)*, one of the most alluring and best-preserved medieval districts in Europe. First stop on anyone's list should be the magnificent Catedral de Barcelona *(p70)*, dedicated to St Eulàlia, one of the city's patron saints, who is buried in an alabaster sarcophagus in the crypt. A lift will carry you up to the rooftop to admire the gargoyles and the stunning views over the ancient city. Back on the ground, wander over to nearby Museu Frederic Marés *(p81)* to enjoy a break in its charming outdoor café. As you cross the enormous Plaça de la Seu, stop outside El Col·legi d'Arquitectes de Catalunya to admire the friezes on the façade created by Norwegian artist Carl Nesjar from drawings made by Picasso, before walking across to Plaça Catalunya, the city's main hub. From here, amble up the Passeig de Gràcia, the wide artery of the elegant Eixample district that was laid out in the late 19th century to accommodate the horse-drawn carriages of the city's aristocrats. Have your camera at the ready: this neighbourhood is full of picture-perfect Modernista mansions, bakeries and pharmacies, many with hand-painted wooden signs, gorgeous stained glass, delicate tiles and filigree ironwork.

Afternoon

Pause for a midday meal at El Nacional *(p117)*, where myriad bars and restaurants are gathered under one gorgeous roof. This former warehouse has been spectacularly renovated to become a stylish gourmet hub and is perfect for lunch. Tuck into tapas and a refreshing glass of cava, then continue your stroll back up the Passeig de Gràcia to admire the façades of some of the city's most iconic Modernista buildings. First is the famous Illa de la Discòrdia *(p116)* area, which features mansions by Barcelona's most important Modernista architects. Casa Lleó i Morera is by Lluís Domènech i Montaner, also responsible for the Palau de la Música Catalana *(p76)*, while three doors down is Casa Amatller by Josep Puig i Cadafalch, who created Casa de les Punxes. The most famous is the colourful Casa Batlló *(p112)*, with its undulating rooftop designed to resemble a scaly dragon's back – unmistakably the work of Antoni Gaudí. Continue walking up the Passeig de Gràcia to reach another of his imaginative creations, La Pedrera *(p114)*, an extraordinary apartment building with a swirling, chimney-capped façade. Finish on a sweet note, with a quick diversion to the Rambla de Catalunya and sample delicious cakes and pastries at Mauri *(pasteleriasmauri.com)*, founded in 1929.

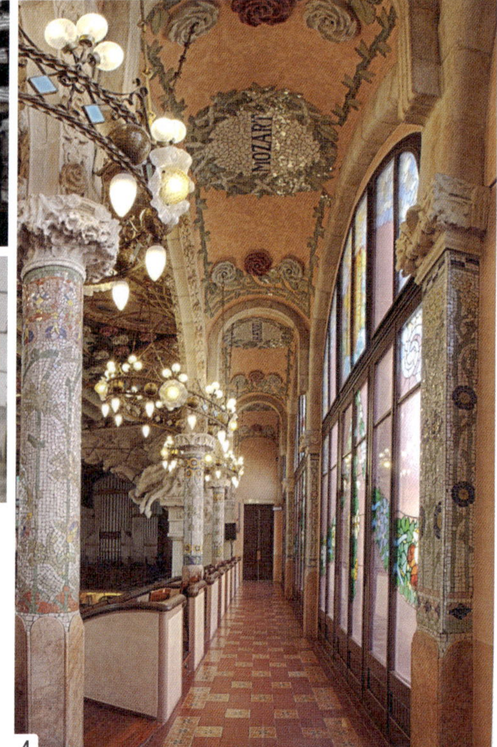

→

1 A lively night out in Gràcia's Carrer de Joan Blanques.

2 Giving thanks on the bronze doors to Sagrada Família.

3 An elaborate handmade cocktail at Paradiso.

4 Dazzling interior of Palau de la Música Catalana.

2 DAYS

in Barcelona

Day 1

Morning Begin with breakfast at the Modernista tavern Els 4 Gats *(p37)*, former haunt of artists including Picasso (who painted the menu). The early Modernista building by Puig i Cadafalch will whet your appetite for a tour of Palau de la Música Catalana *(p76)*, a Modernista masterpiece by Domènech i Montaner. The façade is a riot of colourful mosaics, tiled garlands and sculptures – the enormous inverted skylight of stained glass in the auditorium is breathtaking.

Afternoon Linger over delicious tapas at the tiny Bar del Pla *(p90)* – don't miss the freshly grilled octopus. Later, head to the Museu Picasso *(p78)*. Housed in five graceful Gothic palaces on medieval Carrer de Montcada *(p83)*, the collection focuses mainly on the artist's early years. Afterwards, stop in at La Vinya del Senyor *(p83)* for a glass of wine; the best seats are on the terrace in front of Santa Maria del Mar *(p86)*, an exemplar of Catalan Gothic.

Evening For dinner, head to much-lauded Cal Pep *(p90)*. You could eat in the dining area at the back, but the best seats are at the bar, where the congenial Pep holds court. Fill up on *trifàsic* (a platter of fried calamari, whitebait and prawns) and *crema catalana*, a version of crème brûlée. Follow up the feast with cocktails at Paradiso *(p83)*, a "secret" bar at the back of a pastrami shop. After such a glorious day, fall into bed at the Hotel Duquesa de Cardona *(p93)*.

Day 2

Morning Drift back in time wandering the enticing narrow streets of the medieval Barri Gòtic *(p98)*. Explore the ruins of old Bàrcino, the original Roman settlement, in the bowels of Museu d'Història de Barcelona *(p80)*; here remain streets rutted by Roman cartwheels and vats still stained with dye after two thousand years. Later, emerge, blinking into the light, and head down La Rambla, Barcelona's most famous promenade, to the glorious Boqueria market, properly known as Mercat de Sant Josep *(p72)*. The colourful stalls are a perfect opportunity to brighten any photo album – and there are inviting counter bars for a tasty lunch.

Afternoon After lunch, head to Gaudí's awe-inspiring, albeit unfinished, Sagrada Família cathedral *(p106)* to marvel at the rainbow-tinted nave. Ascend the lift to the rooftop for spectacular views – and brace yourself for the spiral staircase that will bring you back down. Seek refreshment on your return to ground level at Chill Bar *(chillbarcelona.com)*, a friendly, arty little spot with a well-chosen wine list.

Evening Dine at Botafumeiro *(p159)*, one of Barcelona's best seafood restaurants, where long-aproned waiters bear platters of just-caught shellfish. After a post-prandial stroll through Gràcia, catch a live gig at Heliogàbal *(heliogabal.com)*, one of the city's smallest and most atmospheric music venues.

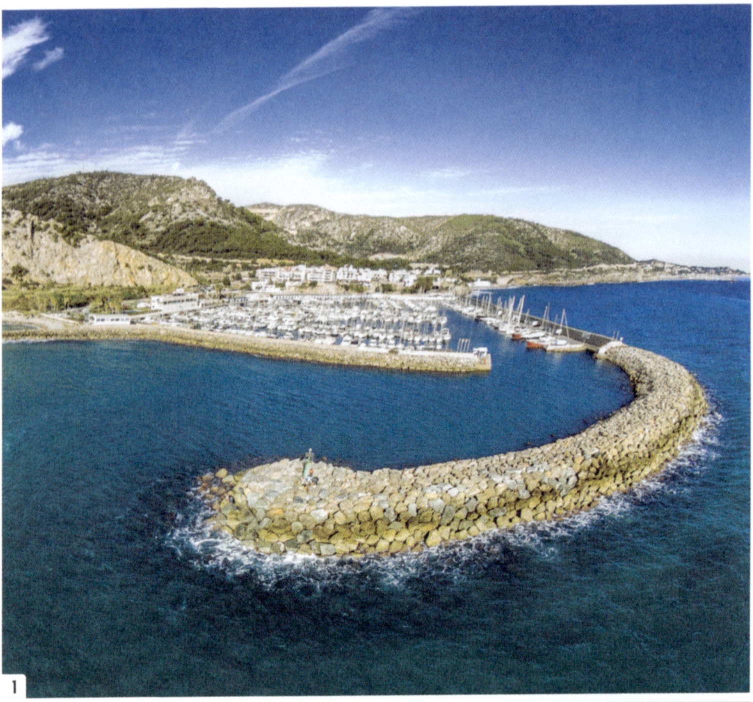

←

1 Clear skies above the curved spit of Garraf marina.

2 Glinting light over Tortosa's historic centre.

3 Exploring Tarragona's Roman history.

4 A table laden with freshly made *suquet de peix*.

3 DAYS

in southern Catalonia

Day 1

Morning Start things off with a leisurely walk around the old fishing village of Garraf, before heading into the wild with a hike through the *matollar* *(p188)* at nearby Parc Natural del Garraf. When you emerge from the outdoors, make a beeline for La Cúpula *(lacupulagarraf.com)* near the beach and experience what these coastal towns do best – seafood. Keep it Catalan with a *suquet de peix* (fish stew).

Afternoon The warm sea is perfect for a quick dip before the ten-minute train ride to lively Sitges *(p197)*. Wander through its charming narrow streets down to the seemingly endless Passeig Marítim promenade. Tear yourself away from the epic sea views to snap a picture of the impressive Sant Bartomeu i Santa Tecla.

Evening Indulge in tasty tapas plates at Komokieras *(p199)* in the Old Town, then return to the seafront for some beachside cocktails at Pub Voramar *(p197)*. As the night wears on, move the party to El Piano *(p197)* to round things off with live music and an unbeatable friendly atmosphere.

Day 2

Morning Breakfast in Sitges before catching a train to Tarragona to immerse yourself in the city's Roman ruins *(p174)*, a World Heritage Site. A walk past the Balcó del Mediterrani viewing point, where the vast ocean stretches away, takes you to the amphitheatre ruins, the epicentre of Roman Tarraco. Find a neighbourhood café for a leisurely *l'hora del vermut* (vermouth hour), sipping the local drink and nibbling *seitons* (pickled sardines), a Catalan delicacy.

Afternoon Grab some *clotxa* (bread stuffed with herring, onions, tomatoes and garlic) from a stall along the Rambla Nova then dive into the winding streets of the Old Town for an on-the-spot tour of the fascinating Roman sights all around.

Evening Bring yourself back to the present day at laid-back El Llagut *(p175)*, where fresh local produce is showcased in the Catalan dishes. A restful night awaits at the Hotel Astari *(hotelastari.com)*.

Day 3

Morning A classic tapas-style *esmorzar de forquilla* breakfast at Cafè Clàssic *(cafeclassic.cat)* is perfect fuel for a jaunt to the Delta de L'Ebre *(p198)*, a paradise for nature lovers. Bring binoculars: birds flock here in their thousands. When hunger strikes, Lo Pati D'Agustí *(restaurantlopatidagusti.com)* in El Poblenou del Delta has delicious *rossejat*, a local speciality made with seafood and rice.

Afternoon Leave the park behind and visit the city of Tortosa *(p198)*, a microcosm of Catalonian history. Explore its labyrinthine streets on foot, stopping first at the impressive cathedral where a Roman temple, a Moorish mosque and an earlier 12th-century cathedral have all stood.

Evening Before sunset, make your way to the Castell de la Suda, the remnants of a Moorish fort. Set high above the city, it's a superb spot to watch dusk settle over the Riu Ebre with a glass of wine in the parador that now occupies the site.

1

2

3

5 DAYS
in Barcelona and Catalonia

Day 1

Morning Set out on foot to explore Barcelona's medieval heart. The narrow streets of ancient El Born *(p100)* are awash with enticing boutiques and cafés. Stop at Hidden Coffee Roasters *(hiddencoffee roasters.com)* for freshly brewed coffee before turning down Carrer de Montcada *(p83)* to marvel at medieval Catalan Gothic-style mansions and courtyards.

Afternoon Lunch on *pulpo al hierro* (grilled octopus) in the retro-chic Elsa y Fred *(p90)*, then swing by the Palau de la Música Catalana *(p76)*, a Modernista concert hall, to pick up tickets for later. Spend the afternoon at the arty MACBA *(p83)*.

Evening After a music-filled evening, head down to the Eixample neighbourhood for reinterpreted Catalan cuisine at Mordisco *(p117)*. Finally, a sumptuous bed awaits at the Serras Hotel *(p93)*.

Day 2

Morning Begin the day with a plunge in the hotel's rooftop pool, then stroll down the city's most famous road, La Rambla *(p72)*, to Gaudí-designed Palau Güell *(p74)*. Don't miss the rooftop, a forest of colourfully tiled chimneys – the photo opportunities are epic.

Afternoon Enjoy a traditional lunch at a counter bar in La Boqueria market *(p72)*, then carry on up the Passeig de Gràcia to another Gaudí masterpiece, the fairy-tale Casa Batlló *(p112)*, dubbed "the House of Bones" for its curiously shaped windows. Gaudí's rooftop was apparently inspired by the scaly back of the dragon killed by Sant Jordi, Catalonia's patron saint.

Evening Wander into shadowy Montjuïc to rub shoulders with a loyal following of locals as you sample the menu of *montaditos* (tapas on bread) at Quimet i Quimet *(p133)*; its 500-strong wine list means you'll always find a perfect pairing.

Day 3

Morning Leave the city behind for hilly Sant Pol de Mar *(p192)*, a whitewashed maze of streets behind a string of sandy beaches. Dip your toes in the sea, then window shop through chic boutiques and art galleries.

4

5

6

1 The plump *El Gato de Botero* in arty El Raval. ↑

2 Tucking into tapas at Elsa y Fred in El Born.

3 Sunbathing at the beach near Sant Pol de Mar.

4 Brewing the perfect coffee at Espresso Mafia.

5 Pristine white façade of Barcelona's MACBA.

6 Colourful narrow houses lining the water in Girona.

Afternoon For lunch, tuck into Catalan dishes at Cuina Sant Pau *(cuina-santpau.cat)*. Then, follow the coast to clifftop Tossa de Mar *(p190)*, a warren of white-washed 13th-century lanes.

Evening Climb the narrow streets behind the marina to tiny La Lluna *(972 34 25 23)*, to feast on *sipia a la planxa* (pan-fried cuttlefish) and *rossejat negro* (squid-ink pasta with allioli), a Catalan speciality.

Day 4

Morning Follow the winding coastal road along the Costa Brava *(p191)* past gorgeous turquoise coves, pausing in summer months for a dip in the sea.

Afternoon Arrive in Girona *(p172)* in time for a plate of *vegetals fideuà*, a vegetarian take on the Catalan paella with pasta, at Amaranta *(amarantavegetal.cat)*. The old city's enticingly tangled streets, recognizable to *Game of Thrones* fans, are an easy place to get lost and found again.

Evening Splash out at El Celler de Can Roca *(book well in advance; p173)* and follow the Roca brothers on a culinary adventure. Tastebuds tingling, head back to a night at Hotel Històric *(hotelhistoric.com)*, in the heart of the Old Town.

Day 5

Morning Kick-start the day at Espresso Mafia *(espressomafiagirona.com)*; the expertly made coffee will power you to Figueres *(p187)*, 15 minutes north by train. Take a surreal turn at Salvador Dalí's eye-popping "theatre-museum", packed with his extraordinary artworks.

Afternoon Continue to picture-perfect Cadaqués *(p186)* and grab some *pa amb tomàquet* (garlicky, tomato-rubbed grilled bread) to take to the beach that dusts the tip of this wild and beautiful Cap de Creus headland. Dalí's former home in tiny Port Lligat offers a fascinating guided tour.

Evening As dusk settles, make your way to harbour-front Casa Nun *(casanun.com)*. Ask for the romantic table on the tiny upstairs balcony and watch the boats bob in the harbour as you enjoy fresher-than-fresh seafood accompanied by sparkling cava and memories of the last five days.

On the Trail of Great Artists

The homes and haunts of some of Spain's most revered artists, including Pablo Picasso and Salvador Dalí, have been converted into museums where artworks are complemented by a fascinating glimpse into the artists' process. In Barcelona, check out the Els 4 Gats tavern *(4gats.com)* where Picasso held his first exhibition, then wander over to the nearby Museu Picasso *(p78)* to see the artist's early output. Across the city, marvel at Miró's colourful and unique style at the light-filled Fundació Joan Miró *(p128)*, which he designed with architect Josep Lluís Sert. Up the coast, get lost in the "Dalí Triangle" - comprising the Theatre-Museu Dali in Figueres *(p187)*, his enchanting former home in Port Lligat and his wife Gala's medieval castle in Púbol - where Surrealist daydreams come to life.

→

Admiring the vibrant tapestries at the Fundació Joan Miró

BARCELONA AND CATALONIA FOR ART LOVERS

A dynamic hotbed of creativity for centuries, Catalonia is brimming with groundbreaking art. From remarkable Romanesque wall paintings in remote Pyrenean churches and Gothic masterpieces in world-class museums, to Barcelona's Modernisme marvels and the wild public art of Gaudí and Tàpies, there's so much Catalan art to discover.

Take to the Streets

From murals to stunning statues, graffiti to light installations, Catalonia's public art is a great way to indulge in some culture on the cheap. Stroll Port Olímpic *(p91)* to see Roy Lichtenstein's colourful *Barcelona Head*, then head to the beach to take in Rebecca Horn's charming sculpture *The Wounded Star*. In El Raval *(p82)* snap Fernando Botero's much-loved *El Gato*, and in the Parc de Joan Miró *(p151)* take a selfie with the artist's curvaceous sculpture *Woman and Bird*. These artworks are complemented by a vibrant street art scene: Street Art Barcelona *(streetartbcn.com)* highlights some of the city's best graffiti art.

Roy Lichtenstein's Pop art *Barcelona Head* sculpture in Port Olímpic

TOP 5 GALLERIES IN BARCELONA

CaixaForum
This converted factory hosts superb temporary exhibitions *(p132)*.

Fundació Joan Miró
The world's largest Miró collection in a stunning building *(p128)*.

Museu Can Framis
Contemporary Catalan art at a remodelled factory complex *(p157)*.

Foto Colectania
Diverse photography exhibitions held in a small gallery *(fotocolectania.org)*.

Projecte SD
Uptown gallery with a focus on artists' books *(projectesd.com)*.

← Honing skills with Life Drawing Barcelona

Creating Art

Each September, the Museu Picasso *(p78)* organizes the Big Draw, with drawing workshops hosted at venues across the city. During the rest of the year, try your hand at drawing with Life Drawing Barcelona *(lifedrawingbarcelona.com)*. Alternatively, capture the city on a tour of the Old Town led by a professional photographer with Shutter Kings BCN *(shutterkingsbarcelona.com)*.

World-Class Museums

Pop into Barcelona's glorious MNAC *(p130)* to admire Romanesque murals gathered here from remote Pyrenean churches and a millennium of Catalan art. The dazzling MACBA *(p83)* holds world-class modern and contemporary art, including pieces by Antoni Tàpies. Further afield, the Espai Carmen Thyssen *(espaicarmenthyssen.com)* in Sant Feliu de Guíxols has a fine collection of 19th- and 20th-century Catalan art.

Striking modern architecture of Barcelona's MACBA museum

On Fizz and Terroir

From earthy reds to fizzy cava, the wines of Catalonia make the taste buds sing. Embark on a tour of the vineyards of Clos Figueras *(closfigueras.info)* in Tarragone province, then quaff a glass of red made from local Cariñena and Garnacha grapes. For something more bubbly, head to Penedès to tour some revered cava cellars, including Codorníu *(codorniu.com)* with its charming Modernista cellar.

Wine tasting at the small Castell Roig winery in the Penedès region

BARCELONA AND CATALONIA FOR FOODIES

Whether you're sampling avant-garde gastronomy, tucking into tasty home-cooking at a family-run country inn or just enjoying some mouthwatering sardines fresh from the grill by the beach, the culinary delights of Catalonia are a feast for both the belly and the soul.

CATALAN DISHES

Pa amb tomàquet
Bread rubbed with garlicky tomatoes and seasoned with olive oil.

Escudella i carn d'olla
A meat and vegetable stew with pasta or rice.

Esqueixada
A fresh salad with tomatoes and salted cod.

Coca Catalana
Flatbread served with any number of toppings.

Crema Catalana
Similar to crème brûlée, but with cinnamon and lemon zest.

Super Street Food

Street food fanatics can head to events organized by Eat Street *(eatstreet.barcelona)*, covering everything from taco festivals and barbecues to classic street food. Across town, check out the trendy Palo Market Fest *(palo marketfest.com)*, or visit the Mercantic vintage market *(mercantic.com)* in Sant Cugat for Catalan classics.

→

Busy food stalls at Barcelona's monthly Palo Market Fest

Third-Wave Coffee Bars

Coffee culture has hit Catalonia in a big way, with Scandi style and the aroma of fresh-roasted beans wafting through hip coffee joints on every urban corner. Looking for Barcelona's best java, carefully roasted and brewed by meticulous baristas? Get your caffeine fix at Nømad *(nomadcoffee.es)* in El Born or Dalston Coffee *(dalstoncoffee.com)* in El Raval. In Girona, check out La Fábrica *(lafabricagirona.com)* on the edge of the Jewish Quarter.

↑ Enjoying a coffee break in a colourful Barcelona café

Nueva Cocina

Catalonia's "new cuisine" is the brainchild of chef Ferran Adrià, whose restaurant El Bulli *(elbullifoundation.com)* has been transformed into a "museum to culinary invention" that recounts the story of the world's most renowned restaurant and its mythical chef.

← A creative dessert of chocolate bonbons and blackcurrant sorbet

Traditional Catalan Cuisine

Pa amb tomàquet (toasted bread rubbed with fresh tomato and drizzled with olive oil) is found everywhere, from food stalls to gourmet restaurants. In Vic *(p193)*, sample a platter of *embutits* (charcuterie) and tasty *escalivada* (garlicky roast aubergine and peppers). On the coast, try the local version of surf 'n' turf, *sípia amb mandonguilles* (squid with meatballs).

→ Fried white beans and sausage, a typical Catalan dish

Awesome Entertainment

Take the kids up to Tibidabo *(p154)*, on the outskirts of Barcelona, for thrills and spills at one of Spain's oldest and prettiest funfairs while you soak up the views over the city. Come evening, wow the kids with Montjuïc's Font Màgica *(p134)*, where dancing fountains are lit up with a colourful sound and light show - always a hit.

Young and old enjoying the spectacle at Montjuïc's Font Màgica

BARCELONA AND CATALONIA FOR FAMILIES

In a country that welcomes children with open arms, Catalonia is a perfect family destination. An abundance of theme parks, castles, museums, waterfalls and nature reserves means there's something for everyone. The fun-packed Barcelona has it all, including almost 5 km (3 miles) of city beaches.

TRAVELLING WITH YOUNG CHILDREN

Expect to see kids out and about until late, particularly during the summer. Barcelona's metro and bus network are almost completely pushchair-friendly, but you may struggle with the Old Town's uneven streets. Bring a booster seat, as taxis rarely have them and they can double as high-chairs. Getting around the city can be fun: take a cable car to Montjuïc or a modern funicular up to Tibidabo.

Little Artists

The city that inspired Gaudí, Picasso and Miró has plenty to keep budding young artists happy. The museums offer plenty of child-friendly activities and workshops, or you could introduce them to street art with a tour from Kids&Cat *(kids-cat.com)*, which includes an optional painting workshop.

→

Kids taking part in the Big Draw at the Museu Picasso

↑ Snapping photos for the family album at Park Güell in Barcelona

Open-air Fun

Barcelona has play areas on virtually every block to help energetic kids burn off steam. Looking for more space to run wild? Head to Parc de la Ciutadella *(p88)*, the city's largest green space, where you can also take a rowing boat out on the lake. Park Güell *(p144)* is another good bet, combining a little culture with the great outdoors. Alternatively, venture into Val d'Aran *(p177)*, in the Spanish Pyrenees, to play hide-and-seek in shady forested groves.

INSIDER TIP
Time for Dinner

Many restaurants don't open until 8:30 or 9pm, but there are tapas bars - with child-sized portions - to fill the gap. The city centre has restaurants that are open all day, look for signs saying *"cocina ininterrumpida"*.

Wet and Wild

When the summer months heat up, you can cool off at one of Catalonia's epic water parks. Slip down twisting water slides and splash in the wave pool at Illa Fantasia *(illafantasia.com)*, the closest to Barcelona. Picnic areas and a free shuttle bus service from the city are handy perks. Further down the coast, make a splash at the Caribe Aquatic Park, part of PortAventura World *(portaventuraworld.com)* theme park.

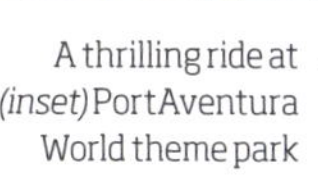

A thrilling ride at *(inset)* PortAventura World theme park ↑

Great Bookshops

The main hub of the Spanish publishing industry, Catalonia has an array of enticing bookshops. In Barcelona, browse shelves of rare tomes at the Librería Anticuaria Farré; then cross the city to Altaïr, a charming bookshop-cum-café with an excellent travel literature section.

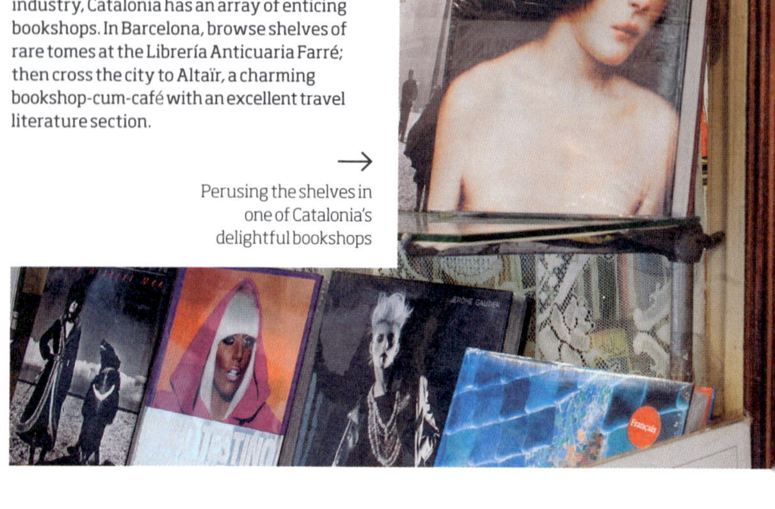

Perusing the shelves in one of Catalonia's delightful bookshops

BARCELONA AND CATALONIA FOR BOOKWORMS

Delve into Catalonia's rich literary history, which ranges from the atmospheric intrigue of *The Shadow of the Wind* to the critically acclaimed exposé of the Spanish Civil War in *Homage to Catalonia*. Join Catalan bibliophiles at independent festivals, in quirky bookshops, and on the hunt for literary locales.

Fiesta Time!

Book-loving Catalonia is a treat for bookworms, hosting scores of fabulous literary festivals throughout the year. One of the best is Kosmopolis *(kosmopolis.cccb.org)*, Barcelona's biennial festival hosted by the Centre de Cultura Contemporània de Barcelona; meet top writers from around the world, attend author panels and discover what's hot on the literary scene. On La Diada de Sant Jordi (23 April), which is Catalonia's literary answer to Valentine's Day, exchange books with the one you love.

Street activity during Barcelona's biennial Kosmopolis festival

Barcelona-born writer and journalist Manuel Vázquez Montalbán

Homage to Barcelona

Few cities have captured the imagination quite like the Catalan capital. Let Colm Tóibín's *Homage to Barcelona* lead you through the best of its art and architecture. Dive down a different alley with Manuel Vázquez Montalbán's series featuring gourmet detective Pepe Carvalho. Use the story as inspiration for a Catalan feast across the city.

HOLIDAY READS IN BARCELONA

The Shadow of the Wind (Carlos Ruiz Zafón)
This tour-de-force describes a young boy's discovery of a unique book in the Cemetery of Lost Books.

Homage to Catalonia (George Orwell)
A riveting and widely read account of Orwell's experiences fighting for the Republicans during the bloody Spanish Civil War.

Cathedral of the Sea (Ildefonso Falcones)
This dreamy novel recounts the long construction of the beautiful church of Santa Maria del Mar.

Plaça de Catalunya, one of Barcelona's literary locales

Literary Tours

Books come to life in the streets of Barcelona through the fantastic self-guided literary tours created by Barcelona's tourist office *(barcelonaturisme.com)*. Our favourite takes in all the locations featured in George Orwell's *Homage to Catalonia*. Led by literary historians, conèixerBcn *(coneixerbcn.com)* also runs excellent guided literary tours focusing on Catalan classics, such as *The Shadow of the Wind* by Carlos Ruiz Zafón.

Exploring the Cadafalch

With its Neo-Gothic spikes and sculptures, Josep Puig i Cadafalch's architecture recalls Catalonia's years of maritime power in the Middle Ages, when it ruled a vast Mediterranean empire. Check out the imposing façade of Casa Terrades, which has needle-thin turrets *(p119)*. Cadafalch also designed Casa Amatller, the home of wealthy chocolatier Antoni Amatller i Costa, to resemble a Gothic palace, covered in sculptures of animals making and eating chocolate. Take a tour of the residence, climbing the grand staircase to the family's private apartments, before dipping a biscotto into a steaming cup of hot chocolate.

→ Whimsical exterior of Cadafalch's Casa Terrades, with its soaring spires

BARCELONA AND CATALONIA FOR MODERNISTA MARVELS

Modernisme - sometimes called Catalan Art Nouveau - transformed Barcelona's skyline between the late 19th and early 20th centuries. Although Gaudí is the best-known proponent of the style, Lluís Domènech i Montaner and Josep Puig i Cadafalch also left their marks on the city.

Oh My Gaudí!

From the vast, as yet unfinished, spires of the Sagrada Família *(p106)* to the luxuriant gardens of the Park Güell *(p144)*, guarded by a pair of fairy-tale pavilions, Gaudí is everywhere you look in Barcelona. As well as these large-scale public works, he designed several imaginative private homes for wealthy patrons, many of which offer visiting experiences beyond the norm. Sip a glass of cava to the sound of a string quartet on the otherworldly roof of Palau Güell *(p74)*, take an augmented reality tour of Casa Batlló *(p112)* or join Gaudí himself - or Mrs Ramoneta, the family's maid - on a kids' tour of La Pedrera, with an actor *(p114)*.

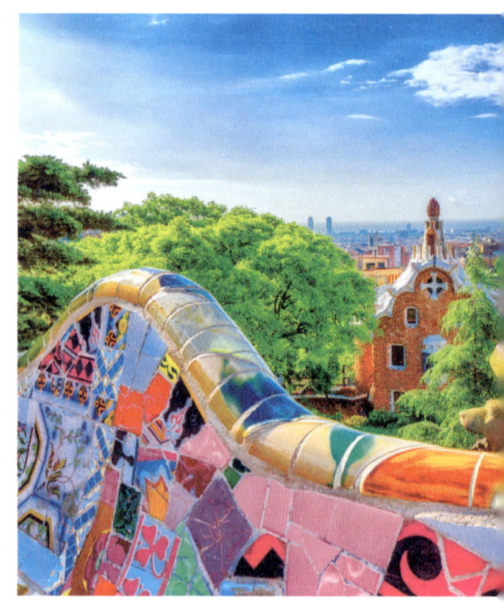

→ Looking over the city from Gaudí's psychedelically tiled bench, Park Güell

Climbing the Montaner

Lluís Domènech i Montaner is often described as the father of Modernisme. He designed two of Barcelona's most glorious and iconic buildings – the Palau de la Música Catalana *(p76)* and Hospital de la Santa Creu i de Sant Pau *(p118)*. Guided tours are available for both of these buildings, but catching a concert under the stained glass in the Palau de la Música Catalana or in the grand gardens of what is now the Recinte Modernista de Sant Pau is an absolutely unforgettable experience.

← Statues of muses on a mosaicked wall in the Palau de la Música Catalana

DRINK

Els 4 Gats

Picasso's favourite watering hole has grand Modernista proportions.

Carrer de Montsió 3
4gats.com

London Bar

Enjoy a tipple under this tiny bar's sweeping signage.

Carrer Nou de la Rambla 34
938 08 21 87

Café de l'Òpera

Once La Mallorquina chocolate shop, this café is decorated with opera-themed mirrors.

La Rambla 74
cafeoperabcn.com

↑ Beautiful stained-glass doorway of the Farmàcia Bolós

Ruta del Modernisme

As well as covering the big-name sights – and entitling you to discounts – this self-guided walking tour will lead you to the city's hidden Modernista gems *(rutadelmodernisme.com)*. Pick up a guide from any of Barcelona's tourist offices and follow the red plaques to some of the 120 buildings. Browse the wooden shelves of the charming Farmàcia Bolós *(Rambla de Catalunya 77)* after snapping a picture of its stained-glass doorway, or admire the cathedral-like Casa Martí before enjoying a drink in the tiled Els 4 Gats on the ground floor.

Kilometre Zero

The "kilometre zero" concept grew out of the slow food movement: the premise is to produce, sell and eat locally grown and sourced food. You'll see signs in shops and restaurants where Kilometre Zero (often shortened to "KM0") food is available. Good bets for finding KM0 food in Barcelona include the small Flax & Kale restaurant group and Gat Blau in the Sant Antoni neighbourhood.

Fine dining in Barcelona's restaurants linked to the slow food movement

BARCELONA AND CATALONIA THINK GREEN

The Catalan capital has proven its commitment to sustainability, from promoting public transport and cycling to establishing a sustainability education centre. Elsewhere in Catalonia, there are organic and biodynamic farms, wineries and olive oil producers, and farmer's markets in many towns.

EAT

Rasoterra

Tuck into innovative veggie and vegan dishes at this slow food favourite.

Carrer Palau 5
rasoterra.cat

Flax & Kale Passage

Delicious and nutritious veggie and vegan food served in a chic setting.

Carrer de Sant Pere Més Alt 31-33
flaxandkale.com

Two Wheels

Barcelona has about 300 km (186 miles) of bike paths stretching across the city, part of a broad initiative backed by the city to make it greener, less polluted and quieter. Among the scores of places that rent bikes is Un Cotxe Menys *(biketoursbarcelona.com)*, which means "one less car". Bikes are allowed on regional trains so you can also travel easily around Catalonia.

Cycling through an allée in the Passeig de Lluís Companys

Biodynamic Wineries

Catalan wines have enjoyed a renaissance since the 1990s. The most recent shift has been towards more organic and biodynamic wines, often produced by boutique wineries. Biodynamic farming is a holistic way of production that goes beyond organic farming and aims to improve the land. Many producers are happy to invite visitors for tastings. You can also take a tour, such as the ones offered by Feel By Doing *(feelbydoing.com)*, which include grape harvesting and vineyard picnics, plus tastings of artisan cheeses and organic wines.

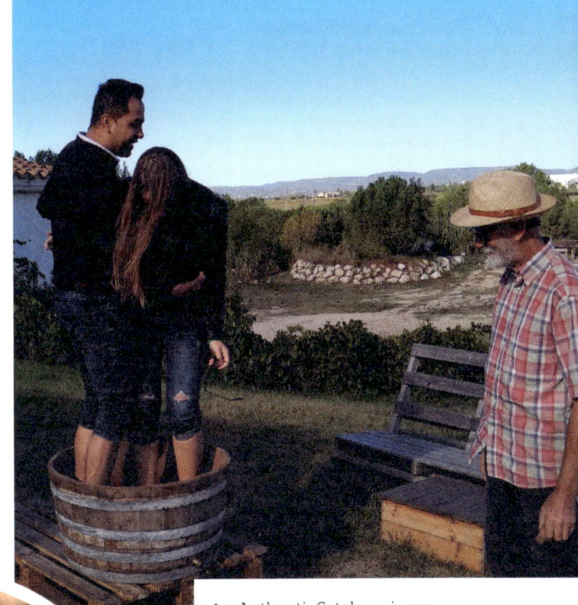

↑ Authentic Catalan winery experiences on a tour with Feel By Doing

Plastic-Free Shopping

Across Barcelona you'll find several waste-free shops where you can bring your own containers to fill with goodies. Among them are the Yes Future Positive Supermarket *(yesfuture.store)* in Sant Antoni and Gra de Gràcia's three stores in Gràcia.

← Bring-your-own-container shopping at Yes Future Positive Supermarket

Eco-Tours

These days, tour companies are offering trips around Barcelona and Catalonia that focus on sustainability. Among them is El Brogit *(elbrogit.com)*, a local company that runs a wide range of guided and self-guided tours including hiking, biking, star-gazing, photography, and visits to organic and biodynamic wine and olive oil producers.

→ Visiting local producers on an eco-tour with El Brogit

Spectacular Panoramas

After a day of sightseeing in Barcelona, get above the crowds at Bunkers del Carmel, a Civil War-era anti-aircraft battery. Tucked away in a quiet suburb, it's the perfect spot to relax over a glass of fizzing cava while gazing down at the city. There are more gorgeous, Barcelona-wide views to be had from the Torre Bellesguard *(p155)*, a less famous edifice in Gaudí's portfolio.

People taking in the impressive city views at Bunkers del Carmel ↑

BARCELONA AND CATALONIA OFF THE BEATEN TRACK

Barcelona's extraordinary history and idiosyncratic style can overshadow the wealth of unexpected gems waiting to be found across Catalonia. Whether you're after a tour with a twist or an escape into solitude, here we uncover the best of Catalonia's hidden treasures.

TOP 3 PARKS AND NATURE RESERVES

Serra de Collserola
A deliciously shady wilderness in the hills behind Barcelona *(parcnatural collserola.cat)*.

Parc Nacional d'Aigüestortes
The only national park *(p180)* in Catalonia, located high in the Pyrenees, with spectacular lakes and waterfalls.

Zona Volcànica de la Garrotxa
Hiking paths and green, long-extinct volcanoes set in forest *(en.turisme garrotxa.com)*.

Templar Treasures

In the Middle Ages, the Knights Templar owned vast swathes of territory in Catalonia. Take the ferry across the Ebro to marvel at their castle at Miravet - one of the largest and best preserved in Europe, attesting to their power. The order was disbanded by the pope in 1312, but you can track down more Templar remains in Tortosa *(p198)*, where the castle is now a parador, and Lleida *(p196)*, where Castell Templer de Gardeny has a fascinating museum of the knights' history.

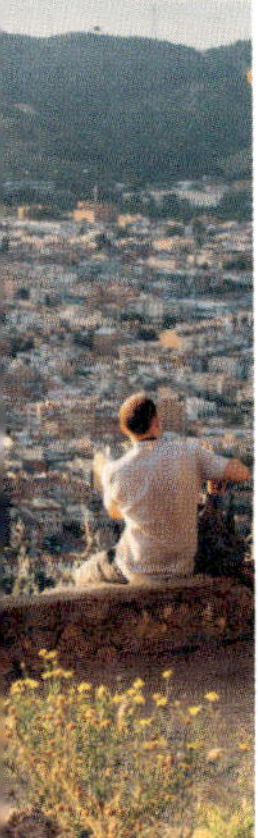

The Art of Death

More marvellous than macabre, two cemeteries in Barcelona stand out for their funerary art. The Montjuïc cemetery is replete with lavish Modernista tombs; pay your respects to Joan Miró and other luminaries. The Neo-Classical Poblenou cemetery has beautiful sculptures; look out for Jaume Barba's *Petó de la Mort* (*Kiss of Death*, 1930).

The *Kiss of Death* marble sculpture located at El Poblenou cemetery

Quirky Tours

Take to the skies in a hot-air balloon tour with Vol de Coloms *(voldecoloms.cat)* to see the volcanic landscape of the Garrotxa from above. If a tour on water is more your thing, enjoy a cruise through pink clouds of flamingos in the Delta de l'Ebre *(creuersdeltaebre.com)*.

Gorgeous flamingos in the Delta de l'Ebre nature reserve

↑ The Knights Templar castle at Miravet on the Ebro river

Eccentric Collectors

The sculptor Frederic Marès gathered a remarkable collection of curios, now beautifully displayed in the Museu Frederic Marès *(p81)*. In nearby Sitges, the hotchpotch of items in the Museu del Cau Ferrat *(p197)* was brought together by Modernista artist Santiago Rusiñol.

↑ Beautiful sculptures in the Museu Frederic Marès

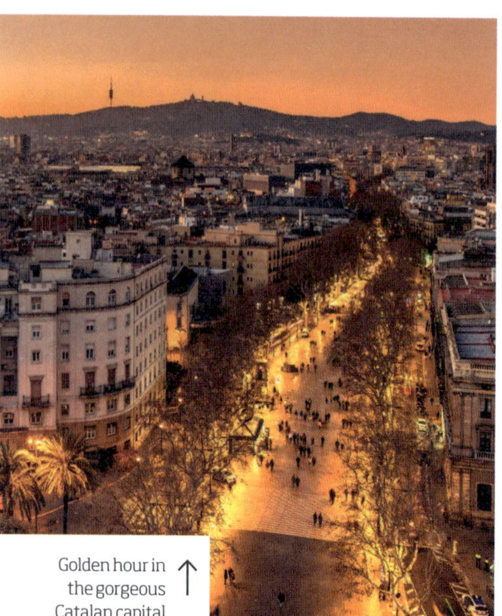

Golden hour in the gorgeous Catalan capital

Ode to the Setting Sun

To memorialize the golden hour in Barcelona, you need to head to the hills. You'll get some of the best panoramic shots of the city from the ramparts of Castell de Montjuïc *(p138)*, in the west, where you can place other landmarks in the frame. For stunning rooftop views from the heart of the city, climb up to the walkways above the Catedral de Barcelona *(p70)* - the carved stone of the central spire radiates warmth in the glow of the setting sun, a fantastic juxtaposition to the metal girders of the walkway. Down the coast, in Tarragona, crouch in the shadow of the slopes to use the setting sun to silhouette the soaring arches of the iconic Les Ferreres Aqueduct.

BARCELONA AND CATALONIA FOR PHOTOGRAPHERS

Full of dreamy landscapes and stunning architecture, Catalonia is a nirvana for shutterbugs. Its photogenic streets and dramatic vistas are the perfect backdrop for its colourful culture. All you need is a camera.

Lights, Camera, Capture!

As dusk falls, Barcelona becomes a sea of twinkling lights, adding a dreamlike quality to any snap. Set your shutter speed for a long exposure to get fluid, draping shots of fountains like the Font Màgica *(p134)* - lit with brilliant colour, it's majestic at night. Climb to the rooftop of Las Arenas, in Plaça d'Espanya *(p138)*, and use the same technique with a tripod for a fleeting shot of the vehicles whizzing around the central roundabout below.

Font Màgica in Montjuïc, impressively lit up at night

A Slice of Life

Catalonia's streetscapes beg to be photographed. In Barcelona, use the buildings around the cathedral as an intriguing frame; Carrer del Dr Joaquim Pou is the most picturesque. Then head to La Rambla *(p72)* and let the bustling scene unfold before you. In Calella de Palafrugell, you'll find dazzling white houses and rustic fishers' cottages. Idle on Port Bo, at the curving beach, to snap the catch of the day being hauled up onto shore.

↓ Fishing boats stranded on Barques beach in Calella de Palafrugell

Gaudí Inside and Out

Synonymous with Catalan Modernisme, Gaudí's buildings are achingly photogenic. The immense, nearing-complete Sagrada Família *(p106)* is emblematic of his signature style. Snap its exterior from Plaça de Gaudí across the road, where the cathedral is perfectly mirrored in a small lake. At Casa Batlló *(p112)* go inside, wide-angle lens at the ready, to capture its incredible interiors.

← Jesus on the cross above the altar of the majestic Sagrada Família basilica

Enter the Heartland

Rural Catalonia offers shutterbugs spectacular scenery, from picturesque villages where time seems to stand still to stunning mountainscapes. Follow the trail cut into the cliffs above the Congost de Mont-rebei to frame images of the gorge and the river below – for a dramatic sense of scale, try to catch someone walking along the path. Later, go south to Penedès for the perfect symmetry of hills corduroyed with vineyards, then pause for a while at the epic wine cathedral in the village of El Pinell de Brai *(p195)*.

→ Kayaking in the dramatic Congost de Mont-rebei

Wonderful Wetlands
Catalonia has two extensive marshlands that are home to an extraordinary array of bird life. Bring your binoculars to the Parc Natural dels Aiguamolls de l'Empordà *(parcsnaturals.gencat.cat/ca/xarxa-de-parcs/aiguamolls-emporda)*, a mosaic of marshland, lagoons and dunes on the Costa Brava, to spot white storks and Cetti's warblers from bird hides and a viewing tower. The Delta de l'Ebre *(p198)* protects a landscape of endless beaches, rice fields and marshes. Cruise it with a shallow-bottomed punt from Lo Mas de la Cuixota *(lomasdelacuixota.com)* and see the mesmeric dance of resident flamingos up close.

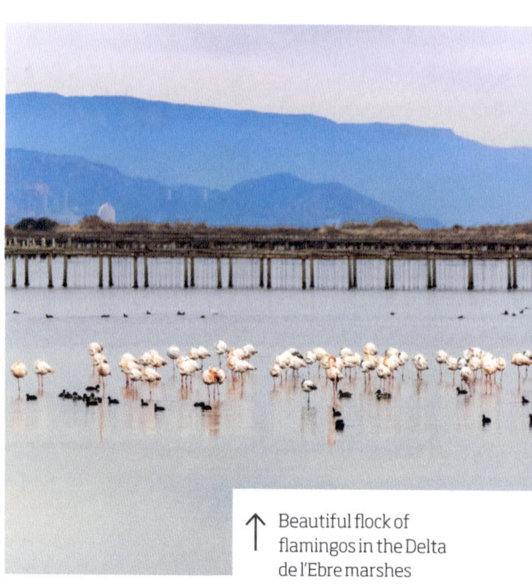

↑ Beautiful flock of flamingos in the Delta de l'Ebre marshes

CATALONIA FOR WILD SPACES

Catalonia is home to a vast array of landscapes, with plenty of opportunities to get into the wild. Hike or sail around rugged headlands, watch myriad birds in beautiful wetlands, dive in pristine waters, stargaze in remote canyons or try your hand at mushrooming (a Catalan passion): the choice is yours.

"Twisted Waters"
Catalonia's only national park, the Parc Nacional d'Aigüestortes *(p180)* encompasses gorgeous scenery. Set your sights on the hundreds of miles of "twisted waters" – the streams and waterfalls tumbling through its meadows and valleys. Glorious for a spot of wild swimming, these pristine waterways also offer prime wildlife-watching opportunities, including the elusive brown bear. Less than 40 km (25 miles) southeast, Paddle in Spain *(paddleinspain.com)* runs kayaking trips for the whole family down the Río Noguera Pallaresa.

Emerald waters of Estany Tort de Peguera in Parc Nacional d'Aigüestortes

Sky High

Looming over the northern edge of Catalonia, the Pyrenees mountain range is criss-crossed with perfect ski slopes. Skiing enthusiasts will have a brilliant time at Boí Taüll *(boitaullresort.com)*, the highest ski slopes in the Pyrenees at a soaring 2,751 m (9,025 ft), which transform into tranquil hiking and cycling trails come summer. In the Montsec mountain range, an hour outside Lleida on Catalonia's western border, you can hike across dramatic *congostos* (gorges) carved into the mountains. Arguably the most dramatic is the Congost de Mont-rebei, a dizzying trail etched into the cliffside. Since 2013 Montsec has been designated a Starlight Reserve area, thanks to its exceptional conditions for enjoying the night sky. After a long day of hiking, galactic panoramas await during a guided nighttime visit to the Parc Astronòmic del Montsec *(parcastronomic.cat)*, thanks to the retractable cupola at the observatory.

← Multimedia planetarium at the Parc Astronòmic del Montsec

TOP 3 HIKING TRAILS

Sitges to Vilanova i la Geltrú
Enjoy a stroll along the clifftops between Sitges *(p197)* and Vilanova i la Geltrú, stopping off for a refreshing dip.

Trans-Pyrenean Hike (GR11)
A demanding and immensely rewarding hike that spans the Pyrenees to the Basque Lands, beginning in Cadaqués *(p186)*.

Montserrat
Most famous for its basilica, Montserrat *(p168)* also offers panoramic hiking and climbing routes.

Into the Woods

Hike in the undulating landscape formed by long-extinct volcanoes in the Zona Volcànica de la Garrotxa natural park, covered in woodland *(en.turismegarrotxa.com)*. One of the most spectacular areas of the park is the Fageda d'en Jordà, a majestic beech forest growing on a plain formed by an ancient lava flow from the Croscat volcano, which is particularly beautiful in autumn.

← Lush, forested landscape of the Fageda d'en Jordà and La Garrotxa

Medieval Mercantile Empire

Barcelona was the centre of a vast empire built on maritime trade that stretched as far as Sicily and Greece during the Middle Ages. Huge galleys were built in the Drassanes (shipyards), now converted into the excellent Maritime Museum *(p96)*. The church of Santa Maria del Mar *(p86)* was built with donations by local merchants and shipbuilders.

→

Striking façade of the Gothic Basílica de Santa Maria del Mar

BARCELONA AND CATALONIA FOR HISTORY BUFFS

Phoenicians, Greeks, Romans and many other peoples have left their mark in Catalonia. From the ancient Greek settlement of Empúries to the splendid royal mausoleum at Poblet, the region is rich in historic treasures, while Barcelona's Gothic Quarter is one of the largest surviving medieval cities in Europe.

CATALONIA AND THE WAR OF SUCCESSION

In the early 18th century, the Catalans backed the losing side in the Spanish War of Succession, and Barcelona fell after a 14-month-long siege. The Bourbon victors abolished Catalan rights and institutions; a huge swathe of the El Born neighbourhood was demolished and a vast fortress built in its place. The ruins dating from this period have been preserved in the excellent El Born Centre de Cultura i Memória *(p90)*, which is now ground zero for the Catalan independence movement.

Spanish Civil War

There are few vestiges of the Spanish Civil War in Catalonia, but you can visit a bomb shelter in Poble Sec, while the anti-aircraft battery on the Turó de la Rovira (also known as Bunkers del Carmel) is now a cultural centre. Nick Lloyd runs a superb Civil War tour *(info@spanishcivilwartours.com)* for history buffs.

→

Admiring Barcelona from the Turó de la Rovira anti-aircraft battery

Did You Know?

An estimated 45,000 foreign nationals came to Catalonia to help in the fight against Franco.

The Olympic Effect

The 1992 Olympic Games, held in Barcelona, were responsible not just for putting the city firmly on the tourist map but for pulling Spain out of its Francoist isolationism. Barcelona was transformed: the rotting warehouses that once lined the seafront were replaced with a pleasure port (the Port Olímpic) and a residential district (the Vila Olímpica) and many sporting facilities were built. Relive the 1992 Games at the enjoyable Olympic Museum *(p138)* on Montjuïc.

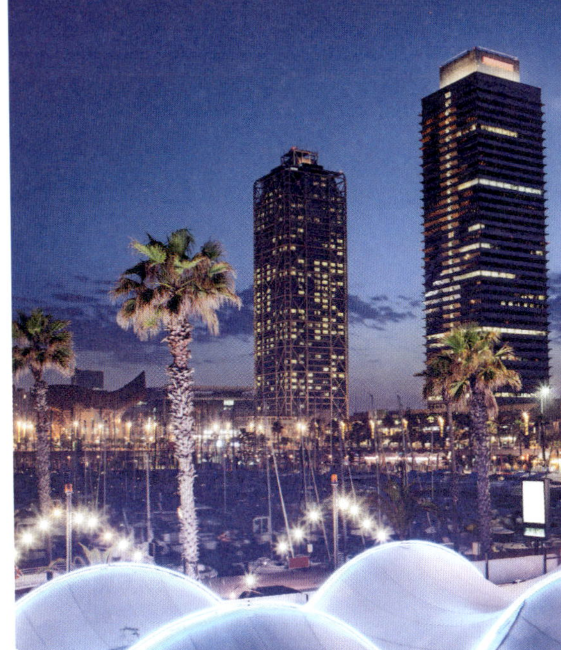

→ Bright lights of Port Olímpic's promenade at night

← Vivid prehistoric rock painting in the Roca dels Moros

Extraordinary Cave Art

Discover a remarkable record of early humanity across Catalonia. In the Delta de l'Ebre *(p198)* you can see more than 400 dynamic sketches of hunting and battle; start at the interactive Abrics de l'Ermita visitors' centre at Ulldecona. In the Roca dels Moros *(p196)*, near Lleida, male and female figures dance in vivid red and black, hair whipping with energy as animals look on.

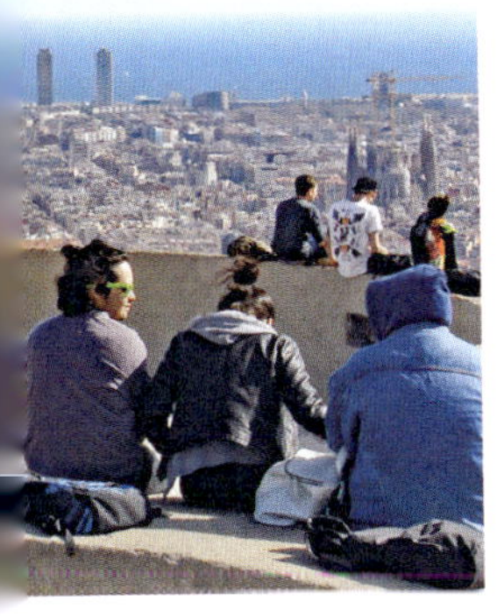

Roman Barcino

The remains of the Roman settlement of Barcino can be seen beneath the MUHBA *(p80)* in Barcelona's Old Town, the cart-rutted streets still resonant after two millennia. Nearby, the columns of the Temple of Augustus still stand, engulfed in the medieval walls, as well as ancient Roman sarcophagi in the Plaça de la Villa de Madrid.

→ Ancient Roman columns of the Temple of Augustus

The Rhythm Takes Control

Beloved by Catalans, flamenco *tablaos* (literally "flamenco floorboards") attract aficionados across Barcelona and beyond. Head to the Tablao Flamenco Cordobés *(tablaocordobes.es)* and Tablao de Carmen *(tablaodecarmen.com)* to see some of the best flamenco performers in action.

An emotional live performance at the Tablao Flamenco Cordobés

BARCELONA AND CATALONIA AFTER DARK

Vivacious by day, Barcelona really lights up after sunset. From underground clubs to cocktails with a view, the city's got you covered. Outside the capital, Girona has a great student scene, Sitges is an LGBTQ+ hotspot and, in summer, the seaside resorts fill up as people flock to the sands to dance till dawn.

TOP 3 NIGHTLIFE ON THE COSTA BRAVA

Lloret de Mar
Quiet by day, the beaches and bars of Lloret de Mar (one of the busiest resorts on the "wild coast") break loose as soon as the sun sets.

Begur
This sun-drenched coastal town shines after dark, especially at popular dusk-till-dawn spot La Lluna *(972 62 20 23)*.

Platja d'Aro
As the stars emerge, bars spill onto the beach and dance club Mala Vida *(651 84 04 98)* draws night owls like moths to a flame.

Full of Pride

Cornerstones of Catalonia's LGBTQ+ scene, Barcelona and Sitges are the destinations for LGBTQ+ nightlife. Pick from scores of fantastic bars and clubs in Barcelona's "Gaixample" *(p116)*. Sitges's Pride parade in mid-June is one of the biggest in all Spain, and the town is packed with LGBTQ+ spots - the best are clustered around Carrer 2 de Mayo, nicknamed "Sin Street".

Revellers filling the streets for Sitges's Pride parade

Music in the Air

In the summer months through to September, grab a glass of perfectly chilled cava and catch jazz concerts on the spectacular rooftop of La Pedrera *(p114)*, flanked by stunning citywide views. On ground level, take a picnic supper and a blanket to lay on the grass in municipal parks across the city. There are also free outdoor concerts at all of Barcelona's popular neighbourhood festivals, of which Gràcia's (in mid-August) is the biggest.

↑ Jazz performance on the roof of Antoni Gaudí's Casa Mila

Jazz in the Night

Barcelona's jazz scene is legendary. Jazz lovers flock into town during the Barcelona Jazz Festival *(jazz.barcelona)* in October to see some of the world's greatest talent play across the city. Alternatively, catch live bands at the iconic Harlem Jazz *(harlemjazzclub.es)*, or hop over to Girona's Sunset Jazz Club *(sunsetjazz-club.com)* for some of the finest Catalan jazz.

← A jazz band on stage at Barcelona's Harlem Jazz club

Mixology Masters

Catalonia has long been home to potent liquors, from ratafia to vermouth. Learn how to shake, stir and whip these herb-infused brews into ever-changing creative concoctions at Collage Art & Cocktails Social Club *(collagecocktailbar.com)*, in a class taught by expert mixologists, then sample the results. Or, sit back and let the professionals take the reins at Paradiso *(p82)*, a swanky watering hole that's consistently ranked amongst the World's 50 Best Bars.

→ A creative cocktail from Barcelona's Collage Art & Cocktails Social Club

Get Up to Speed

From motorbikes to rallycross, motorsport has left its mark in Catalonia. Join fans in April to cheer on rallycross competitors at the Circuit de Barcelona-Catalunya *(circuitcat.com)* in Montmeló. In May, embrace your inner speed demon at the Spanish Grand Prix. The F1 race used to wind through the roads of Montjuïc in Barcelona; this racing past is now evoked in the Espíritu de Montjuïc *(espiritu demontjuic.com)* in March.

→

Racing cars lining up for the Espíritu de Montjüic

BARCELONA AND CATALONIA FOR SPORTS FANS

Sports-obsessed Catalans have more than FC Barcelona to choose from. Locals are just as likely to cheer on their volleyball and basketball teams, embrace the need for speed at the Spanish Grand Prix, spend winter week-ends zipping down Pyrenees slopes or dive into watersports all summer long.

Snow Party

When the mercury drops, Catalans flock to ski resorts dotted across the Catalan Pyrenees. Go full glam at Baqueira-Beret *(p176)*, where you might find yourself sharing the piste with Spanish royalty. Travelling with the kids? Get them out on the bunny slopes or making friends and snow-people at family-friendly Vall de Núria *(valldenuria.cat)*; the resort has a host of activities for all ages.

→

Heading for the slopes at the popular Baqueira-Beret resort

Wet, Wet, Wet

The stunning Mediterranean coastline offers a superb range of aquatic activities. Try your hand at paddle-boarding anywhere in the calm seas along the Costa Brava, then cross over to the marine nature reserve of the Illes Medes on the Costa Brava to dive beneath the waves with Aquàtica *(aquatica-sub.com)*. Alternatively, you can take a sailing lesson offered by the Barcelona Sailing School *(barcelonasailing school.com)*, which is based in the very marina constructed for the 1992 Olympics.

←

Clear blue waters of the Illes Medes on the Costa Brava

TOP 4 TRAILS FOR RUNNING AND CYCLING

Carretera de las Aigües
This track above Barcelona is the top spot for running and biking.

Banyoles
A lake ringed by a path perfect for gentle family strolls or bike rides.

Montserrat
The "jagged mountain" has some challenging mountain biking routes.

Montseny
A leafy nature reserve with wonderful biking and running routes.

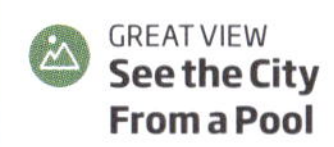

GREAT VIEW
See the City From a Pool

Built in 1929, the Piscina Municipal de Montjuïc is an outdoor pool with great city-wide views. It was one of the sporting venues renovated for the 1992 Olympic Games, when it hosted the diving events.

Beautiful Games

Catalonians are fervent football fans. While there are local teams and leagues across the province, Barça, as FC Barcelona *(fcbarcelona.com)* is commonly known, is the stuff of footballing legend. Grab tickets for a home game, or pay a visit to the club's museum at Camp Nou *(p146)* and admire the array of glittering trophies.

→

Passionate FC Barcelona fans at Camp Nou

Sand in the City

Bang in the heart of the city, Barceloneta is the perfect city break beach. Dotted with *xiringuitos* (beach bars), it has sun loungers for rent and scores of bars and restaurants within easy reach. South of the capital, L'Arrabassada has Blue Flag waters, golden sands and a promenade with little pop-ups great for picking up a refreshing *granizado de limon* (a lemon slushy).

The famous golden sands of the Platja de l'Arrabassada on the Costa Daurada

BARCELONA AND CATALONIA FOR BEACHES

Catalonia's 800 km (497 miles) of coastline are dotted with breathtaking beaches, from endless sweeps of golden sand to magical turquoise coves. Beaches for for partying, beaches for families, and beaches for water-sports – you'll find them all along this gorgeous stretch of the Mediterranean.

Escape the Crowds

Retreat to scores of tiny untouched coves tucked into the ochre cliffs of Catalonia's rugged coast. Find a quiet spot in the camping grounds outside Tossa de Mar, then hike the coastal path to Cala Llevadó, a sandy haven wedged between sea and pine woodland. Alternatively, you can walk the Camí de Ronda from Tamariu to reach the perfectly pebbly shores of secluded Cala Marquesa.

→

Motorboat lolling in the turquoise sea cove of Cala Marquesa

LGBTQ+ Beaches

All the beaches in Barcelona are welcoming of the LGBTQ+ community, but Mar Bella is the best. Its *xiringuitos* have live DJs and a party atmosphere all summer. In Sitges, visit Bassa Rodona, the main LGBTQ+ beach. The cliff walk south of the city has a couple of fab beach bars perfect for cocktails and sea views.

INSIDER TIP
Camins de Ronda

Walking the scenic paths known as Camí de Ronda is a great way to explore the stunning Catalan coastline, whether you opt for a leisurely hour's stroll or a week-long hike.

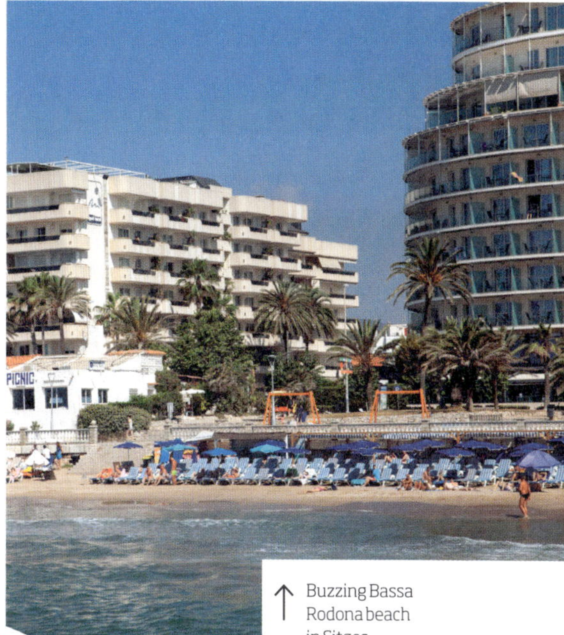

Buzzing Bassa Rodona beach in Sitges

Fun for the Family

The pretty little beach of Garraf is a great option for kids, with pedaloes and rock pools; it's easily reached by train from Barcelona. On the Costa Brava, head to Tamariu's shallow beach flanked by pine-shaded cliffs or the endless sugary sands of Platja del Canadell in Calella de Palafrugell.

Calella de Palafrugell's large Platja del Canadell, popular with families

Beach Activities

Many of Barcelona's beaches offer watersports facilities; the Nova Icària beach, next to the Port Olímpic, has beach volleyball pitches and a city-run sailing school *(velabarcelona.com)*. On the Costa Brava, pick up the paddles with Kayaking Costa Brava *(kayakingcostabrava.com)* to reach hidden coves.

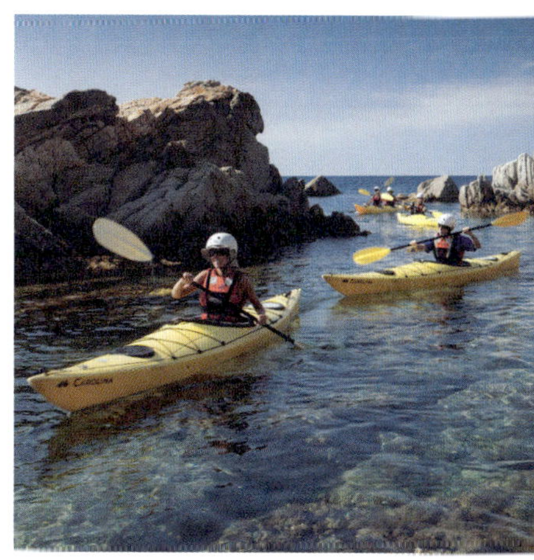

Kayaking adventures along the Costa Brava

Of Giants and Fatheads

Catalan *gegants* (giants) and their sidekicks, the *capgrosses* (fatheads), have formed part of local festivities since the Middle Ages. Made of wood and papier-mâché, the *gegants* usually depict historical figures and dance in festival parades. The *capgrosses*, often caricatures of contemporary figures, create havoc for laughs. Get up close to these uncanny creations at La Casa dels Gegants in Lleida, then see them in action at the town's Festa Major in May.

→ Traditional Catalan *gegants* parade through Barcelona

BARCELONA AND CATALONIA FOR TRADITIONS

From fire-running to fatheads, human towers to the "dance of death", Catalan traditions are testament to the region's vibrant culture. Experience it all at the fun-filled fiestas that take place in every town and city in Catalonia, usually during the summer months.

TÍO DE NADAL

Every December, the kids in Catalonia bring out Tío de Nadal – a log painted with a smiling face that is usually wearing a jaunty *barretina* (the red Catalan beret) – and they fatten it up by "feeding" it vegetables. On Christmas Eve, a blanket is thrown over Tío de Nadal and the children beat the log with a stick while singing a traditional song that urges it to "poo" out sweets. The blanket is whipped away to reveal small gifts and *turrones* (traditional Catalan nougat that is served at Christmas).

Firestarters

Easily the most spectacular event at any local festival, *correfoc* (fire-running) has its roots in pagan rituals. Hit the crowd-packed streets as fire-spitting dragons lumber along, surrounded by leaping packs of *demonis* (demons) holding sparklers and Catherine wheels that whizz out fiery little sparks. Be sure to dress in old clothing and don't forget to cover any exposed skin.

→ Fun times during a Catalan fire-running performance

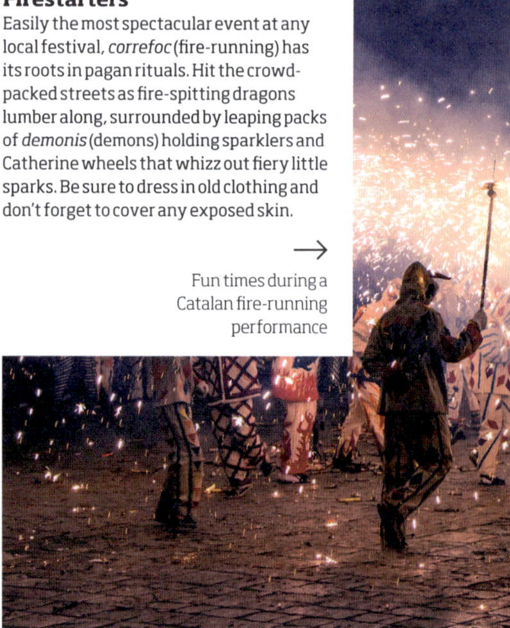

The Band Plays On

Catalonia's national dance – the Sardana – emerged in earnest during the Renaixença (Catalan cultural revival). Look for it at any *festa*, as *sardanistas* (dancers) link hands with raised arms, forming circles that grow bigger and bigger as more people join in. When the circle gets too big, the dancers form more circles. Circles usually break off for novices, so you can join in as the *cobla* band plays on. Too shy to give it a go? Head to Montjuïc *(p124)*, where you can practise your moves with the Monument a La Sardana, a ring of stone dancers commemorating solidarity.

Catalans performing the Sardana

TRADITIONAL FESTIVALS

Patum de Berga (end of June)
Drums beat and townspeople dressed as mythical beasts dance through Berga in this ancient festival.

Dansa de la Mort (Easter week)
The Dance of Death in Verges is part of the town's Easter celebrations.

Corpus Christi (June)
The feast of Corpus Christi is beautifully celebrated with elaborately designed "carpets" of flowers in Sitges.

Race to the Top

Nothing encapsulates the egalitarian spirit of the Catalans like the *colles castellers*, teams of townspeople who stand on each other's shoulders in an effort to build the highest *castell* (human tower). Cheer them all the way to the top in Vilafranca del Penedès at the town festival in August or during Barcelona's La Mercè festival in September.

↑ Human towers built by teams of locals during Barcelona's city holiday, La Mercè

A YEAR IN BARCELONA AND CATALONIA

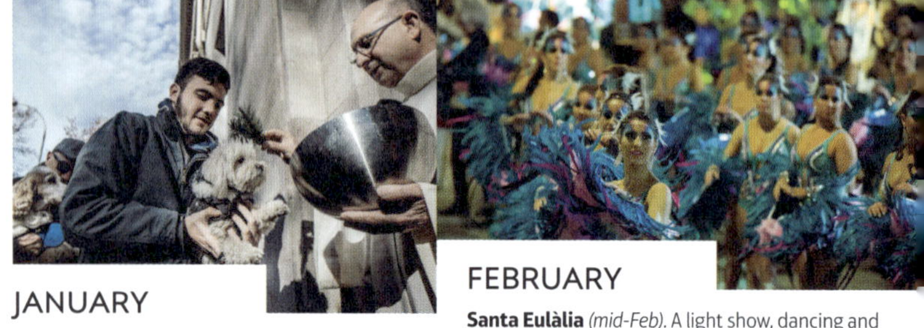

JANUARY

△ **Els Tres Tombs** *(17 Jan)*. Pets are blessed in honour of St Anthony, patron saint of animals.

Gran Festa de la Calçotada *(end Jan)*. The air fills with the scent of grilling *calçots* (spring onions); eat them off a clay roof tile with romesco sauce.

FEBRUARY

Santa Eulàlia *(mid-Feb)*. A light show, dancing and *gegant* (giant) parades honour the patron saint of Barcelona in the Old Town.

△ **Carnestoltes** *(late Feb)*. All of Catalonia erupts in a confetti of sequins, feathers and fun to celebrate *dijous gras* (Mardi Gras).

MAY

△ **Fira de Sant Ponç** *(11 May)*. Stock up on aromatic and medicinal herbs and honey at this ancient fair on Barcelona's Carrer de l'Hospital.

Nit dels Museus *(mid-May)*. Barcelona's museums throw their doors open at night in celebration of International Museums Day.

JUNE

Corpus Christi *(May/Jun)*. Lay flowers and dance with *la patum* (dragon) in Berga to honour the Eucharist.

Primavera Sound *(late May–early Jun)*. World-famous music acts up the tempo across Barcelona.

△ **Revetlla de Sant Joan** *(23 Jun)*. Catalan towns come alive with fireworks, music, street parties and beach bonfires during the vibrant festival of Saint John.

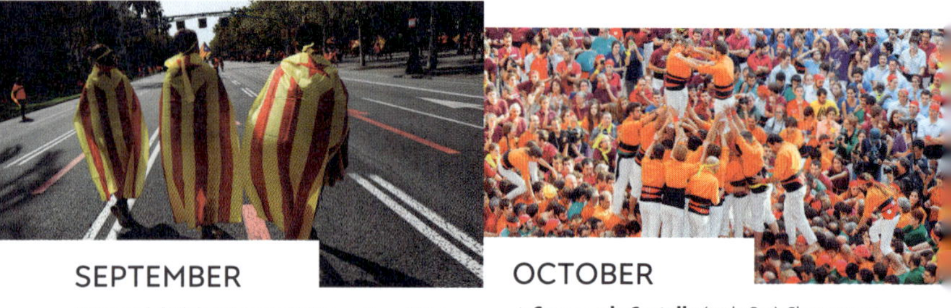

SEPTEMBER

Mostra del Vi de l'Empordà *(1st weekend)*. Raise a glass to Figueres's exquisite wine heritage, with workshops, vineyard tours and tastings.

△ **La Diada** *(11 Sep)*. Catalonia's national day mourns its lost autonomy and celebrates Catalan identity.

La Mercè *(24 Sep)*. Barcelona's annual festival honours *Nostra Senyora de la Mercè* (Our Lady of Mercy) in a week of concerts, masses and dances.

OCTOBER

△ **Concurs de Castells** *(early Oct)*. Cheer on as *castellers* (human towers) triumph in Tarragona.

Sitges Film Festival *(early Oct)*. Actors and directors gather to celebrate the fantasy genre.

Cavatast *(1st weekend)*. Corks are popped across Catalonia in this effervescent festival.

El Festival Internacional de Jazz de Barcelona *(late Oct)*. The hottest ticket in international jazz.

MARCH

De Cajón! Flamenco Festival *(Feb–Mar). Bailaors* and *bailaoras* (flamenco dancers) stamp-tap through concerts and classes held in venues across Barcelona.

Festa de Sant Medir *(3 Mar).* The sweetest festival of the year, with epic parades in Barcelona's Gràcia district that pepper the crowds with free sweets.

△ **Jazz Terrassa** *(two weeks mid-Mar).* Music lovers get into the groove at this internationally renowned festival, with jazz concerts in venues around the town of Terrassa.

APRIL

Setmana Santa *(Mar–Apr).* All across Catalonia, villages and towns erupt in Holy Week events in the seven days leading up to Easter.

△ **La Diada de Sant Jordi** *(23 Apr).* Roses and books are exchanged during the Feast of St George, patron saint of Catalonia, known locally as *el dia del llibre* (book day).

Feria de Abril *(end Apr).* Barcelona's Parc del Fòrum comes alive with flamenco dancing and concerts. Tapas stalls and attractions for kids add to the fun.

JULY

Grec Festival *(Jun–Jul).* Performers from Catalonia and around the world flock to Barcelona to delight crowds in a six-week series of events.

Cantada d'Havaneres *(1st Sun).* Singers belt out *havaneres* (sea shanties), fuelled by *cremat* (coffee and rum); see the best at Calella de Palafrugell.

△ **Santa Cristina** *(24 Jul).* The people of Lloret de Mar honour their patron saint.

AUGUST

Porta Ferrada *(Jul–Aug).* The Costa Brava village of Sant Feliu de Guíxols becomes a centre of the arts.

△ **Circuit Festival** *(early–mid-Aug).* Thousands storm the beaches of Barcelona for this huge LGBTQ+ party.

Aquelarre de Cervera *(last weekend).* Be enchanted as witches and the Mascle Cabró (a satyr) take over the town of Cervera.

NOVEMBER

△ **Tots Sants** *(1 Nov).* The streets fill with the scent of roasted chestnuts and baked sweet potato as All Saints' Eve dawns. The next day, Dia dels Difunts (All Souls' Day), people visit loved ones' graves.

Nice One Barcelona *(end Nov).* Gaming nerds from across the country flex their controller thumbs over three days of Spanish video game industry reveals, forums and launches.

DECEMBER

△ **Fira de Santa Llúcia** *(late Nov–23 Dec).* Barcelona's oldest Christmas market sees hundreds of stalls set up around Catedral de Barcelona selling handmade gifts.

Fira de l'Avet d'Espinelves *(1st two weeks).* The fir trees at this busy Christmas market steal the spotlight as they are the best in the region. There are also stalls full of crafts and gifts.

Reveillón *(31 Dec).* All over Spain on Reveillón (New Year's Eve) people try to eat 12 grapes – one between each chime of the midnight bell.

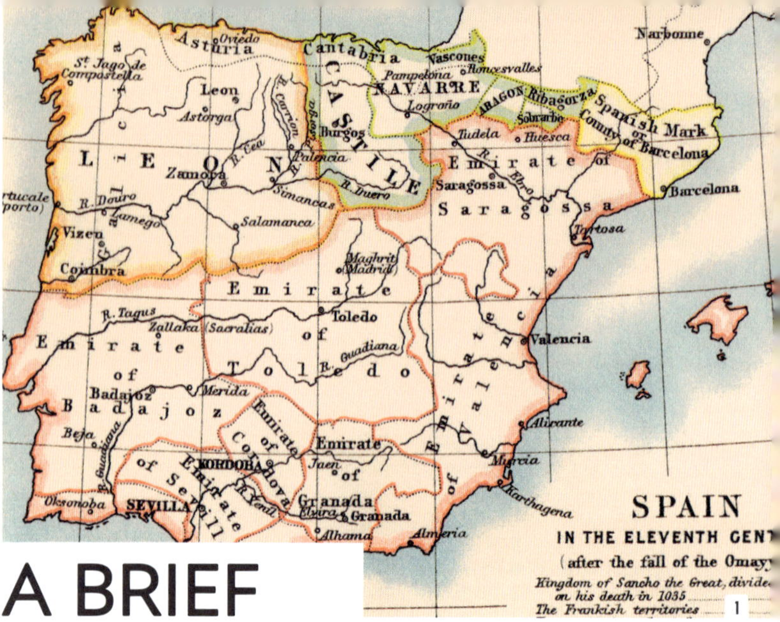

A BRIEF HISTORY

First united under the House of Barcelona, Catalonia has a distinct culture and language thanks to frequent spells of autonomy. Its history is a long tug-of-war between independence and Spanish rule that continues to this day.

Early Catalonia

First inhabited around 8000 BCE by cave-painting hunter-gatherers, Catalonia was more permanently settled by the Laietani and Iberians around 1000 BCE. Greek and Carthaginian trading ports, established around 550 BCE, were absorbed by the Romans, who arrived at Empúries in 218 BCE. They repressed the Iberians and established Tarraco (Tarragona) as their capital.

Visigoths and Moors

Following the collapse of the Roman Empire, the Visigoths moved their base from Toulouse in France to Spain, where they stayed

801 CE

Louis the Pious, son of Charlemagne, reclaims Barcelona from the Moors.

Timeline of events

2000–1500 BCE

Megalithic monuments are built throughout Catalonia.

550 BCE

Greeks establish a trading settlement at Empúries.

218 BCE

Romans arrive at Empúries to take Spain.

531 CE

Visigoths establish themselves in Barcelona after the fall of Rome.

717

Moors take control of Catalonia.

until the Moors stormed Spain's southern shores in 711. Moving north with impressive speed, the Moors captured Barcelona six years later, but their control was short-lived. At the start of the 9th century Charlemagne reclaimed Barcelona and established the Marca Hispanica, a buffer state to separate Moorish al-Andalus to the south from his own northern kingdom. It was put under the control of local lords and a Catalan nation began to emerge.

Consolidation and Expansion

In 878, Guifré el Pilós (Wilfred the Hairy), the first count of Barcelona, brought the Catalan counties of Barcelona, Cerdanya, Conflent, Osona, Urgell and Girona under his control, and established hereditary rule. Catalonia began to assert more independence and towards the end of the 11th century it established the first constitutional government in Europe with a bill of rights. The region's boundaries pushed south past Tarragona, and united with Aragon, to the north, in 1137. Under the long reign of Jaume I the Conqueror (Jaime I, in Castilian) there was an explosion of Catalan prosperity and maritime expansion. He established the Corts (Catalan Parliament), and promoted Catalan language and literature.

1 Map of the Iberian Peninsula in the 11th century, after the fall of the Moorish caliphate. ↑

2 Finely tiled Roman mosaic of Mnemosyne, mother of the Muses, in Tarragona.

3 Visigothic writing once used on the Iberian Peninsula, set in stone.

4 The conquest of the island of Majorca, under Jaume I of Aragon.

801

Moors are driven out of Catalonia by Charlemagne, who establishes the Marca Hispanica.

1060

The constitution, the Usatges, is drawn; the word "Catalan" is first recorded.

878

Guifré el Pilós (Wilfred the Hairy) consolidates the eastern Pyrenees and gains autonomy.

1300s

The Corts (Catalan Parliament) is established.

1137

Barcelona unites with neighbouring Aragon by royal marriage.

The Catholic Monarchs

Spain was united in 1469 when Fernando II of Catalonia-Aragon married Isabel of Castile, a region which by then had absorbed the rest of northern Spain. In 1492, they reclaimed Granada, the last Muslim-controlled area of the peninsula. Then, in a fever of righteousness, they also drove out the Jewish population. This had a disastrous effect on the economy of Barcelona and Girona. That same year, explorer Christopher Columbus set foot in America, opening up trade routes that promised unprecedented wealth and prosperity for Spain as European colonialism began to ravage the Americas. However, Barcelona was shut out from the economic potential when Seville and Cádiz were awarded a monopoly over trade with the Americas. As a result of this economic delimitation, Barcelona went into a period of decline and the seeds were sown for centuries of tensions between Catalonia and Castile.

War of Spanish Succession

During the Thirty Years' War, Catalonia eventually allied with France rather than Spain, heightening tensions between Spain

CATALAN ROMANESQUE

From the 11th century, the thick stone and striking decoration of Romanesque architecture flourished in the region, especially in a proliferation of small, beautiful churches in the narrow Vall de Boí. Their most characteristic feature is the tall, square belfry (as seen at Sant Climent de Taüll), with high, columned windows and radiating chapels.

Timeline of events

1469

Fernando II of Catalonia-Aragon marries Isabel of Castile, uniting Spain under one ruling house.

1492

Columbus lands in the Americas; Barcelona is barred from trade with the Americas.

1494

Supreme Council of Aragon brings Catalonia under Castilian control.

1659

The end of the Thirty Years' War sees the redrawing of the border with France; Roussillon cedes to France.

3

4

5

and the Catalan state. In the end, Spain's Felipe IV laid siege to and defeated the region. A second confrontation with Madrid arose during the War of Spanish Succession, when Barcelona allied with England to back the Habsburgs, who eventually lost the Spanish crown to the Bourbons. Following this defeat, Barcelona fell to Felipe V's forces on 11 September 1714. This marked a turning point for Catalonia as Felipe proceeded to annul Catalan independence and privilege. The Catalan language was banned, Catalonia's universities were closed and Felipe built a citadel to keep an eye on the population.

The Catalan Renaixença

Catalonia's fortunes changed once more as Barcelona became the first city in Spain to industrialize in the 1800s. Immigrant workers arrived and the population grew rapidly, eventually bursting out of its medieval city walls. Industrialization led to wealth and prosperity, which inspired the Renaixença, a renaissance of the Catalan culture that had been suppressed for over a hundred years. As well as traditional customs and a return to the Catalan language, Catalan art and literature flourished.

1 Isabel of Castile and Fernando of Catalonia-Aragon with their daughter Joanna.

2 Drawing of the siege of Barcelona by the forces of the Spanish King Felipe V (1714).

3 Engraving of the War of Spanish Succession (1701–1714).

4 Painting of the Sert and Sola Brothers (1882) by Antonio Regalt.

5 *The Working Girl* (1885) by Catalan painter Joan Planella i Rodríguez.

1714

Barcelona is sacked by Felipe V of Bourbon; Catalan universities close and the Catalan language is banned.

1778

The ban on Catalonian trade with the Americas is lifted, bringing new wealth.

1808–14

Peninsular War: Girona is besieged, Barcelona is occupied and Montserrat monastery is sacked.

1823–6

The French occupy Catalonia.

1

2

3

Catalanism and Modernisme

As part of the region's momentum towards autonomy, Felipe V's citadel, a symbol of Madrid's hold on Catalonia, was razed in the 1840s and replaced by a vast public park. In 1887 the first home-rule party, the Lliga de Catalunya, was founded as disputes with the central government continued. Meanwhile, Barcelona continued to expand. The new district of Eixample (Catalan for "expansion") was created on a grid system. Architects such as Antoni Gaudí and Lluís Domènech i Montaner developed Modernisme, an architectural style that captured the essence of Catalan identity; it is now considered synonymous with Catalonia.

Civil War and the Franco Era

As Catalonia's re-emerging national identity inspired calls for full independence, momentum was stopped in its tracks by the Spanish Civil War. All of Spain was ravaged from 1936 until 1939. Catalonia was bombed by German aircraft and Italian warships, as both countries sided with Francisco Franco's Nationalist cause. After the Nationalist victory, Franco installed himself as dictator of Spain. Engulfed by what the Catalans call the *negre nit* (dark

↑ Portrait of famous Spanish architect Antoni Gaudí

Timeline of events

1849

Spain's first railway links Barcelona and Mataró.

1859

A revival of Jocs Florals's poetry feeds a revival of Catalan culture.

1888

Universal Exhibition, held in Parc de la Ciutadella, showcases the Modernista style.

1936–9

Spanish Civil War. Nationalist victory sees the suppression of Catalan language, culture and identity.

1960s

Package holidays across the Costa Brava create a boom in tourism.

4

night), Catalonia was stripped of its autonomy, its language outlawed yet again, and any public displays of separatist sympathy were brutally suppressed. Barcelona was left short of resources and largely neglected by the government.

Catalonia Today

Despite Franco's oppressive regime, the 1960s brought an economic boom in the form of tourism along the Costa Brava and Costa Daurada. When Franco died in 1975, constitutional democracy was restored to Spain and Catalonia regained a considerable degree of independence. Barcelona was rejuvenated in 1992 for the Olympic Games. The global economic crisis of the early 2000s hit Catalonia hard and led again to calls for complete separation from Spain. An independence referendum held in 2017 was declared illegal by the Constitutional Court of Spain. The political crisis continues to simmer, but a more conciliatory approach from the PSOE government, which won the 2019 Spanish general elections, and disagreement among the main pro-independence parties in Catalonia on how to achieve their goals, has led to a dip in popular support for independence from Spain.

1 Aerial view of the grid formation of Eixample. ↑

2 Unique rooftop of Gaudí's famous La Pedrera in Barcelona, built between 1906 and 1910.

3 Crowds waiting in the streets to greet General Francisco Franco's troops.

4 The Estelada (Catalan separatist flag) flying at a protest calling for independence.

1975

Franco dies; King Juan Carlos ascends the throne, restoring the Bourbon line.

1979

Partial autonomy is granted to Catalonia.

1986

Spain joins the European Community (now the European Union) and NATO.

2015

Ada Colau is elected mayor of Barcelona, the first woman to hold the office.

2022

Barcelona becomes the first city to win the Biosphere Platinum certificate for sustainable tourism policies.

EXPERIENCE

Ambling along Barcelona's La Rambla

Early morning light dappling Barri Gòtic's quiet Carrer del Bisbe

OLD TOWN

Barcelona's Ciutat Vella (Old Town) is where the city itself came into being. Settled by the prehistoric Laietani, the area stretching between the Besòs and Llobregat river deltas was chosen by the Romans around 15 BCE to be the site of their new *colonia* (town): Barcino. They surrounded the town with defensive walls, the ruins of which can still be seen today. The Roman forum on the Plaça de Sant Jaume was replaced by the medieval Palau de la Generalitat in 1596, the seat of Catalonia's government, and the Casa de la Ciutat, the city's town hall. Close by are the 14th-century former royal palace and the Gothic cathedral, dedicated to St Eulàlia, the city's first patron saint.

As the medieval town grew wealthy from trade across the Mediterranean, it expanded out into El Born and, later, rural El Raval. In the 18th century, Barceloneta was developed into a fishing quarter. The medieval walls surrounded the city until the mid-19th century, when they were torn down for an urban expansion project which saw the creation of neighbouring Eixample.

Today, the Old Town remains the beating heart of the Catalan capital, particularly its main artery La Rambla, a vibrant street that draws tourists from around the world and pulses with life,

OLD TOWN
EIXAMPLE
p102
EL RAVAL
BARRI GÒTIC
SANT PERE
LA RIBERA
MONTJUÏC
p124
PORT VELL
BARCELONETA
Museu d'Art Contemporani (MACBA)
Mercat de Sant Josep
La Rambla
El Raval
Gran Teatre del Liceu
Palau Güell
Catedral de Barcelona
El Call
Museu Frederic Marès
Museu d'Història de Barcelona (MUHBA)
MUHBA El Call
Palau de la Generalitat
Palau de la Música Catalana
Casa de la Ciutat
Carrer de Montcada
Moco Museum
Basílica de Santa Maria del Mar
La Llotja
Museu de Cera
Museu Marítim and Drassanes
Mirador de Colom
Pailebot Santa Eulàlia
Moll de Barcelona
Dàrsena Nacional
Marina Port Vell
Aquàrium
Maremàgnum
Port Vell
Museu d'Història de Catalunya
Barceloneta
World Trade Centre
Torre Jaume I
Torre Sant Sebastià
Transbordador del Port - Estació Sant Sebastià
Universitat
Catalunya
Urquinaona
Sant Antoni
Liceu
Jaume I
Paral·lel
Drassanes
Barceloneta
RONDA DE LA UNIVERSITAT
RONDA DE SANT ANTONI
RONDA DE SANT PAU
GRAN VIA DE LES CORTS CATALANES
RAMBLA CATALUNYA
PASSEIG DE GRÀCIA
CARRER DE VALÈNCIA
CARRER D'ARAGÓ
CARRER DE ROGER DE LLÚRIA
PLAÇA DE CATALUNYA
CARRER DELS TALLERS
CARRER DE PELAI
CARRER DE VALLDONZELLA
CARRER DE JOAQUIN COSTA
PLAÇA DE VICENÇ MARTORELL
CARRER DE PEU DE LA CREU
C. D'EN XUCLÀ
CARRER DEL CARME
PLAÇA DE PEDRO
CARRER DE L'HOSPITAL
RAMBLA DEL RAVAL
C. D'EN ROBADOR
CARRER DE SANT PAU
CARRER DE LA UNIÓ
CARRER NOU DE LA RAMBLA
AVINGUDA DE LES DRASSANES
CARRER DE L'ARC DEL TEATRE
C. DEL CID
AVINGUDA DEL PARAL·LEL
LA RAMBLA
CARRER DE FONTANELLA
VIA LAIETANA
AVDA DEL PORTAL DE L'ÀNGEL
C DE SANTA ANNA
C DE LA CANUDA
PLAÇA DE LA VILA DE MADRID
PLAÇA DE LLUÍS MILLET
PLAÇA D'ANTONI MAURA
RONDA DE SANT PERE
CARRER DE SANT PERE MES ALT
CARRER DE SANT PERE MITJA
CARRER DE SANT PERE MES BAIX
PLAÇA DE SANT AGUSTÍ VELL
CARRER DE LA PRINCESA
CARRER DE FERRAN
PLAÇA REIAL
CARRER D'AVINYÓ
PLAÇA DELS TRAGINERS
C DELS ESCUDELLERS
C. NOU DE SANT FRANCESC
C. DE CODOLS
CARRER AMPLE
CARRER DE LA MERCÈ
PLAÇA D'ANTONI LÓPEZ
PASSEIG DE ISABEL II
CARRER DE JOSEP ANSELM CLAVÉ
PLAÇA DEL DUC DE MEDINACELI
PASSEIG DE COLOM
MOLL DE FUSTA
PLAÇA DEL PORTAL DE LA PAU
PLAÇA DE LES DRASSANES
RAMBLA DE MAR
MOLL D'ESPANYA
PLAÇA DE PAU VILA
PASSEIG JOAN DE BORBÓ
PLAÇA DE POETA BOSCÀ
E
F
G
H
5
6
7
8
9

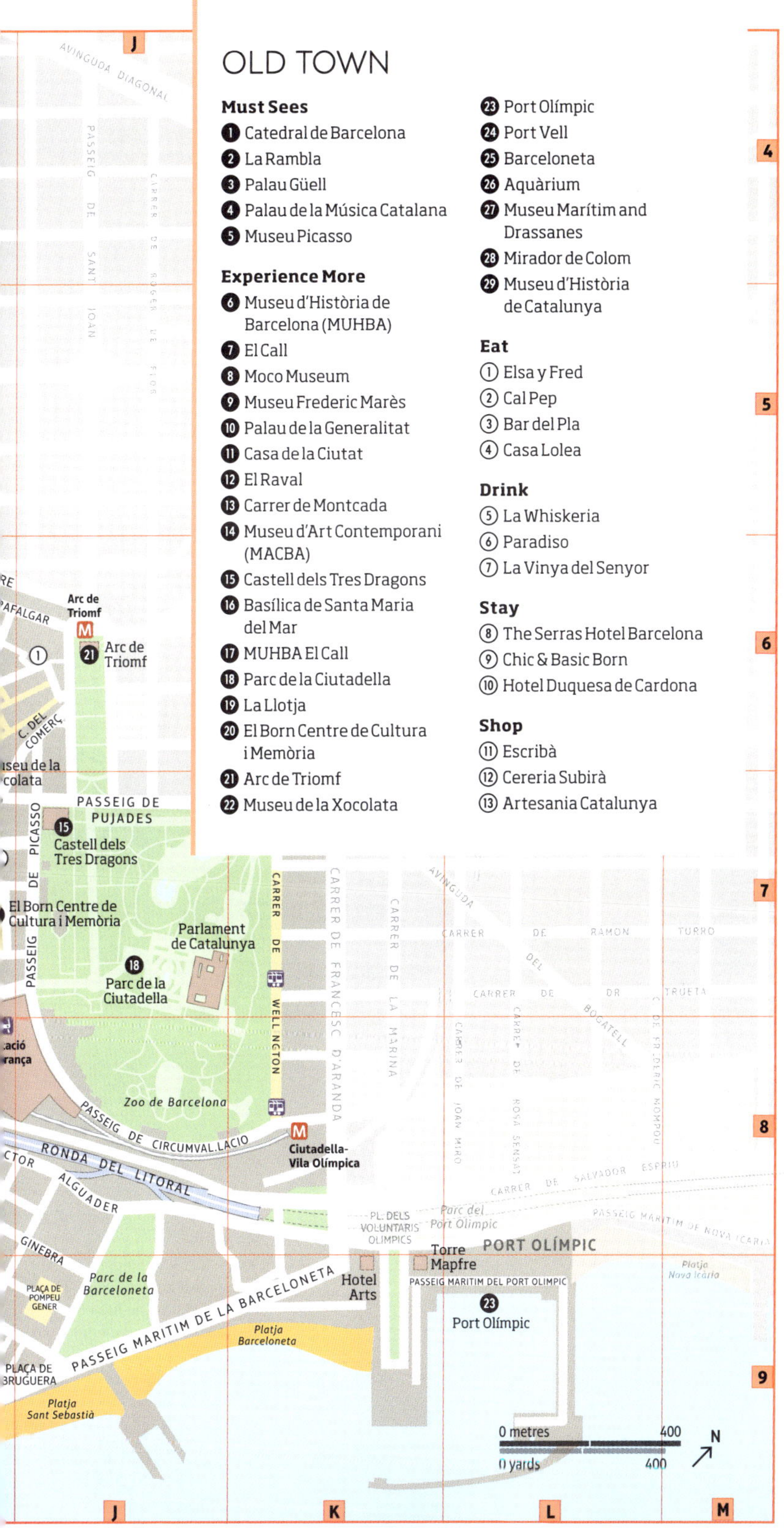
OLD TOWN
Must Sees
1 Catedral de Barcelona
2 La Rambla
3 Palau Güell
4 Palau de la Música Catalana
5 Museu Picasso
Experience More
6 Museu d'Història de Barcelona (MUHBA)
7 El Call
8 Moco Museum
9 Museu Frederic Marès
10 Palau de la Generalitat
11 Casa de la Ciutat
12 El Raval
13 Carrer de Montcada
14 Museu d'Art Contemporani (MACBA)
15 Castell dels Tres Dragons
16 Basílica de Santa Maria del Mar
17 MUHBA El Call
18 Parc de la Ciutadella
19 La Llotja
20 El Born Centre de Cultura i Memòria
21 Arc de Triomf
22 Museu de la Xocolata
23 Port Olímpic
24 Port Vell
25 Barceloneta
26 Aquàrium
27 Museu Marítim and Drassanes
28 Mirador de Colom
29 Museu d'Història de Catalunya
Eat
1 Elsa y Fred
2 Cal Pep
3 Bar del Pla
4 Casa Lolea
Drink
5 La Whiskeria
6 Paradiso
7 La Vinya del Senyor
Stay
8 The Serras Hotel Barcelona
9 Chic & Basic Born
10 Hotel Duquesa de Cardona
Shop
11 Escribà
12 Cereria Subirà
13 Artesania Catalunya
J
K
L
M
4
5
6
7
8
9
AVINGUDA DIAGONAL
PASSEIG DE SANT JOAN
Arc de Triomf
Arc de Triomf
C. DEL COMERÇ
PASSEIG DE PUJADES
Castell dels Tres Dragons
PASSEIG DE PICASSO
El Born Centre de Cultura i Memòria
Parlament de Catalunya
Parc de la Ciutadella
CARRER DE WELLINGTON
Zoo de Barcelona
PASSEIG DE CIRCUMVAL.LACIO
Ciutadella-Vila Olímpica
RONDA DEL LITORAL
ALGUADER
GINEBRA
PLAÇA DE POMPEU GENER
Parc de la Barceloneta
PASSEIG MARITIM DE LA BARCELONETA
Platja Barceloneta
PLAÇA DE BRUGUERA
Platja Sant Sebastià
CARRER DE FRANCESC D'ARANDA
CARRER DE LA MARINA
AVINGUDA
CARRER DE RAMON TURRO
CARRER DE PERE IV
CARRER DE SALVADOR ESPRIU
PASSEIG MARITIM DE NOVA ICARIA
PL. DELS VOLUNTARIS OLIMPICS
Parc del Port Olímpic
PORT OLÍMPIC
Torre Mapfre
Hotel Arts
PASSEIG MARITIM DEL PORT OLIMPIC
Port Olímpic
Platja Nova Icària
0 metres 400
0 yards 400
N

CATEDRAL DE BARCELONA

G7 Plaça de la Seu Jaume I 17, 19, 45 9:30am-6:30pm Mon-Fri (last adm: 5:45pm); 9:30am-5:15pm Sat (last adm: 4:30pm); 2-5pm Sun (last adm: 4:30pm) catedralbcn.org

With its intricate façade and inviting interior, Barcelona Cathedral is a beguiling sight. Treading beneath the nave's soaring vaults, you may feel as if you are stepping back in time.

One of the city's few churches spared from destruction in the Civil War, this compact Gothic cathedral was begun in 1298 under Jaime (Jaume) II on the foundations of a site dating back to Visigothic times, but was not finished until the late 19th century. This interruption has lent Barcelona Cathedral a distinct look compared to the rest of the Barri Gòtic. The cathedral is dedicated to St Eulàlia, the city's patron saint, whose alabaster sarcophagus is located in the crypt. Take your time to explore the exceptional interior, as well as the lofty roof terrace and shady cloisters.

Twin octagonal bell towers, dating from 1386 to 1393

Viewpoint offering 360-degree views of the Catalan capital

The Catalan Gothic-style interior, with a single wide nave that has 28 side chapels

Beautifully carved choir stalls, which date from the 15th century

The Capella del Santíssim Sagrament

Timeline

877

▲ St Eulàlia's remains brought here from Santa Maria del Mar.

1046–58

▼ Romanesque cathedral built under Ramon Berenguer I.

1298

Start of the construction of the present Gothic building, which was consecrated in 1339.

1889

▼ Main façade completed, based on plans dating from 1408 by architect Charles Galters.

1 The cathedral's central spire was finally completed in 1913.

2 The shaded Gothic cloisters are especially popular with visitors.

3 The cathedral's crypt is home to the alabaster sarcophagus of St Eulàlia.

The crypt, where St Eulàlia's tomb is found

The Capella de Sant Benet, a chapel dedicated to the founder of the Benedictine Order and patron saint of Europe, is home to a magnificent altarpiece

Porta de Santa Eulàlia, the entrance to the cloisters

Cloisters, with a fountain decorated with a statue of St George

The Sacristy Museum, which houses a small treasury

Capella de Santa Llúcia

↑ The distinctive Barcelona Cathedral, set in the city's Old Town

Did You Know?

Thirteen geese live in the cloister, representing St Eulàlia's age at her martyrdom.

2

LA RAMBLA

F6 Drassanes, Liceu, Catalunya Catalunya

The historic avenue of La Rambla splits the Old Town in half as it stretches from Plaça de Catalunya to Port Vell. Newsstands, flower stalls, tarot readers, musicians and mime artists line the wide, tree-shaded central walkway around the clock, but La Rambla is particularly frenetic in the evenings and at weekends.

The name of this long avenue, known as Les Rambles in Catalan, comes from the Arabic *ramla*, meaning "the dried-up bed of a seasonal river". The 13th-century city wall followed the left bank of such a river that flowed from the Collserola hills to the sea. Convents, monasteries and the university were built on the opposite bank in the 16th century. As time passed, the riverbed was filled in and those buildings demolished, but they are remembered in the names of the five consecutive Rambles that make up the great avenue.

The first of these, Rambla de Canaletes, is named after an extravagant fountain; and Rambla dels Estudis after a university established here in the 16th century. Along the latter, you'll find the Palau Moja, which occasionally hosts temporary exhibitions in its Baroque salons. Next comes Rambla de Sant Josep, where a monastery dedicated to the saint was demolished to make room for the market better known as "La Boqueria" – the place where *boc* (goat) is sold. Don't miss the Palau de le Virreina, which hosts free exhibitions. Rambla dels Caputxins and Rambla de Santa Mònica also recall a long-gone monastery and convent.

→ A street performer, dressed as a golden monster, striking a pose on La Rambla

EAT

Mercat de Sant Josep
"La Boqueria" is Barcelona's most colourful food market. Seek out Bar Quiosc Modern for its seafood.

Plaça de la Boqueria Sun
boqueria.barcelona

Rocambolesc
The ice cream at this kiosk is served up by the Roca brothers, who are regularly voted the best chefs in the world.

La Rambla 51-59
rocambolesc.com

↑ Sampling dishes at the busy food stalls inside La Boqueria

Did You Know?

The poet Lorca said La Rambla was "the only street in the world that I wish would never end".

↑ Tree-lined La Rambla snaking through the heart of Barcelona towards distant hills

3

PALAU GÜELL

F7 Nou de la Rambla 3-5 Liceu Apr-Oct: 10am-8pm Tue-Sun; Nov-Mar: 10am-5:30pm Tue-Sun 1, 6 & the last week of Jan, 25 & 26 Dec palauguell.cat

Half-hidden on a narrow side street off La Rambla, Antoni Gaudí's first major building in Barcelona quickly established his international reputation for outstanding, original architecture. It was built in 1889 for the industrialist Eusebi Güell, who would go on to become Gaudí's lifelong patron.

Unusually for Gaudí, this austere grey house is characterized by straight horizontal and vertical lines. All that hints at his future style are the parabolic arches on the doorways; the spire-like chimneys behind the parapet on the roof; and the spiral cobbled ramp that swoops down to the basement, where large stone arches reach from torch-shaped columns to support the roof.

Güell made it known that there would be no limit to the budget at Gaudí's disposal, and Gaudí took him at his word, using only the best materials and crafters. The most notable feature of the house is its very high central room on the main floor. Something between a sitting room and a covered courtyard, this central room rises three floors and is spanned by a cupola. The other rooms are grouped around it.

INSIDER TIP
Les Nits del Palau Güell

On Saturday nights in July, the Palau Güell transforms into a performance space for a diverse programme of musicians. Concertgoers can go up to the rooftop for cava and nibbles before showtime.

Upper galleries are richly decorated with carved wood and cofferwork

→ Cut-away illustration of Antoni Gaudí's rather modest Palau Güell

Dramatic Cupola

▼ A dramatic three-storey cupola covering the central salon, inspired by Islamic architecture, gives the illusion of stars.

Spiral Ramp

The spiral carriage ramp is an early sign of Gaudí's predilection for curved lines.

Highlights

Decorated Chimneys

▲ The colourful glazed tiles that decorate the chimneys became one of the trademarks of Gaudí's later work.

Parabolic Arches

Parabolic arches, used extensively by Gaudí, beginning in the Palau Güell, show his interest in Gothic architecture.

→

Highly decorative wrought-iron gates leading into the main hall

Did You Know?

The Palau's concert hall is the only one in Europe lit by natural light.

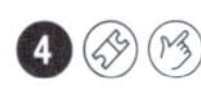

PALAU DE LA MÚSICA CATALANA

H6 Carrer Palau de la Música 4-6 Urquinaona 9am-3:30pm daily and for concerts palaumusica.cat

This is a true monument to music, a Modernista celebration of tilework, sculpture and stained glass. Designed by Lluís Domènech i Montaner, it was completed in 1908. Its red-brick façade is elaborate, but it's the main auditorium that is truly inspiring.

The Palace of Catalan Music was built in 1891 for the Orfeó Català, a choral society that played an important role in the Catalan cultural movement known as the Renaixença. The building's façade is richly decorated with colourful murals, as well as an enormous sculptural group depicting "Catalan Song" and Sant Jordi, the Catalan patron saint.

Inside, the main auditorium is one of the most beautiful in the world, lit by an inverted dome of stained glass portraying angelic choristers. Sculptures of Richard Wagner and Antoni Clavé adorn the proscenium arch above the stage, with a charming group of dancing muses. An underground concert hall and an outdoor square for summer concerts were later added, consolidating the Palau's reputation as Barcelona's most loved music venue.

PICTURE PERFECT

On the Balcony

Book a tour in advance to gain access to the site's balcony. It's the ideal spot to snap the gorgeous stained-glass skylight framed by the auditorium. The colourful tiled pillars are also worth a close-up shot.

Interior of the Palau's sublime concert hall, beneath its inverted stained-glass dome

THE SARDANA

Catalonia's national dance is more complicated than it appears. The success of the Sardana depends on all of the dancers accurately counting the complicated short- and long-step skips and jumps, which accounts for their serious faces. Music is provided by a *cobla*, an 11-person band consisting of a leader playing a three-holed flute *(flabiol)* and a little drum *(tambor)*, five woodwind players and five brass players. When the music starts, dancers join hands and form circles. The Sardana is performed at most local *festes* and the Palau de la Música Catalana occasionally stages performances.

American jazz singer Madeleine Peyrou performing in the Palau

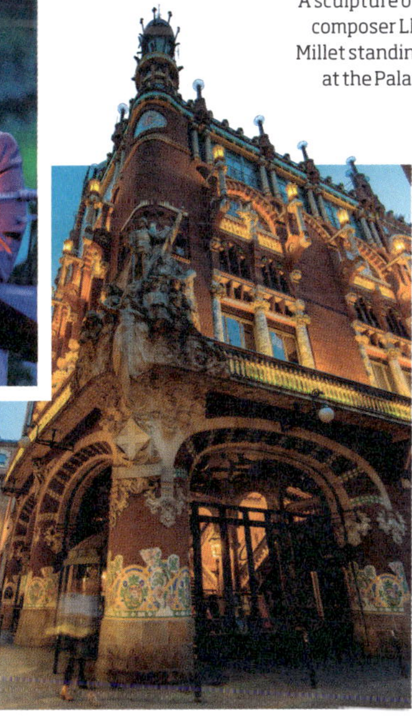

Ornate, pillared façade of the Palau, lit up at dusk

A sculpture of the composer Lluís Millet standing at the Palau

Did You Know?

Picasso's full name is 20 words long and includes the names of several saints.

Exploring the inner courtyard of the Museu Picasso in Barcelona ↑

5

MUSEU PICASSO

H7 Carrer de Montcada 15-23 Jaume I Mid-Apr-mid-Oct: 9am-8pm Tue-Sun (to 9pm Thu-Sat); mid-Oct-mid-Apr: 10am-7pm Tue-Sun museupicasso.bcn.cat

One of Barcelona's most popular attractions, this is the first museum dedicated to the artist's work. It is housed in five adjoining medieval palaces: Berenguer d'Aguilar, Baró de Castellet, Meca, Mauri and Finestres. The collection focuses on Picasso's early work, showcasing his development and the influence of the city that was his home for many years.

The core of the Picasso museum's collection is a large donation made in 1963 by the artist's secretary and great friend, Jaume Sabartés. Given that Picasso had publicly sworn that he wouldn't set foot in Spain while Franco lived, it was known as the Sabartés Collection for many years (as a museum using the artist's own name would have been met with censorship). Following Sabartés' death in 1968, Picasso himself donated further paintings, including early examples. These were later complemented by graphic works, left in his will, and 141 ceramic pieces given by his widow, Jacqueline.

The setting of the museum itself makes for a unique experience. Visitors are able to wander through stone archways, into pretty courtyards and up well-preserved staircases as they take in the artworks.

The strength of the 4,200-piece collection, which includes sketches, paintings, sculptures and ceramics, is Picasso's early works. These show how, even at the ages of 15 and 16, he had prodigious talent, while the haunting paintings of his Blue Period evoke the misery and hopelessness of the beggars and sex workers he encountered on Barcelona's streets. The highlight of the museum's collection, however, is Picasso's extraordinary suite of 58 paintings, which he created in response to Velázquez's masterpiece, *Las Meninas* (1656).

← Portrait of Picasso in his later years

↑ One of the paintings in Picasso's *Las Meninas* series (1957)

PABLO PICASSO IN BARCELONA

Picasso (1881-1973) was born in Málaga and was almost 14 when he came to Barcelona. He enrolled in the city's art academy and was a precocious talent among his contemporaries. Amid the prostitutes of Carrer d'Avinyo, Picasso found inspiration for his *Les Demoiselles d'Avignon* (1906-7). He left Barcelona for Paris in his early twenties and returned several times, but after the Civil War his opposition to Franco kept him in France.

EXPERIENCE MORE

6 

Museu d'Història de Barcelona (MUHBA)

G7 Plaça del Rei Jaume I 10am-7pm Tue-Sat, 10am-8pm Sun 1 Jan, 1 May, 24 Jun, 25 Dec museuhistoria.bcn.cat

A building of great historical importance, the Palau Reial (Royal Palace) is an apt location for Barcelona's multi-sited Museu d'Història. It was the residence of the counts of Barcelona from its foundation in the 13th century. It was here that Isabel and Fernando received explorer Christopher Columbus after his return from the Americas, in the 14th-century Gothic Saló del Tinell, a vast room with arches spanning 17 m (56 ft). This room is also the site of the Holy Inquisition, the proponents of which believed the walls would move if lies were told. Built into the Roman city wall is the royal chapel, the Capella de Santa Àgata, with a painted wood ceiling and an altarpiece by Jaume Huguet. Stairs on the right of the altar lead to the 16th-century tower of Martí the Humanist (who reigned from 1396 to 1410), the last ruler of the 500-year dynasty of the count-kings of Barcelona. The tower is not open to visitors.

The museum's highlight lies below ground. Entire streets of old Barcino (Roman Barcelona) are accessible via a lift and walkways suspended over the ruins. The site was discovered when the Casa Clariana-Padellàs, the Gothic building from which you enter, was moved here, stone by stone, in 1931, as depicted in a photo of the original dig. The water systems, homes with mosaic floors and even the old forum now make up the most extensive subterranean Roman ruins in the world.

7

El Call

G7 Jaume I, Liceu

Named for the Hebrew word *kahal*, meaning community or congregation, El Call remains the centre of Jewish life in Barcelona. Segregated in 1243 following a wave of anti-Semitic violence, it had been abandoned by its Jewish community long before the expulsion of the Jews in 1424 by Catholic rulers Isabel and Fernando.

Today, nestled in the Old Town's Barri Gòtic, the lively

BARCELONA'S EARLY JEWISH COMMUNITY

First documented in Barcelona in 889, evidence suggests the first synagogue was founded in the 5th century. Barcelona's Jewish community grew to 15 per cent of the city's population by the 14th century, providing doctors and the first seat of learning. Chronic violent anti-Semitism led to the Jews being consigned to El Call. The area was abandoned in 1401, 91 years before Judaism was fully outlawed in Spain.

The square outside the Museu d'Història de Barcelona (MUHBA)

neighbourhood once again flourishes, while remnants of the medieval Jewish character of these narrow streets remain. Descend into the basement of the Café Caelum to see ancient Jewish baths. Around the corner, in the wall at No 5 Carrer de Marlet, a 14th-century Hebrew tablet reads: "Holy Foundation of Rabbi Samuel Hassardi. His soul will rest in Heaven".

The 5th-century remains of the city's oldest synagogue, lost as a place of worship in the 15th century, was restored and reopened for special events in 2002.

Moco Museum

H7 Carrer de Montcada 25 Jaume I 10am-8pm daily (last adm: 7pm) mocomuseum.com

This museum has a wonderful collection of modern and contemporary works, as well as street art, displayed in the Palau Cervelló, a beautiful building constructed in the 15th and 16th centuries. A giant Mickey Mouse sculpture by Brian Donnelly, known professionally as "Kaws", greets visitors in the Gothic courtyard, alongside pieces from many other world-famous artists. The museum also features an exhibition of street art by well-known English artist, Banksy. To see more of his art, visit Moco's sister establishment, the Museu Banksy, which is a 15-minute walk away at Carrer de Trafalgar 34.

Museu Frederic Marès

G7 Plaça de Sant Iu 5 Jaume I 10am-7pm Tue-Sat, 11am-8pm Sun & pub hols 1 Jan, 1 May, 24 Jun, 25 Dec museumares.bcn.cat

The renowned sculptor Frederic Marès i Deulovol (1893–1991) was also a traveller and collector, and this museum stands as a monument to his eclectic taste. As part of the Royal Palace, it was occupied by 13th-century bishops, 14th-century counts of Barcelona, 15th-century judges as well as 18th-century nuns, who lived here until they were expelled in 1936.

Marès, who maintained a modest and small apartment in the building, opened this museum in 1948. In the crypt and on the ground floor are stone sculptures and two complete Romanesque portals. The first floor has Renaissance and Baroque sculpture. The second and third floors feature a more eclectic mix of exhibits, with pieces ranging from children's toys, clocks and costumes to antique cameras, smoking pipes and postcards.

Stone arches, and *(inset)* exhibits at the Museu Frederic Marès

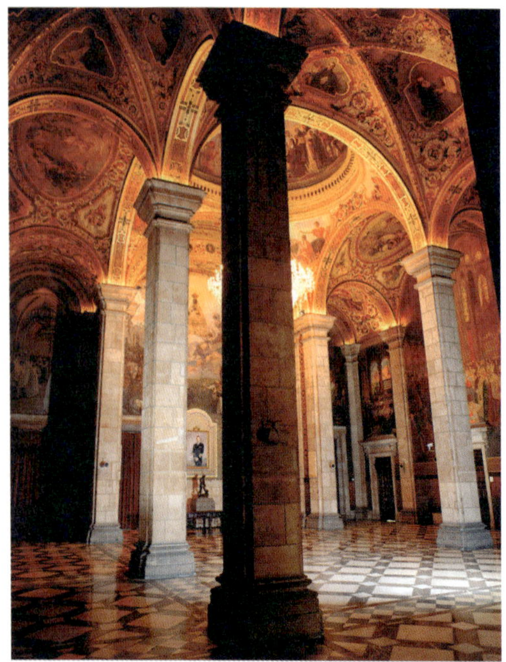

Richly decorated ceiling of the St Jordi chapel in the Palau de la Generalitat

10 Palau de la Generalitat

G7 Plaça de Sant Jaume 4 Jaume I Sep-Jul: 10:30am-1:30pm 2nd & 4th Sat & Sun of month by appt only; passport needed for entry presidencia.gencat.cat

Since 1403, the Generalitat has been the seat of the Catalonian government. The Catalan president has offices here and in the next door Casa dels Canonges. The *casa* (house) and the Generalitat are connected across Carrer del Bisbe by a 1928 bridge modelled on the Bridge of Sighs in Venice.

A statue of Sant Jordi (St George) – the patron saint of Catalonia – and the dragon stands guard above the entrance. The late Catalan Gothic courtyard and the fine Gothic chapel of St Jordi are both by Marc Safont, while the Italianate Saló de Sant Jordi is by Pere Blai. The Palau holds three open days a year: 23 April, and 11 and 24 September.

At the back, above street level, lies the Pati dels Tarongers (Orange Tree Courtyard) by master builder Pau Mateu, which has a bell tower built by Pere Ferrer in 1568.

11 Casa de la Ciutat

G7 Plaça de Sant Jaume 1 934 02 70 00 Jaume I, Liceu 10am-1pm Sun; 23 Apr & 30 May: 10am-8pm

The magnificent 14th-century Ajuntament *(town hall)* faces the Palau de la Generalitat. Flanking the entrance are statues of Jaume I, who granted the city rights to elect councillors in 1249, and Joan Fiveller, who levied taxes on court members in the 1500s. Inside is the council chamber, the 14th-century Saló de Cent, built for the city's 100 councillors. The first-floor Saló de les Cròniques was commissioned for the 1929 International Exhibition and decorated by Josep Maria Sert with murals of events in Catalan history.

12 El Raval

E6 Catalunya, Liceu

The district of El Raval lies west of La Rambla *(p72)* and includes the area near the port, once known as Barri Xinès (Chinese Quarter).

From the 14th century, the city hospital was located in Carrer de l'Hospital, which still has several herbal and medicinal shops today. Gaudí *(p84)* was brought here after being fatally hit by a tram in 1926. The buildings now house the Biblioteca de Catalunya (Catalonian Library), but you can visit the elegantly restored former dissecting room.

Towards the port on Carrer Nou de la Rambla is Gaudí's Palau Güell *(p74)*. At the end of Carrer Sant Pau is the city's

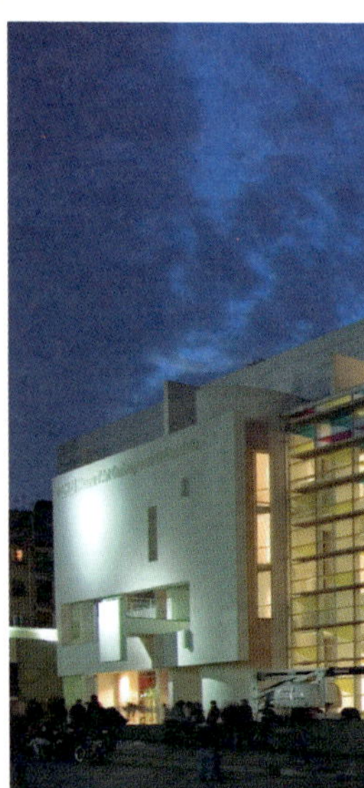

Barcelona's Museu d'Art Contemporani, aglow with colourful lights at night

most complete Romanesque church, the 12th-century Sant Pau del Camp, with a charming cloister featuring exquisitely carved capitals.

Carrer de Montcada

H7 Jaume I

The most authentic medieval street in the city, this narrow lane is overshadowed by gargoyles and roofs that almost touch overhead. The Gothic palaces that line it date back to Catalonia's expansion in the 13th century. Almost all of the buildings were modified over the years, particularly during the 17th century. Only Casa Cervelló-Guidice at No 25 retains its original façade.

HIDDEN GEM
Casa de la Seda

A ten-minute walk from Carrer de Montcada is the Casa de la Seda *(casadelaseda.com)* or "House of Silk", the former headquarters of the silkmakers' guild. Visit to take a tour through sumptuously decorated rooms.

Museu d'Art Contemporani (MACBA)

F6 Plaça dels Àngels 1 Universitat, Catalunya 11am-7:30pm Mon & Wed-Fri, 10am-8pm Sat, 10am-3pm Sun 1 Jan, 25 Dec macba.cat

This glass-fronted building designed by renowned American architect Richard Meier was opened to the public in November 1995. Its light, airy galleries serve as the hub of the city's contemporary art scene. The permanent collection of mainly Spanish painting and sculpture from the 1950s onwards is complemented by temporary exhibitions by international artists, among them South African photojournalist David Goldblatt.

Next to the MACBA is the **Centre de Cultura Contemporània de Barcelona** (CCCB), a lively arts centre.

Centre de Cultura Contemporània de Barcelona

Montalegre 5 11am-8pm Tue-Sun cccb.org

DRINK

La Whiskeria

Choose from a list of 250 whiskies and cocktails at this historic haunt with a jazzy vibe.

F6 Carrer de Casp 39 lawhiskeria.es

Paradiso

Accessed through a refrigerator door, this hidden speakeasy has inspired cocktails.

H7 Carrer Rera Palau 4 paradiso.cat

La Vinya del Senyor

A tiny wine bar with a sprawling terrace, this is a relaxing pit stop in the heart of El Born.

H7 Plaça de Santa María 5 lavinyadelsenyor.es

GAUDÍ'S CITY

Barcelona bears the indelible mark of Catalonia's most famous son, Antoni Gaudí i Cornet, who transformed the city's skyline into an architectural masterpiece. Drawing on Persian and Japanese arts, Mudéjar architecture, and the natural world, Gaudí reinvented the already adventurous art and architectural style known as Catalan Modernisme. A highly dexterous architect, Gaudí designed or collaborated on designs in almost every known medium. He combined bare, undecorated materials - wood, rough-hewn stone, rubble and brickwork - with meticulous craftwork in wrought iron, stained glass and elaborate mosaics. Every Gaudí creation is unique, but they are united by their skill and romanticism.

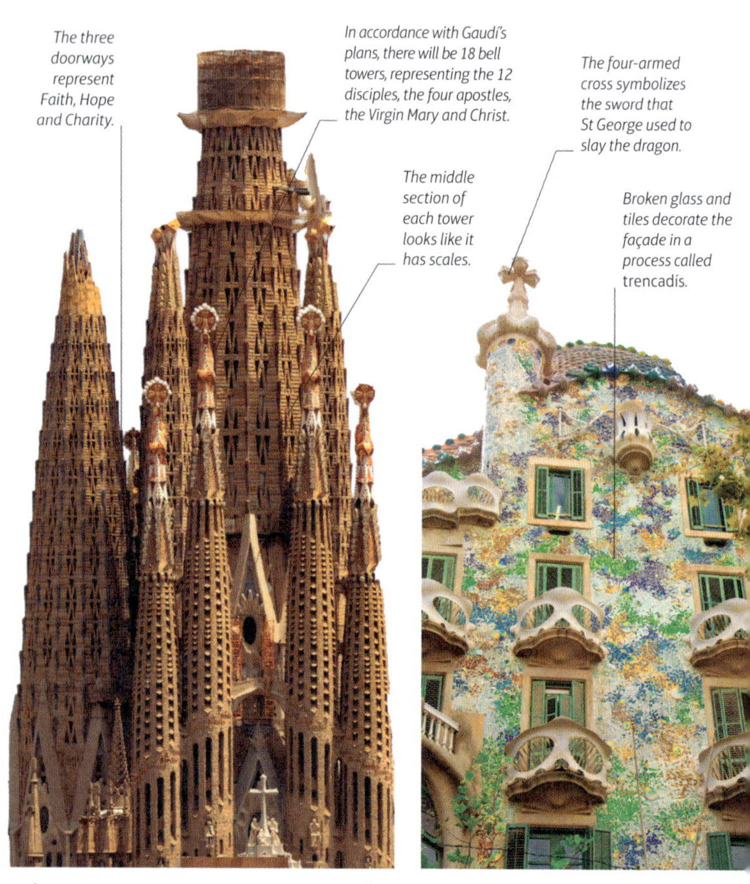

The three doorways represent Faith, Hope and Charity.

In accordance with Gaudí's plans, there will be 18 bell towers, representing the 12 disciples, the four apostles, the Virgin Mary and Christ.

The middle section of each tower looks like it has scales.

The four-armed cross symbolizes the sword that St George used to slay the dragon.

Broken glass and tiles decorate the façade in a process called trencadís.

Gaudí Highlights

Sagrada Família

▲ After Gaudí took over the construction of the Sagrada Família *(p106)* in 1883, it became his lifelong obsession. The soaring interior and the Nativity façade reference both biblical events and the natural world. Although he did not live to see its completion, the cathedral is still being built to his vision.

Casa Batlló

▲ Industrialist Josep Batlló gave Gaudí complete creative freedom to reform this late-19th-century house. Completed in 1906, Casa Batlló *(p112)* is an evocation of artistic joy. The façade acted as an exuberant and marine-inspired canvas, while the roof ripples like a dragon in flight. Inside, light pours in through effervescent stained glass, while the central patio ensures natural light reaches every room.

Did You Know?

Shortly before he died, Gaudí was mistaken for a beggar because of his unkempt appearance.

↑ Gaudí's famous salamander, covered in brightly coloured mosaics, at Park Güell

Gaudí's predilection for curved lines is evident in La Pedrera's wavy façade.

Bizarrely decorated chimneys became one of the trademarks of Gaudí's later work.

The twisting wrought-iron balconies were designed by Josep Maria Jujol.

The influence of nature on Gaudí is seen in the mushroom-shaped dome.

One of the pavilions is topped with a four-armed cross.

The stone façade of the pavilion is crowned by a mosaic-covered roof.

La Pedrera

▲ The last private residence to be designed by Gaudí, rough-hewn La Pedrera *(p114)* raised eyebrows in its time due to its undulating stone façade, abstract roof sculptures and look like seaweed against the walls. The entrance doors, designed to facilitate both people and vehicles, are made up of smaller panes of glass in irregular shapes, based on animals and plants, with larger, more luminous pieces at the top.

Park Güell

▲ Part of Gaudí's naturalist phase, Park Güell *(p144)* represents the architect's fanciful style. The stone-built pavilions, with their brightly tiled gingerbread roofs, are like something from a fairy tale. One of these lodges was designed to be the Casa del Guarda (Caretaker's House). Park Guell was initially conceived as a garden city for Barcelona's wealthy families, but only two plots were purchased.

SHOP

Escribà
Find cakes, chocolates and other Wonka-esque delights at this decades-old patisserie.
F6 La Rambla 83
escriba.es

Cereria Subirà
Pick up beautiful handmade wax creations at this lovely candlemaker's.
G7 Baixada de la Llibreteria 7
cereriasubira.cat

Artesania Catalunya
The best artisanal products of the region are available here.
G7 Carrer des Banys Nous 11 bcncrafts.com

15

Castell dels Tres Dragons

J7 Passeig de Picasso 932 56 22 00 Arc de Triomf, Jaume I To the public

At the entrance to the Parc de la Ciutadella *(p88)* is the fortress-like Castell dels Tres Dragons (Castle of the Three Dragons), probably named after a play by Serafí Pitarra (Frederic Soler). A classic example of Catalonia's Modernista architecture, this crenellated brick edifice was built by Lluís Domènech i Montaner for the 1888 Universal Exhibition. He later used the building as a workshop for Modernista design, and it became a focus of the movement. Shortly afterwards it housed the History Museum and was later the home of the Biology Museum. The building now serves as a laboratory of the Science Museum and is open only to researchers.

16 

Basílica de Santa Maria del Mar

H7 Pl Sta Maria 1 Jaume I 10am-8:30pm daily santamariadelmarbarcelona.org

This beautiful building, the name of which translates to Our Lady of the Sea, is the city's favourite church. It has superb acoustics for concerts and is the only example of a church entirely in the Catalan Gothic style. Completed in 1383, the basilica took only 55 years to build, with money donated by local merchants and shipbuilders. This speed – unrivalled in the Middle Ages – gave it a unity of style both inside and out. The west front features a 15th-century rose window of the *Coronation of the Virgin*. More stained glass from the 15th to

Crenellated Castell dels Tres Dragons rising from the trees

The spectacular Church of Santa Maria del Mar ↑

the 18th centuries lights the wide nave and high aisles. Though the choir stalls, the Baroque altar and furnishings were burned in the Civil War, their simple restoration creates a sense of space. The rooftop viewing terraces offer the chance to get closer to features such as the gargoyles and the rose window. The 360-degree views are breathtaking.

17 

MUHBA El Call

G7 Placeta de Manuel Ribé 3 Jaume I, Liceu 11am-2pm Wed, 11am-3pm & 4-7pm Sat & Sun barcelona.cat/museuhistoria/en/heritages/els-espais-del-muhba/muhba-el-call

One of the many branches of the Museu d'Història de Barcelona *(p80)*, this information centre occupies a modern building over what was once the home of Yusef Bonhiac, a medieval weaver. Its small collection includes artifacts from medieval life in El Call, Barcelona's former Jewish quarter, such as two tombstones inscribed with Hebrew. The touch-screen information panels and exhibitions give an excellent overview of the area and the lives of its inhabitants. The centre also offers occasional activities, which might include walking tours, or fascinating lectures on medieval Barcelona.

BLOODY SUNDAY

Much of the city's medieval Barri Gòtic remains remarkably unscathed following the violence of the Spanish Civil War, but it was not entirely untouched. Just north of MUHBA El Call, in El Call Major, Plaça Sant Felipe Neri was one of the bloodiest sites of the conflict. On Sunday 30 January 1938, two bombs were dropped by Italian forces during a bombardment in support of Franco's Nationalist regime. Of the 42 fatalities, most were children – orphaned refugees escaping the fighting in Madrid – who had taken shelter in the basement of the church of Sant Felipe Neri. Its Baroque façade is still stippled with shrapnel marks from the explosion. For years after the end of the war, Franco's supporters spread false rumours that the shrapnel scars were bullet holes left by rebels as they massacred the church's priests.

→ Parc de la Ciutadella's epic fountain, and *(inset)* its pleasant boating lake

18

Parc de la Ciutadella

J7 Passeig de Picasso 1 Barceloneta, Ciutadella-Vila Olímpica 7am-10:30pm daily

Colourful parrots take flight from the tops of palm trees and orange groves dotted about this popular park. A perfect picnic spot, the city's largest central green space was once the site of a massive star-shaped citadel, built for Felipe V between 1715 and 1720 following a 14-month siege of Barcelona. The fortress was intended to house soldiers to keep law and order, but was never used for this purpose. It was converted into a prison and became notorious during the Napoleonic occupation, and, during the 19th-century liberal repressions, it was much-hated as a symbol of centralized power.

In 1878, under General Prim, whose statue stands in the middle of the park, the citadel was pulled down and the park given to the city to become, in 1888, the venue of the Universal Exhibition. Three buildings survived: the Governor's Palace, now a school; the chapel; and the arsenal, which remains home to the Catalan parliament.

The park offers more cultural and leisure activities than any other in the city, and is particularly popular on Sunday afternoons when people gather to play instruments, dance, relax, head out onto the boating lake for a punt or enjoy a visit to the zoo.

The **Zoo de Barcelona** was laid out in the 1940s to what was, at the time, an enlightened design; although the enclosures are not large, the animals are separated by moats instead of bars. In recent years, the zoo has turned increasingly to conservation and protection, returning more than 30 per cent of animals born there to their natural habitats.

Standing by the zoo's entrance is a replica of an 1885 sculpture by Catalan artist Roig i Soler, *The Lady with the Umbrella*, which has become a symbol of Barcelona (the original statue is stored by the council). The zoo has a plethora of family-friendly activities, including interactive animal experiences and a face-painting area, ideal for smaller children.

Works by Catalan sculptors, such as Marès, Arnau, Carbonell, Clarà, Llimona, Gargallo, Dunyach and Fuxà, can be found across

INSIDER TIP
Laps of the Lake

On a sunny day, there's nothing nicer than renting a rowing boat and heading out on the lake in the middle of the Parc de la Ciutadella. It's especially popular on Sunday afternoons; go early to beat the crowds.

the park, alongside pieces by contemporary artists such as Tàpies and Botero.

Along the park's southern boundary is an imposing Neo-Classical building, designed by the architect Antoni Rovira i Trias. Now home to the **Museu Centre Martorell d'Exposicions**, a branch of the Science Museum, it hosts a small exhibition on animal natural history. Nearby, the recently restored Umbráculo del Parque de la Ciutadella – an elegant 19th-century iron-and-glass greenhouse – features a lush array of subtropical and Mediterranean plants.

The northeastern corner of the park features a magnificent fountain, a cascading waterfall topped by a chariot rider spurring on a team of horses and flanked by griffins. It was designed by architect Josep Fontseré, with the help of Antoni Gaudí, who was a young student at the time.

Zoo de Barcelona
Parc de la Ciutadella
Ciutadella-Vila Olímpica
Hours vary, check website
zoobarcelona.cat

Museu Centre Martorell d'Exposicions
Parc de la Ciutadella
Ciutadella-Vila Olímpica
Hours vary, check website
museuciencies.cat/en/the-nat/venues/centre-martorell-dexposicions

19 

La Llotja

H7 Carrer del Consolat de Mar 2 Barceloneta Mid-May-Aug: Sat for guided tours (in Catalan and Spanish only) llotjademar.cat

La Llotja (meaning commodity exchange) was built in the 1380s as the headquarters of the Consolat de Mar. It was remodelled in Neo-Classical style in 1771 and housed the city's stock exchange until 1994, the original Gothic hall acting as the trading floor. The upper floors housed the Barcelona School of Fine Arts.

↑ Neo-Classical interior of the stunning La Llotja

20 El Born Centre de Cultura i Memòria

H7 Plaça Comercial 12 Jaume I, Barceloneta Mar-Oct: 10am-8pm Tue-Sun; Nov-Feb: 10am-7pm Tue-Sat, 10am-8pm Sun elbornculturaimemoria.barcelona.cat

This covered market, with its ornate ironwork and crystal roof, was Barcelona's main market until the early 1970s, when it outgrew its location.

While being remodelled, extensive 18th-century ruins were discovered beneath its foundations. These ruins are now the focal point of the cultural centre, set off by talks, exhibitions and screenings.

The street names here hint at the trade in Barcelona's old mercantile hub: Flassaders was where you would go for a woven blanket; Vidriería was once lit up with glass-blowers' torches. A few of these establishments remain, but they are now significantly outnumbered by chic boutiques.

Much of this area was razed after Barcelona fell to the French-Spanish forces during the War of Succession. This key event is remembered each year on 11 September, with activities focused on a monument dedicated to those who died in 1714, which is located near the market.

21 Arc de Triomf

J6 Passeig Lluís Companys Arc de Triomf

The main gateway to the 1888 Universal Exhibition, which filled the Parc de la Ciutadella *(p88)*, was designed by Josep Vilaseca i Casanovas. It is built of brick in Mudéjar (Spanish Moorish) style, with sculpted allegories of crafts, industry and business. The frieze by Josep Reynés on the main façade represents the city welcoming foreign visitors. Reliefs on one side symbolize agriculture and industry, while those on the other depict commerce and art. Climb to the viewing terrace at the top of the arch during the 48h Open House Barcelona festival, held at the end of October.

22 Museu de la Xocolata

H7 Comerç 36 Jaume I, Arc de Triomf 10am-7pm Mon-Sat, 10am-3pm Sun & public hols 1 & 6 Jan, 1 May, 11 Sep, 25 & 26 Dec museuxocolata.cat

Founded by Barcelona's chocolate- and pastry-makers' union, this museum takes you through the history of one

EAT

Some of the city's best tapas bars are in El Born. Here are our favourites.

Elsa y Fred
J6 Carrer Rec Comtal 11
elsayfred.es

Cal Pep
H7 Plaça de les Olles 8 calpep.com

Bar del Pla
H7 Carrer de Montcada 2
bardelpla.cat

Casa Lolea
H6 Carrer de Sant Pere Més Alt 49
casalolea.com

Richly decorated Arc de Triomf, a major Barcelona landmark

of the most universally loved foods. The chocolatey exhibits cover the discovery of cocoa in South America through to the invention of the first chocolate machine in Barcelona, using old posters, photographs and footage. The real thing is displayed in a homage to the art of the *mona* – a Catalan invention, this was a traditional Easter cake that evolved over centuries into an edible sculpture. Every year, *pastissiers* compete to create finely decorated chocolate versions of landmarks or folk figures with jewels and other materials.

As well as activities for children, the museum hosts workshops for adults. Don't miss the museum's shop, which sells – as expected – all manner of delicious chocolatey treats. For those craving more, Carrer de Petrixol, 1 km (half a mile) away, is known as "sweet street" for its myriad chocolate shops. Locals flock here to indulge in steaming cups of drinking chocolate.

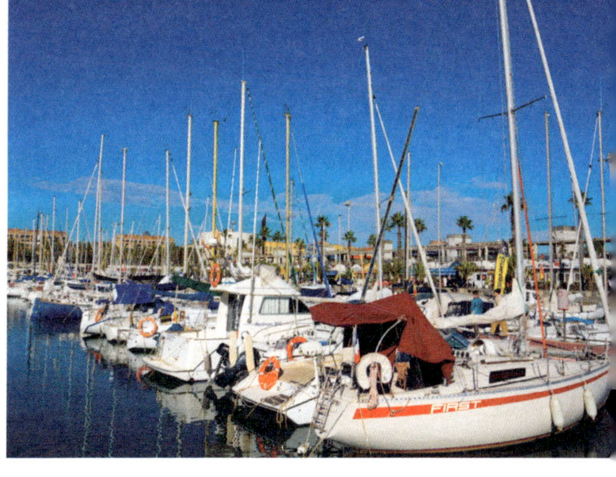

↑ Picturesque marina at Port Olímpic, bustling with small pleasure boats

23   

Port Olímpic

L9 Ciutadella-Vila Olímpica

A gateway to some of the city's best beaches, Port Olímpic was created out of the old industrial waterfront to host sailing events for the 1992 summer Olympics. The dramatic makeover redefined the city's skyline and laid out 4 km (2 miles) of open promenade and pristine stretches of sand. The marina, also built for the 1992 games, is home to one of the city's most eye-catching symbols – *El Peix*, the emblematic golden fish sculpture by Canadian artist Frank Gehry. The spectacular fish stretches, 56 m (184 ft) long, next to the water and its steel scales glimmer in the sunshine.

PICTURE PERFECT

Pailebot Santa Eulàlia

Bobbing in the water at the palm-lined Moll de la Fusta (Timber Quay), this elegant three-mast schooner was originally christened *Carmen Flores*. It first set sail from Spain in 1918. In 1997, the Museum Marítim beautifully restored the ship.

On the seafront are twin skyscrapers, one occupied by offices, the other by the Hotel Arts. They stand beside the former Vila Olímpica built to house athletes. The port has now been transformed into a vibrant public space, with new promenades, improved beach access and a focus on sustainable, sea-linked activities. Nightclubs have given way to a breezy waterfront lined with restaurants offering a range of international cuisines, catering to the tastes of the multitude of visitors who make use of the berthing facilities. The renovated Moll de Gregal is home to a vast gastronomic balcony featuring even more stylish Mediterranean restaurants.

After lunching on plates of fresh seafood, take off your shoes and head onto the sand for a stroll along the string of beaches extending in either direction, edged by the palm-fringed promenade. Behind the promenade, the coastal road winds around a palm-filled park that lies beside another three beaches, each divided by rocky breakwaters. Swimming is safe off the gently sloping, sandy strands. For those seeking a more energetic experience, several of the marina's charter firms offer boating excursions, "taster" sailing trips, kayaking and paddle-surfing.

24 Port Vell

 **G9 Barceloneta, Drassanes**

Barcelona's marina is located at the foot of La Rambla *(p72)*, just beyond the old customs house. This house was built in 1902 at the Portal de la Pau, the city's former maritime entrance. To the south, the Moll de Barcelona serves as the passenger pier for visiting liners. In front of the customs house, La Rambla is connected to the yacht clubs on the Moll d'Espanya by a swing bridge and a pedestrian jetty, known as La Rambla de Mar. The Moll d'Espanya is home to Barcelona's impressive Aquàrium and a vast shopping and restaurant complex, the Maremagnum.

On the shore, the Moll de la Fusta (Timber Wharf) has red structures inspired by the bridge at Arles, in France, painted by Van Gogh in 1888. A huge prawn, designed by Javier Mariscal, sits atop one of them. At the end of the wharf is the colourful *El Cap de Barcelona (Barcelona Head)*, a 20-m- (66-ft-) tall sculpture by renowned Pop artist Roy Lichtenstein. The luxury marina on the other side of the Moll d'Espanya was once lined with warehouses. The former General Stores building is the sole building still standing from Barcelona's Old Port. The stores were designed in 1881 by the engineer Maurici Garrán and were originally intended for use as trading depots. They were refurbished in 1992 and today house the Museu d'Història de Catalunya *(p97)*. Great views of the port can be seen from the top of Mirador de Colom *(p96)*.

GREAT VIEW
Golondrinas

Board a *golondrina* (meaning "swallow") - a small double-decker boat - for a sightseeing trip around Port Vell. The tours take 40 to 60 minutes and offer fantastic from-the-sea views of the steep, castle-topped hill of Montjuïc towards the industrial port.

25 Barceloneta

 **H9 Barceloneta**

Barcelona's historic fishing district lies on a triangular tongue of land jutting into the sea just below the city centre. It is renowned for its little restaurants and cafés, as well as its lively atmosphere. Its beach is also the closest to the city centre and is well equipped with lifeguards, wheelchair access, showers and play areas for children.

The area was designed in 1753 by the architect and military engineer Juan Martín Cermeño to rehouse people made homeless by the construction, just inland, of the Ciutadella fortress *(p88)*. Laid out in an easy-to-navigate grid system with narrow two- and three-storey houses, in which each room has a window looking over the street, it has housed fishers and workers since the 18th century.

In the small Plaça de la Barceloneta is the Baroque church of Sant Miquel del Port, which was also designed by Cermeño. Nearby, the

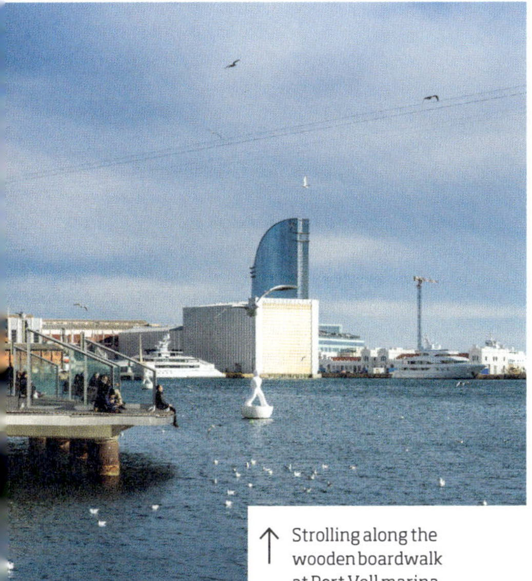

↑ Strolling along the wooden boardwalk at Port Vell marina

neighbourhood's huge main square is dominated by a popular covered market.

Today, Barceloneta's fishing fleet is still based in the nearby Moll del Rellotge (the clock dock), where stands a small clock tower. On the opposite side of this harbour is the Torre de Sant Sebastià, terminus of the cable car that runs right across the port, via the World Trade Centre, to the garden-filled slopes of Montjuïc.

Aquàrium

G9 Moll d'Espanya
Barceloneta, Drassanes
Hours vary, check website
aquariumbcn.com

Populated by over 11,000 creatures belonging to 450 different species, Barcelona's aquarium is one of the biggest in Europe. The three-storey glass aquarium focuses particularly on the marine life of the local Mediterranean coast. Two of Catalonia's nature reserves, the southern Delta de L'Ebre *(p198)* and the Medes isles off the Costa Brava, are given a tank apiece. Tropical seas are also represented and moving platforms ferry visitors through a glass tunnel under an "ocean" filled with toothy sharks, soaring rays and bright schools of sunfish. A large hall provides ample space for children's activities, including an island reached via crawl-through glass tunnels.

↑ Sharks and schools of fish swim above the glass tunnels of the Aquàrium

STAY

The Serras Hotel Barcelona

Youthful Serras is a firm favourite of those in the know. Perks include a rooftop plunge pool.

G8 Passeig de Colom 9 serras barcelona.com

Chic & Basic Born

Great style on a budget, this 19th-century townhouse has small, cleverly designed rooms.

H7 Calle Princessa 50 chicandbasic.com

Hotel Duquesa de Cardona

This luxurious hotel has great port views and a rooftop pool.

G8 Passeig de Colom 12 hduquesade cardona.com

Sandy beach stretching along the city's coast

↑ A complete replica of the *Real*, housed in the *(inset)* Museu Marítim and Drassanes

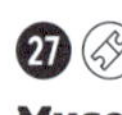

Museu Marítim and Drassanes

F8 Avinguda de les Drassanes Drassanes 10am-8pm daily 1 & 6 Jan, 25 & 26 Dec mmb.cat

The great galleys that were instrumental in making Barcelona a major seafaring power were built in the sheds of the Drassanes (shipyards). Today, the shipyards house the maritime museum, a sprawling exhibition space covering more than 10,000 sq m (108,000 sq ft) and fronted by glass windows. The docks were founded in the mid-13th century, when dynastic marriages uniting the kingdoms of Sicily and Aragón meant that better maritime communications between the two became a priority. Three of the yards' four original corner towers survive. Indeed these royal dry docks are now the largest and most complete surviving medieval complex of their kind in the world.

Among the vessels to slip from the Drassanes' vaulted halls was the *Real*, flagship of Don Juan of Austria, who led the Christian fleet to the famous victory against the Turks at Lepanto in 1571.

Among the vessels to slip from the Drassanes' vaulted halls was the *Real*, flagship of Don Juan of Austria, who led the Christian fleet to the famous victory against the Turks at Lepanto in 1571.

The undoubted highlight of the museum's collection is a full-scale replica of the *Real* decorated in red and gold. The renovated halls also host temporary exhibitions with a maritime theme, as well as displaying other historic boats created right in these shipyards. With many 18th- to 20th-century instruments preserved in the museum's permanent collection, visitors can also track the development of nautical navigation tools from the sextant to the depth gauge.

Included in the admission fee is an audio guide of the museum's collections, as well as a visit to the *Santa Eulàlia* *(p91)*, a restored century-old schooner moored in Port Vell.

Mirador de Colom

F8 Plaça del Portal de la Pau 932 85 38 54 Drassanes 8:30am-2:30pm daily (last adm: 1:30pm)

The Columbus monument at the bottom of La Rambla *(p72)* was designed by architect Gaietà Buigas for the 1888 Universal Exhibition, when Catalans considered the explorer a Catalan rather than an Italian. The bronze statue of the explorer atop the column was designed by Spanish sculptor Rafael Atché. As Columbus's legacy is reconsidered in the 21st century, from the perspective of the peoples he enslaved and exploited, very few modern Catalans are keen to claim him as one of their own, with some calling for the statue to be removed.

The towering monument marks the spot where Columbus stepped ashore in 1493 after returning from his voyage to the Caribbean. The pointing gesture Columbus makes upon his pedestal is not towards the Americas (as is often surmised) but is simply a dramatic pose.

A lift leads to a viewing platform at the top of the monument from where visitors can take in panoramic vistas across the city.

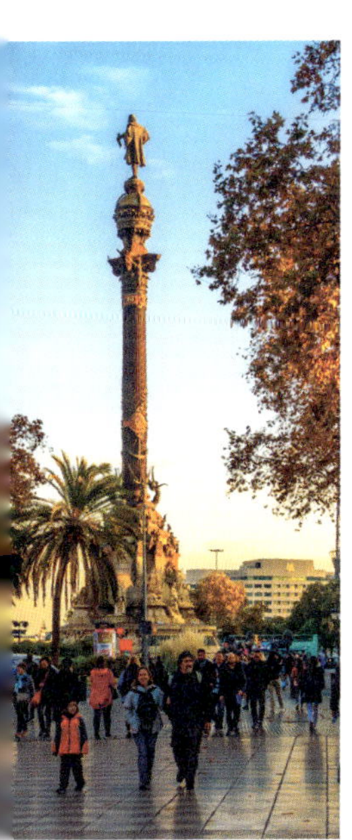

The 60-m- (197-ft-) tall Mirador de Colom in La Rambla

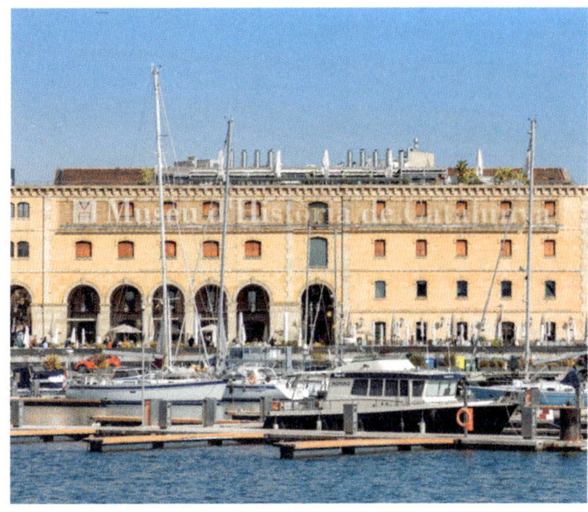

Museu d'Història de Catalunya at the Marina Port Vell, off the Mediterranean coast

29  

Museu d'Història de Catalunya

H8 Plaça Pau Vila 3 Barceloneta, Drassanes 10am-7pm Tue-Sat (to 8pm Wed), 10am-2:30pm Sun & public hols 1 & 6 Jan, 1 May, 10 Jun, 25 & 26 Dec mhcat.cat

Charting the long history of Catalonia, this museum explores the region from Lower Palaeolithic times to its heyday as a maritime power and industrial pioneer. On the second floor, there are interactive exhibits including the Moorish invasion, Romanesque architecture *(p178)*, medieval monastic life and the rise of Catalan seafaring. Third-floor exhibits cover the industrial revolution and the impact of steam power and electricity on the economy. Here visitors can try on medieval armour or climb aboard a 1920s tram. The first floor is reserved for temporary exhibits. A free guide provides information in English.

On the fourth floor is the café-restaurant. Note that you do not need to have a ticket to the museum to sample the menu of tasty seafood dishes, which are served alongside beautiful views over the yacht-filled port from the terrace.

CHRISTOPHER COLUMBUS

The first European to successfully voyage to the Americas in the late 15th century, Christopher Columbus started a period of European conquest and colonization that lasted for centuries. A controversial figure during his lifetime as well as today, he was arrested in 1500 on allegations of brutality towards the Indigenous peoples, after establishing a colony on the Caribbean island of Hispaniola, and brought back to Spain to face indictment. While those charges were later dropped, he was stripped of his titles. In 1502, he set sail for the fourth and last time to explore Central America. He died in Valladolid in 1506 and is buried in Seville's cathedral.

A SHORT WALK
BARRI GÒTIC

Distance 1 km (half a mile) **Nearest metro** Jaume I **Time** 15 minutes

The Barri Gòtic (Gothic Quarter) is the true heart of Barcelona. The oldest part of the city, it was the site chosen by the Romans in the reign of Augustus (27 BCE–14 CE) on which to found a new *colonia* (town), and has been the location of the city's administrative buildings ever since. The Roman forum was on the Plaça de Sant Jaume, where the medieval Palau de la Generalitat, Catalonia's parliament, and the Ajuntament, Barcelona's town hall, now stand. A walk around the area also takes in the Gothic cathedral and royal palace, the latter forming part of the city's complex of history museums. Dip inside the palace's cellars to see the streets and shops of ancient Roman Barcelona, Barcino.

Built on the Roman city wall, **Casa de l'Ardiaca**, *the Gothic-Renaissance arch-deacon's residence, now houses the city's historical archives.*

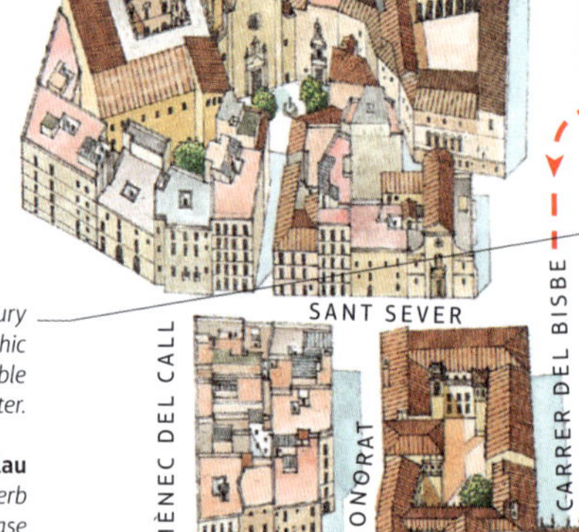

The façade and spire are 20th-century additions to the original Gothic **Cathedral** (p70). *White geese amble around its charming Gothic cloister.*

The seat of Catalonia's governor, the **Palau de la Generalitat** (p82) *has superb Gothic features, including a stone staircase rising to an open-air, arcaded gallery.*

↑ Intricate 20th-century façade and spire of Barcelona Cathedral

To La Rambla

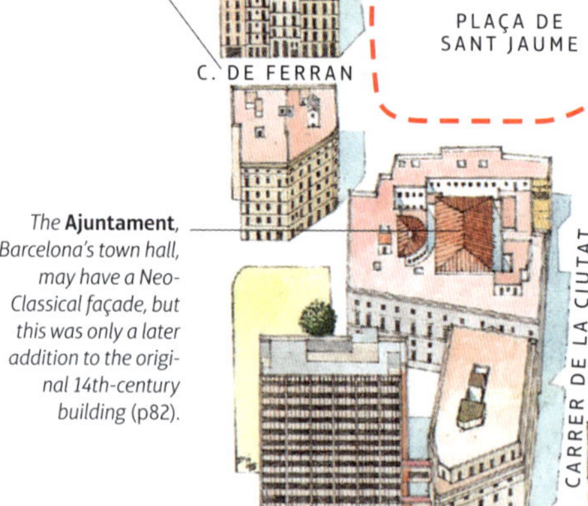

The **Ajuntament**, *Barcelona's town hall, may have a Neo-Classical façade, but this was only a later addition to the original 14th-century building* (p82).

Locator Map
For more detail see p68

Walking under the arches in the internal courtyard of the Museu Frederic Marès

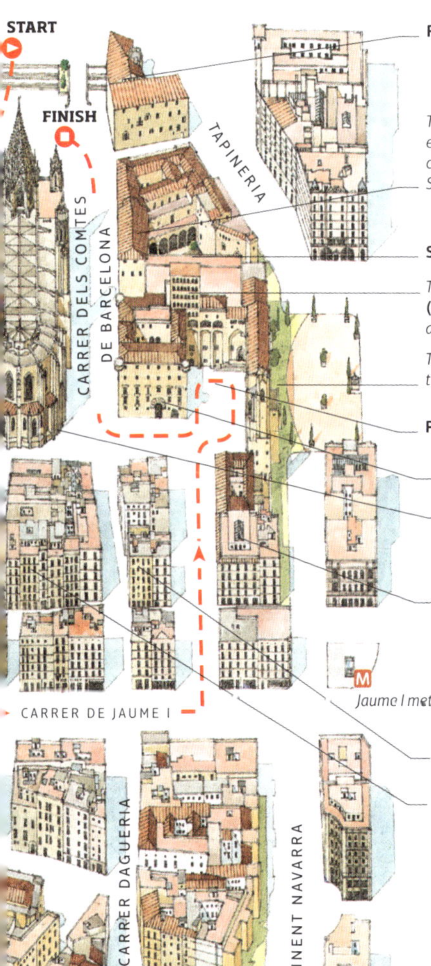

Roman city wall

The mainstay of the **Museu Frederic Mares's** *extraordinarily eclectic and high-quality collections is the extensive display of Spanish sculpture* (p81).

Saló del Tinell

The **Museu d'Història de Barcelona (MUHBA)**, *the former royal palace, has a dramatic exterior* (p80).

The **Capella Reial de Santa Àgata** *is one of the highlights of the MUHBA Plaça del Rei.*

Plaça del Rei

Palau del Lloctinent

Temple of Augustus

This section of **Museu d'Història de Barcelona (MUHBA)** *features the world's most extensive subterranean Roman ruins.*

Cereria Subirà *candle shop*

The **Centre Excursionista de Catalunya** *displays Roman columns from the Temple of Augustus in its entrance courtyard; the site is marked by a millstone in the street outside.*

Did You Know?

The Temple of Augustus was discovered during building work in the 19th century.

A LONG WALK
EL BORN

Distance 1.5 km (1 mile) **Nearest metro** Jaume I **Time** 30 minutes

The tiny district of El Born, across the Via Laietana from the Barrí Gotic, has made a comeback. Close to the waterfront, it flourished in Catalonia's mercantile heyday from the 13th century. The narrow streets still bear the names of the artisans and guilds that set up here. While it retains a medieval air, El Born is a lively area with bars, restaurants, shops and museums.

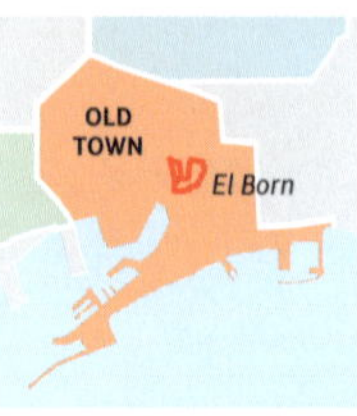

Locator Map
For more detail see p68

From Jaume I metro station in **Plaça de l'Angel**, *set off on a walk down Carrer de l'Argenteria.*

There is a carved head protruding from the wall on the right at the corner of **Carrer dels Miralles**.

Bodega del Born *is one of a handful of old-fashioned taverns that have remained unchanged for decades.*

The charming **Plaça de Santa Maria** *is a perfect place for a coffee or a glass of wine on a café terrace.*

The Neo-Classical **La Llotja** (p89) *was once the city's stock exchange.*

Sunny afternoon on Plaça de Sant Agustí Vell

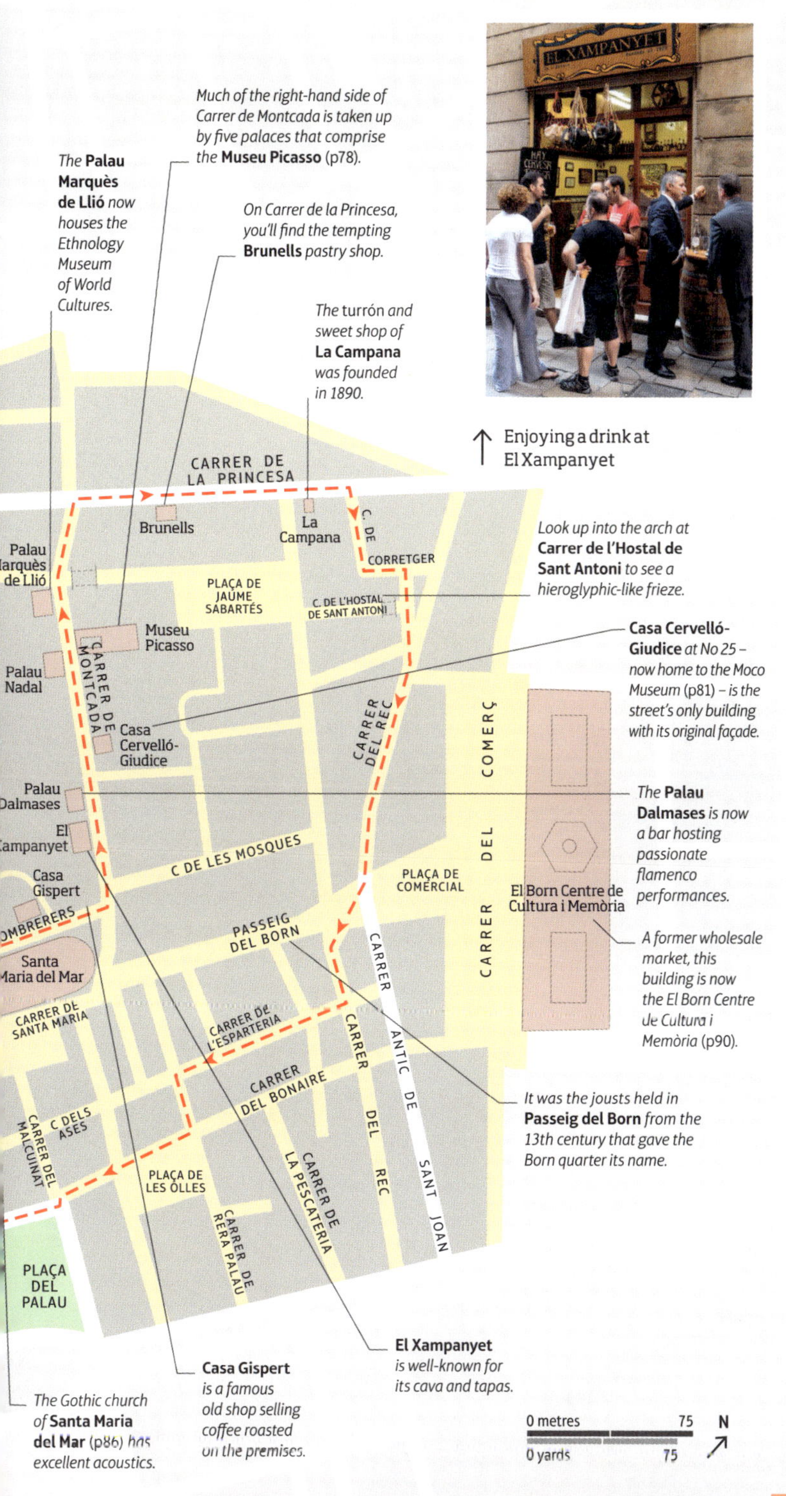

↑ Enjoying a drink at El Xampanyet

A neck-craning view of the central atrium of La Pedrera

EIXAMPLE

Barcelona claims to have the greatest collection of Art Nouveau buildings of any city in Europe. The style, known in Catalonia as Modernisme, flourished after 1854, when the government decided to pull down the medieval walls to allow the city to develop into what had previously been a military zone. The designs of the civil engineer Ildefons Cerdà i Sunyer were chosen for the new expansion *(eixample)* inland. These plans called for a rigid grid system of streets, but at each intersection, the corners were chamfered and cut off at a 45° angle, to allow the buildings there to overlook the junctions or squares. The Modernistes, however, had other ideas for this land, as seen in the Diagonal, a main avenue that runs from the wealthy area of Pedralbes down to the sea, and the Hospital de la Santa Creu i Sant Pau by architect Lluís Domènech i Montaner. He hated the grid system and deliberately angled the hospital to look down the diagonal Avinguda de Gaudí towards Antoni Gaudí's church of the Sagrada Família. The wealth of Barcelona's commercial elite and their passion for all things new allowed them to give free rein to the age's most innovative architects in designing their residences, as well as public buildings, creating a unique cityscape.

In the late 20th century, many shops, bars, clubs and restaurants catering to the LGBTQ+ community sprang up in this fashionable area, creating a sub-neighbourhood known as "Gaixample".

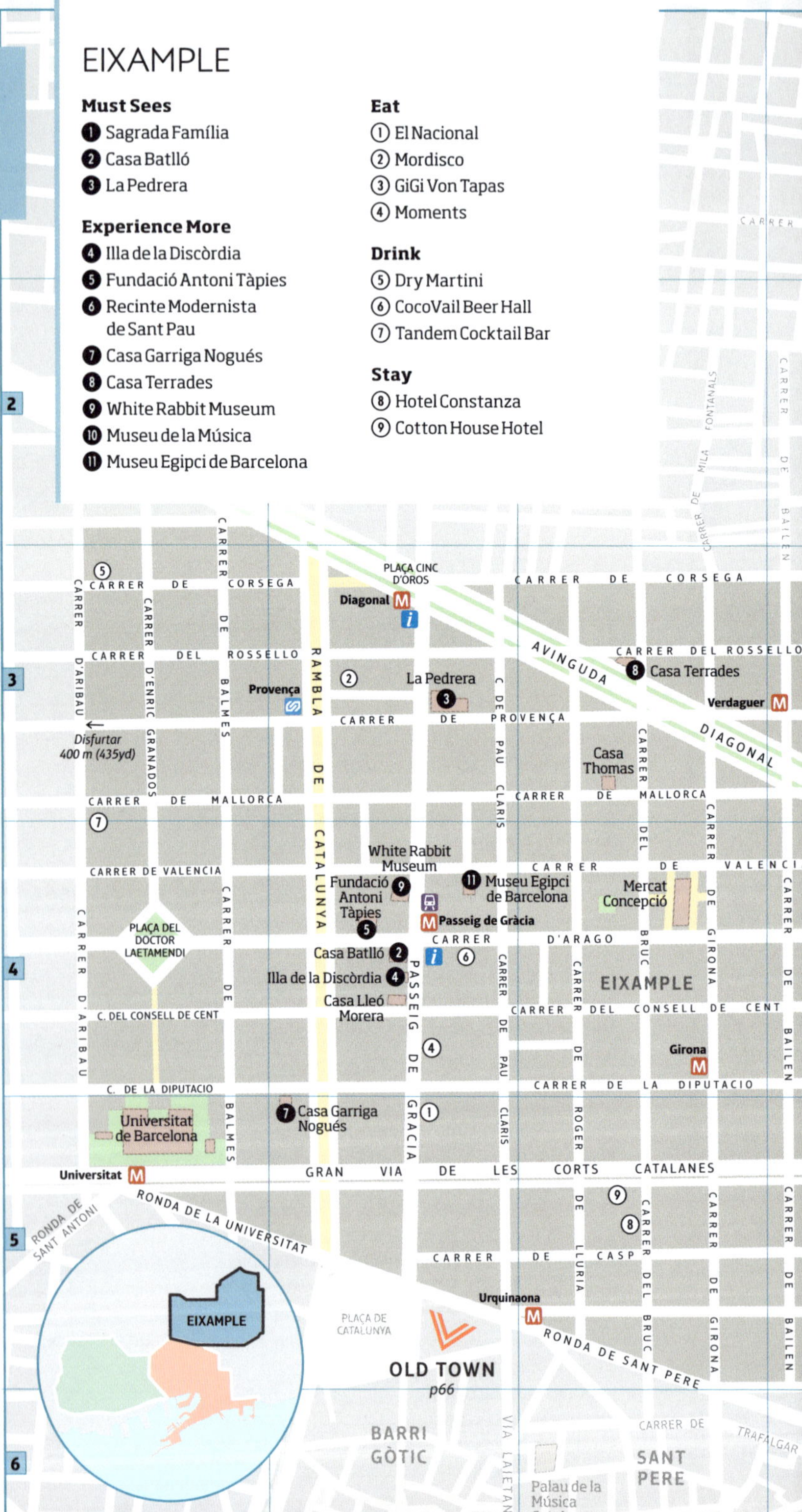

EIXAMPLE
Must Sees
1 Sagrada Família
2 Casa Batlló
3 La Pedrera
Experience More
4 Illa de la Discòrdia
5 Fundació Antoni Tàpies
6 Recinte Modernista de Sant Pau
7 Casa Garriga Nogués
8 Casa Terrades
9 White Rabbit Museum
10 Museu de la Música
11 Museu Egipci de Barcelona
Eat
1 El Nacional
2 Mordisco
3 GiGi Von Tapas
4 Moments
Drink
5 Dry Martini
6 CocoVail Beer Hall
7 Tandem Cocktail Bar
Stay
8 Hotel Constanza
9 Cotton House Hotel
PLAÇA CINC D'OROS
Diagonal
La Pedrera
Provença
Casa Terrades
Verdaguer
AVINGUDA DIAGONAL
Casa Thomas
Disfurtar 400 m (435yd)
RAMBLA DE CATALUNYA
White Rabbit Museum
Fundació Antoni Tàpies
Museu Egipci de Barcelona
Mercat Concepció
Passeig de Gràcia
PLAÇA DEL DOCTOR LAETAMENDI
Casa Batlló
Illa de la Discòrdia
Casa Lleó Morera
EIXAMPLE
Girona
Universitat de Barcelona
Casa Garriga Nogués
Universitat
GRAN VIA DE LES CORTS CATALANES
RONDA DE SANT ANTONI
RONDA DE LA UNIVERSITAT
Urquinaona
PLAÇA DE CATALUNYA
RONDA DE SANT PERE
OLD TOWN p66
BARRI GÒTIC
VIA LAIETANA
Palau de la Música Catalana
SANT PERE
CARRER DE TRAFALGAR

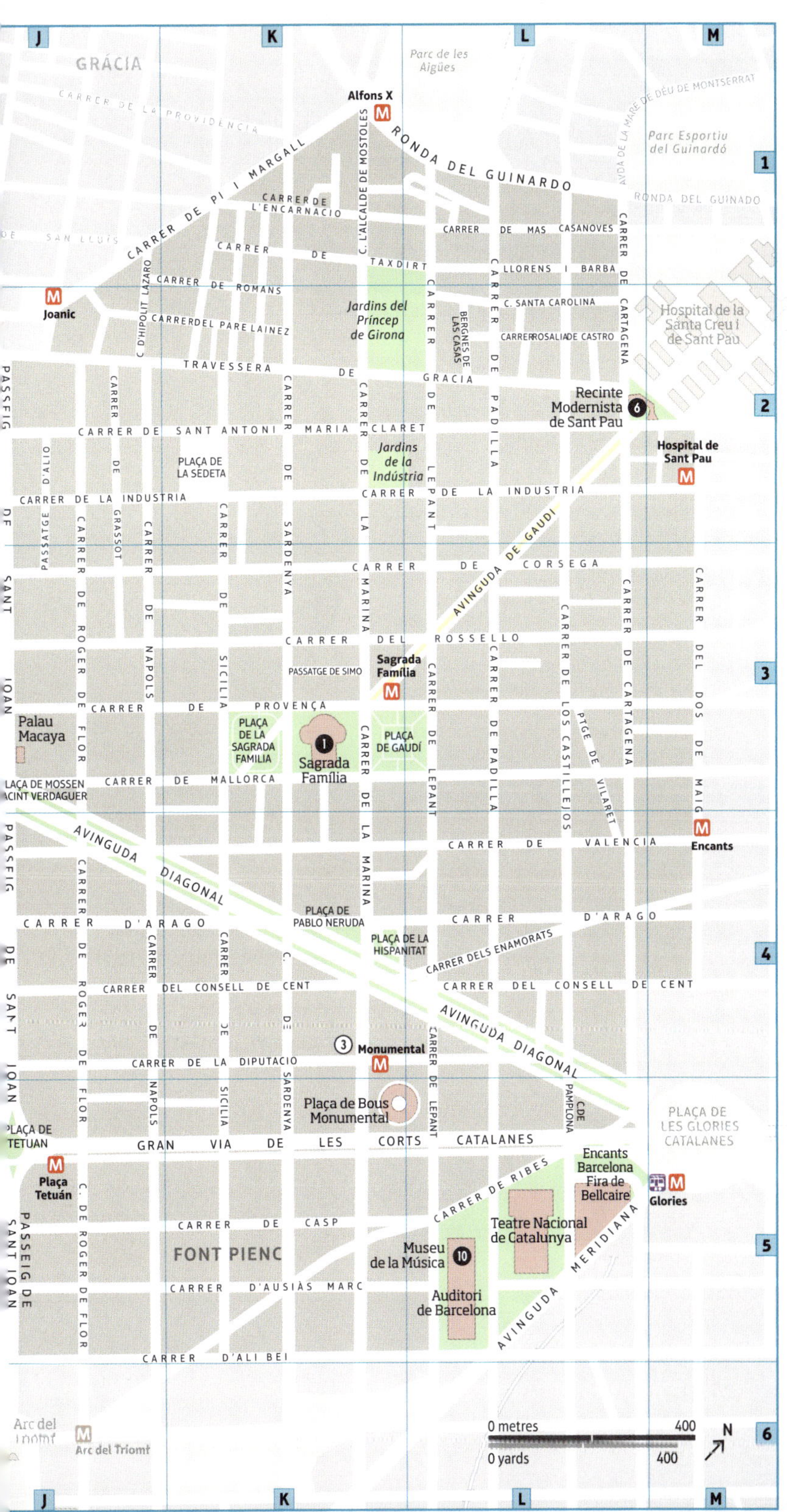

GRÀCIA
Parc de les Aigües
Alfons X
Parc Esportiu del Guinardó
RONDA DEL GUINARDO
Joanic
Jardins del Príncep de Girona
Hospital de la Santa Creu i de Sant Pau
Recinte Modernista de Sant Pau
Hospital de Sant Pau
PLAÇA DE LA SEDETA
Jardins de la Indústria
AVINGUDA DE GAUDÍ
Sagrada Família
Palau Macaya
PLAÇA DE LA SAGRADA FAMILIA
PLAÇA DE GAUDÍ
Sagrada Família
PLAÇA DE MOSSEN JACINT VERDAGUER
Encants
AVINGUDA DIAGONAL
PLAÇA DE PABLO NERUDA
PLAÇA DE LA HISPANITAT
Monumental
Plaça de Bous Monumental
PLAÇA DE LES GLORIES CATALANES
PLAÇA DE TETUAN
GRAN VIA DE LES CORTS CATALANES
Plaça Tetuán
Encants Barcelona Fira de Bellcaire
Glories
Teatre Nacional de Catalunya
FONT PIENC
Museu de la Música
Auditori de Barcelona
Arc del Triomf
0 metres 400
0 yards 400
N

1

SAGRADA FAMÍLIA

K3 Carrer de Sardenya Sagrada Família 19, 43, 51 Apr-Sep: 9am-8pm daily (to 6pm Sat, from 10:30am Sun); Oct & Mar: 9am-7pm daily (to 6pm Sat, from 10:30am Sun); Nov-Feb: 9am-6pm daily (from 10:30am Sun, to 2pm 1 & 6 Jan, 25 & 26 Dec); timed tickets only, advance booking advisable sagradafamilia.org

Europe's most unconventional church, the Templo Expiatorio de la Sagrada Família is an emblem of the city. Crammed with symbolism inspired by nature and striving for originality, it is Gaudí's greatest work and a towering monument to his creativity.

People attending a Mass in the Sagrada Família's soaring nave

Architect Francisco de Paula del Villar i Lozano was initially charged with building a Christian temple in Barcelona. Envisioning a Gothic-style building, he drew up plans for a three-nave church complete with flying buttresses and a pointed bell tower. In 1883, a year after work had begun on a Neo-Gothic church on the site and its crypt had been built, the task of completing it was given to the 31-year-old Gaudí, who changed everything, extemporizing as he went along. He designed it, as a medieval cathedral, to be considered like a book in stone, with each element representing a biblical event or aspect of Christian faith. It's design avoids right angles and uses as few straight lines as possible, paying tribute to the organic shapes found in nature. The building became Gaudí's life's work; he lived on the site for 14 years. At the time of his death (he is buried in the crypt) only one tower on the Nativity façade – dedicated to the apostle Barnabas – had been completed. Work resumed after the Civil War and several more towers have since been finished according to his original plans. Work continues today, financed by a combination of ticket sales and private donations.

> **Crammed with symbolism inspired by nature and striving for originality, it is Gaudí's greatest work and a towering monument to his creativity.**

Timeline

1866

▲ Josep Maria Bocabella founds the Association of Saint Joseph Devout, with the aim to build a temple in the city.

1887

▲ The vicarage is completed. This building becomes Gaudí's work space and is where he spends his last years.

1954

▲ Work begins on the Passion façade, 62 years after it began on the Nativity façade.

2017

▲ On the 135th anniversary of the laying of the foundation stone, 70 per cent of the basilica is finished.

Must See

↑ The awe-inspiring architecture of Gaudí's Sagrada Família

PICTURE PERFECT
Mirror, Mirror on the Floor

The Plaça de Gaudí offers one of the best views of the Sagrada Família. From this garden, you can capture a great shot of the basilica reflected in the lake.

2021

△ The Tower of the Virgin Mary, crowned with a 12-pointed illuminated star, is completed.

2023

△ The Four Evangelist Towers are finished, topped with their sculptural symbols: an ox, lion, eagle and angel.

2026

The next tower to be completed is the Jesus Christ Tower, set to be the tallest structure in Barcelona.

Exploring the Sagrada Família

Gaudí's masterpiece seemingly climbs closer to the heavens as the years progress, its mosaic-covered towers reaching towards the clouds. Of the three decorated façades, the Nativity *(p110)* and Passion *(p111)* have been completed, while the Glory is still a work in progress.

The interior of the basilica more than matches the mesmerizing exterior. Soaring pillars form a canopy-like roof and jewel-hued stained glass creates pools of light on the floor of the nave, giving the effect of walking across a magical forest's floor. The experience culminates at the main altar, which is drenched in natural light. It's a profound expression of the architect's devotion, and a challenge to even the firmest of non-believers to remain unmoved.

After touring the nave and climbing one of the towers, explore the museum in the crypt. Charting Gaudí's career and the development of the basilica, it ends at the foot of his tomb.

2019

The Sagrada Família finally received its official building permit, which Gaudí had applied for in 1885.

Spiral staircases

Towers with lift

13 of the 18 planned towers are complete, with the Jesus Tower due in 2026 and four towers on the Glory Facade to follow.

The altar canopy was designed by Gaudí.

The apse was the first part of the church Gaudí completed. Stairs lead down from here to the crypt below.

The crypt, where Gaudí is buried, was begun by the original architect, Francisco de Paula del Villar i Lozano, in 1882.

The controversial Passion façade was crafted from 1986 to 2000. Its sculpted figures are angular and often sinister.

GREAT VIEW
Get Low

Lie down on the floor of the nave and look up at the ceiling for a unique view of Gaudí's fantastical creation. Does it look like a vibrant coral reef or the inside of a colourful kaleidoscope?

1 Stained-glass windows bathe the nave in multi-coloured pools of light.

2 Spiral staircases lead you to the top of the bell towers, where you'll be rewarded with amazing views of the city.

3 The nave's roof is held up by soaring pillars that branch out at the top to form a canopy.

Finished in 1930, the Nativity façade has doorways which represent Faith, Hope and Charity. Scenes of the Nativity and Christ's childhood are embellished with symbolism.

The nave contains a forest of fluted pillars that support four galleries above the side aisles; a large number of skylights let in both natural and artificial light.

Illustration depicting the magnificent Sagrada Família, still under construction

THE FINISHED CHURCH

Over the years, Gaudí's initial ambitions have been fulfilled using various new technologies to achieve his vision. Still to come is the central tower representing Jesus Christ, which will rise to 172.5 m (566 ft) in the middle of four large towers representing the Evangelists. Four towers on the Glory (south) façade will match the existing four on the Passion (west) and Nativity (east) façades. An ambulatory will skirt the outside of the building. Construction of the church is expected to be completed in 2033.

Soaring bell towers on the honeycomb-like Nativity façade

NATIVITY FAÇADE

Finished according to Gaudí's instructions before his death, the lavish ornamentation on the eastern façade centres around three doors dedicated to Hope (left), Faith (right) and Charity, in the middle.

Hope Doorway

Above this door you'll see Joseph and the child Jesus watched over by Mary's parents, St Ann and St Joachim. The lintel of the door is composed of a woodcutter's two-handled saw and various other tools – all indicative of Joseph's profession

The spire above the doorway is in the form of an elongated boulder, which is an allusion to the holy Catalan mountain of Montserrat *(p168)*. At the base of this boulder sits Joseph in a boat; he bears a resemblance to Gaudí himself and is very likely a posthumous homage.

Did You Know?

The chameleons on this façade represent change, while the turtle signifies stability.

Faith Doorway

The heart of Jesus can be seen set into the lintel above this doorway. The scene on the lower left is the Visitation by Mary to Elizabeth, her cousin and mother of John the Baptist. On the right, Jesus wields a hammer and chisel in his father's workshop.

As it rises, the stonework forms an intricate pinnacle recording the fundamentals of Catholicism, including a lamp with three wicks for the Trinity, bunches of grapes and ears of wheat for the Eucharist, and a hand set with an eye, showing God's omniscience.

Charity Doorway

These double doors are separated by a column recording Jesus's genealogy. The three Magi are on the lower left of the door, with the shepherds opposite them. Out of the Nativity emerges the spiky tail of a many-pointed star, surrounded by a children's choir. Above the star is the Annunciation and the Coronation of the Virgin Mary by Jesus, and on top is a pelican sitting on a crown next to a glass egg bearing the JHS monogram of Jesus.

Stone depiction of the shepherds above the Charity doorway

GLORY FAÇADE

The southern façade is set to be the most monumental of the four and, based on Gaudí's plans, will represent the road to God. It will show humanity's history from Adam and Eve through to the Last Judgement, along with Jesus' teachings on eternal life. A large staircase signifying death, decorated with demons and tombs, will lead to the façade. The seven pillars supporting the structure will depict the seven sins at the base and the seven virtues at the top. Seven doors signify the sacraments that open the way to God. Clouds will rise up the bell towers to a glorious image of God.

PASSION FAÇADE

The Passion façade narrates Christ's final days leading up to the Crucifixion. Designed by Josep Maria Subirachs, whose boxy forms are very unlike the organic shapes on the Gaudí-designed Nativity façade, the Passion façade has divided critics since its completion.

Christ's Passion

The Passion façade depicts the sufferings and execution of Jesus, and its style reflects its subject matter. The statuary has attracted criticism for its angular, "dehumanised" carving, but Gaudí would probably have approved. He is known to have favoured an Expressionist style to give the story of Christ's Passion maximum impact. A great porch, whose roof is held up by six inclined, buttress-like swamp tree roots, shades the 12 groups of sculptures. The first scene (bottom left-hand corner) is the Last Supper, at which Jesus (standing) announces his impending betrayal. Next to this is the arrest in the Garden of Gethsemane. The kiss of betrayal by Judas follows. The numbers of the cryptogram to the side of Jesus add up to 33 in every direction: his age at the time of his death.

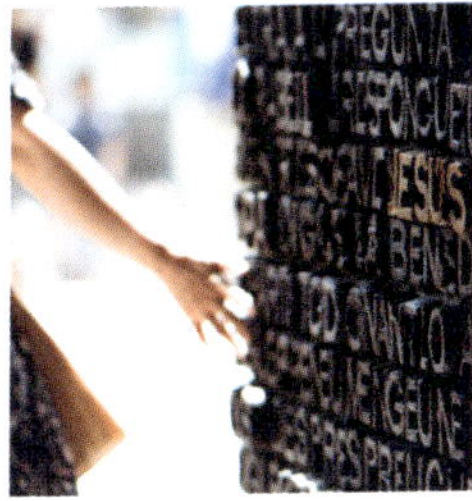

Bronze door carved with the gospel on the Passion façade

The Flagellation

In the Flagellation (between the central doors) Jesus is shown tied to a column at the top of a flight of three steps representing the three days of the Passion. Peter denying Christ is indicated by the cock that will crow three times in fulfilment of Jesus' prophecy. Behind is a labyrinth, a metaphor for Jesus' fate.

The sculptural group on the bottom right shows Christ bound and crowned with thorns. Pilate, overlooked by the Roman eagle, is seen washing his hands, freeing himself of responsibility for Jesus' death. Above, the Three Marys weep as Simon of Cyrene is told by the Romans to pick up the cross.

HIDDEN GEM
School Spirit

To the right of the Passion façade you'll find the Escoles de Gaudí, which the architect designed to be a school. Today, the undulating brick roof shelters a re-creation of Gaudí's office, with displays exploring his craft and aesthetic.

The Holy Shroud

The central sculpture depicts an event not described in the Bible. Veronica holds up her head cloth, which she has offered to Jesus to wipe the blood and sweat from his face. It has been returned, impressed with his likeness.

Next comes a Roman centurion on horseback piercing the side of Jesus with his sword. Above him, three soldiers beneath the cross cast lots for Jesus' tunic. The largest sculpture (top centre) shows Christ hanging from a horizontal cross. At his feet is a skull referring to the place of the Crucifixion, Golgotha. Above him is the veil of the Temple of Jerusalem. The final scene is the burial of Jesus. The figure of Nicodemus, who is anointing the body, is thought to be a self-portrait.

Haunting sculptural figures on the Passion façade depicting Peter's betrayal of Jesus

2

CASA BATLLÓ

G4 Passeig de Gràcia 43 8:30am-10:30pm daily (last adm: 9pm) Passeig de Gràcia casabatllo.es

With its reworked façade of stunning organic forms and its fantastic chimneys and rooftop, Casa Batlló remains as bold and convention-defying today as it was when it was finished in 1906.

Unlike Gaudí's other works, the construction of this block of flats on the prestigious Passeig de Gràcia involved the conversion of an existing structure. The building, commissioned by Josep Batlló i Casanovas, has been said to symbolize the legend of St George killing the dragon, whose scaly back arches above the main façade. The spindly columns across the first-floor windows have since been compared to tibias (lower leg bones), earning Casa Batlló the nickname "House of Bones". Inside, highlights include the blue-hued light well, the skeleton-like attics and the mushroom-shaped fireplace. The building was designated a UNESCO World Heritage Site in 2005.

Did You Know?

Salvador Dalí said that the curving walls and windows represent "waves on a stormy day".

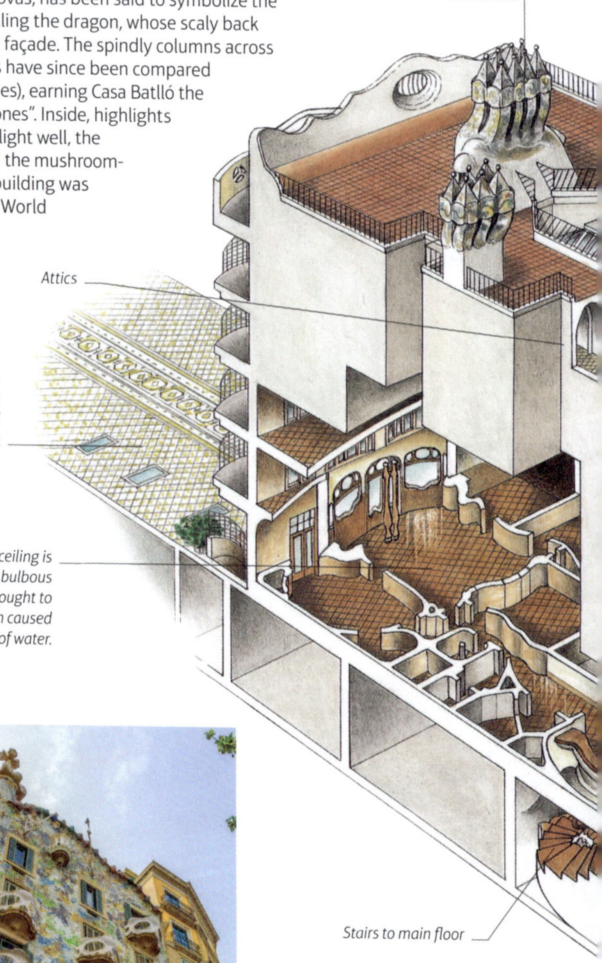

Tightly packed and abstractly patterned chimneys, which became Gaudí's trademark

Attics

Patio and rear façade, with its cast-iron balconies and superbly colourful trencadís work at the top

The dining room ceiling is rippled with bulbous forms that are thought to represent the splash caused by a drop of water.

Stairs to main floor

← Exterior of Casa Batlló, tiled in green and blue

1 The closely packed brick arches of the attics are plastered and painted white, giving the sensation of being inside the skeleton of a large animal.

2 One side of the main drawing room is formed of stained-glass windows looking out over the Passeig de Gràcia.

3 The house is topped with spectacularly patterned chimneys.

←

A look inside Gaudí's intriguing 20th-century Casa Batlló

People walking among the sculptural chimneys on La Pedrera's undulating roof

LA PEDRERA

G3 Passeig de Gràcia 92 Diagonal Hours vary, check website 25 Dec lapedrera.com

There isn't a single straight line in La Pedrera, Gaudí's extraordinary apartment building – the façade ripples like water. The rooftop terrace, with its tiled chimneys and undulating walkways, is one of the city's most popular attractions. What makes the building so special is that every detail bears the hallmark of Gaudí's visionary genius.

Sometimes called Casa Milà, La Pedrera was Gaudí's last work before he devoted himself entirely to the Sagrada Família *(p106)*. Built between 1906 and 1912 for Pere Milà, a wealthy industrialist, La Pedrera completely departed from the construction principles of the time and, as a result, it was strongly attacked by Barcelona's intellectuals. On its completion, it was greeted with both horror and amusement, and was quickly nicknamed "La Pedrera", meaning "the quarry", for its wavy façade of undressed stone.

Here you'll see a restored apartment, as well as the two circular courtyards, before exploring the Gaudí Exhibition on the top floor. The culmination of the visit is the stunning roof terrace, where jazz concerts are held in the summer among the peculiar air ducts and chimneys.

INSIDER TIP

Light Bulb Moment

Book a night tour to see La Pedrera come to life during Pedrera Origins, a spectacular sound and light show held on the roof. After watching the show, you'll be offered a glass of cava and a plate of sweetmeats.

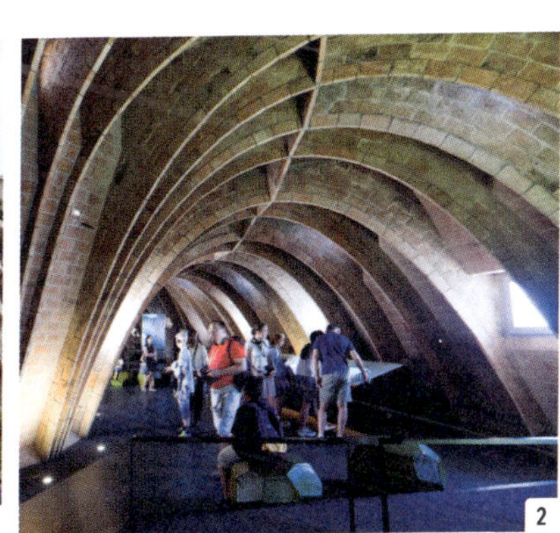

1 The intricate ironwork balconies by Josep Maria Jujol look like seaweed against La Pedrera's wave-like walls of white undressed stone.

2 In the "Whale Attic", the Gaudí Exhibition displays the architect's drawings and models to explain the aesthetics of his designs.

3 The many sculpted air ducts and chimneys on the roof have been dubbed both the "garden of warriors" and "*espanta-bruixes*" ("witch-scarers").

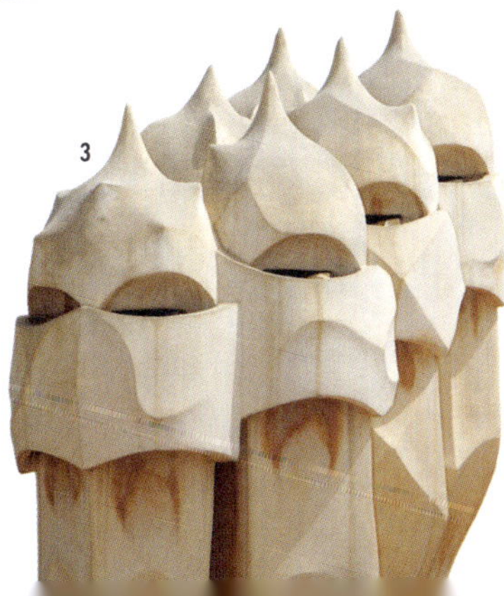

TOP 4 GAIXAMPLE EXPERIENCES

Night Barcelona
A buzzing bar that has a popular Thursday-night happy hour.
nightbarcelona.net

Axel Hotel
The world's first hotel chain aimed specifically at LGBTQ+ travellers.
axelhotels.com

D'Divine
Mediterranean food meets drag shows at this pink-lit restaurant.
ddivine.com

Sauna Casanova
This popular sauna has a steam room, pool and a Jacuzzi.
saunaspases.com/saunacasanova

EXPERIENCE MORE

4 

Illa de la Discòrdia

G4 Passeig de Gràcia, between Carrer d'Aragó and Carrer del Consell de Cent Passeig de Gràcia

Barcelona's most famous group of Modernista *(p36)* buildings illustrates the wide range of styles used by the movement's architects. They lie in an area known as the Illa de la Discòrdia (Block of Discord), in a nod to the startling visual clash between them. The three finest were remodelled in the early 1900s in the Modernista style from existing houses.

At No 35 Passeig de Gràcia, a shop was installed in the ground floor of **Casa Lleó Morera** (1902–6), Lluís Domènech i Montaner's first residential work, in 1943, but upstairs the Modernista interiors have been perfectly preserved. The house is currently closed to the public, but you can still admire the façade and the stained-glass windows from the outside.

Three doors down is **Casa Amatller**, designed by Josep Puig i Cadafalch in 1898. Its façade, under a stepped-gable roof, features a harmonious blend of Moorish and Gothic windows. The entrance patio, with spiral columns and a staircase covered by a stained-glass skylight, can be seen at any time; the rest of the building, including the lovely wood-panelled library and the new immersive digital museum, can be visited on a guided or self-guided tour with an audio guide. On summer evenings, there's also a dramatized tour. On the ground floor, you'll find a lively café and the shop of a renowned jeweller. Also in the block is Antoni Gaudí's Casa Batlló *(p112)*, with its fluid façade evoking marine or natural forms. The bizarrely decorated chimneys became a trademark of Gaudí's later work.

Casa Lleó Morera
Passeig de Gràcia 35 To the public casalleomorera.com

Casa Amatller
Passeig de Gràcia 41 10am-7pm daily amatller.org

Did You Know?

Passeig de Gràcia is the considered home of the most expensive real estate in Barcelona.

← Stunning stained-glass windows of Casa Lleó Morera

Fundació Antoni Tàpies

G4 Carrer d'Aragó 255 Passeig de Gràcia 10am-7pm Tue-Sat, 10am-3pm Sun 1 & 6 Jan, 25 & 26 Dec museutapies.org

Antoni Tàpies (1923–2012) was one of Barcelona's best-known contemporary artists. Strongly inspired by Surrealism, he used a variety of materials in his abstract work, including concrete and metal. The exhibits at the *fundació* provide a comprehensive overview of his work. The collection is housed in Barcelona's first domestic building to be constructed using iron, designed by Barcelona-born Lluís Domènech i Montaner in 1880 for his brother's publishing firm.

↑ Fundació Antoni Tàpies, topped with a cloud of wire

EAT

El Nacional

This gastro temple hosts many bars and restaurants offering everything from fresh oysters to regional charcuterie.

G5 Passeig de Gràcia 24 Bis elnacionalbcn.com

Mordisco

Head here for modern interpretations of classic Catalan cuisine.

G3 Passatge de la Concepció 10 mordisco.com

GiGi Von Tapas

A brunch spot during the day, GiGi Von Tapas offers classics such as eggs Benedict until 4pm. For dinner, the restaurant serves inventive tapas.

K4 Carrer de la Marina 189 gigivontapas.com

Moments

The interiors of this hotel restaurant are as slick as the Michelin-starred food. Try the tasting menu for a truly luxurious experience.

G4 Passeig de Gràcia 38-40 Mon; Tue-Fri & Sun lunch mandarinoriental.com

€€€

INSIDER TIP
La Nit dels Museus

On the "Night of the Museums" *(mid-May)*, several museums in Barcelona, including the Recinte Modernista de Sant Pau, open their doors to the public for free.

Recinte Modernista de Sant Pau

L2 Carrer de Sant Antoni Maria Claret 167 Sant Pau - Dos de Maig Apr-Oct: 9:30am-6:30pm daily (last adm: 6pm); Nov-Mar: 9:30am-5pm daily (last adm: 4:30pm) santpaubarcelona.org

Hospital Sant Pau, Barcelona's main general hospital, was built in the 1400s and expanded in the 17th century. By the end of the 19th century, the city's population had grown enormously and the hospital was no longer suitable. A wealthy banker, Paul Gil, bequeathed funds for the construction of a new hospital. The city approached architect Lluís Domènech i Montaner for this project.

Montaner began designing the new hospital in 1902. He envisioned it as a garden city, as he believed that patients would recover better among fresh air and trees. His innovative scheme consisted of 27 attractive Mudéjar-style pavilions set in large gardens and linked by underground tunnels. The patient wards occupied the pavilions, with lots of light and garden views, while the operating theatres of the main surgery were set below ground. Montaner also believed art and colour to be therapeutic, so each of the pavilions was decorated profusely with colourful tiles, mosaics and charming sculptural decorations; the reception pavilion has mosaic murals and sculptures created by Spanish sculptor and painter Pau Gargallo.

However, Montaner died in 1923, and by then only the first phase of the building's construction was done. The project was finally completed in 1930 by his son, Pere. In 1997, this Modernista masterpiece was named a UNESCO World Heritage Site.

The complex functioned as a hospital until 2009. It was subsequently restored and opened to the public.

Casa Garriga Nogués

G5 Carrer de la Diputació 250 Passeig de Gràcia To the public

The Casa Garriga Nogués is a beautiful mansion designed by Enric Sagnier in a blend of Rococo, Neo-Classical and Modernista styles. The house was completed in 1902 for the wealthy Garriga Nogués banking family, who gave the building its name. Its wide balcony along the façade is supported by four striking columns, designed by sculptor Eusebi Arnau, representing the four stages of life.

Exploring an exhibit housed within a curved tower of the Casa Terrades

Casa Terrades

H3 Avinguda Diagonal 420 Diagonal To the public casalespunxesx cloudworks.com

This free-standing, six-sided apartment block by Catalan Modernista architect Josep Puig i Cadafalch gets its nick-name, "Casa de les Punxes" (House of the Spikes), from the spires on its six corner turrets, which are shaped like witches' hats. A conversion of three existing houses, completed between 1903 and 1905, the building is an eclectic mixture of medi-eval and Renaissance styles. The towers and gables are influenced in particular by the Gothic architecture of northern Europe. However, the floral stone ornamen-tation of the exterior, in combination with the pre-dominant use of red brick, are typically Modernista.

The building serves as a co-working space and is closed to the public.

DRINK

Dry Martini

A bewitchingly old-school cocktail bar, with formal service and an uber modern menu.

F3 Carrer d'Aribau 162 drymartini org.com

CocoVail Beer Hall

This Californian-style beer bar serves snacks and 24 Catalan craft beers on tap.

G4 Carrer d'Aragó 284 cocovailbeer hall.com

Tandem Cocktail Bar

In this elegant bar, sharply suited bartenders mix classic cocktails in a low-lit, intimate setting.

F4 Carrer d'Aribau 86 934 51 43 30

The splendid buildings of the Recinte Modernista de Sant Pau, bright with mosaics

↑ Digital displays, viewed through virtual reality headsets *(inset)* at the White Rabbit Museum

9  

White Rabbit Museum

G4 Passeig de Gràcia 55 Passeig de Gràcia 10am-8pm daily (last adm: 7pm) whiterabbit-theoffmuseum.com

Also known as The Off-Museum, this fully accessible and family-friendly museum is especially popular with creative teens and curious visitors. Created by local artists and designers, it has a playful tone – more funhouse than fine art – and offers a lively, immersive introduction to Catalan identity. Here, humour, storytelling and technology come together in a unique way to reimagine the city's rich culture. Set across ten themed spaces, this museum uses light, sound and digital installations to explore vibrant local traditions such as *castellers* (human towers), street festivals and the *caganer* (Catalan nativity figure). Highlights include an infinity mirror room, a glowing digital art cube and a virtual-reality human tower. There's also a colourful shop and café, offering coffee, ice cream and plenty of quirky gifts.

10  

Museu de la Música

L5 L'Auditori, Calle Lepant 150 Marina, Glòries 10am-6pm Tue-Wed, 10am-9pm Thu, 10am-7pm Fri-Sun ajuntament.barcelona.cat/museumusica

Barcelona's fascinating music museum is located in L'Auditori concert hall. In addition to regular temporary exhibits, the permanent collection contains more than 2,200 instruments from all over the world. At any one time, around 500 of these are usually on display in red velvet cases. Ranging from 17th-century lutes to Indian sitars to Japanese kotos, the exhibits are further enriched by audiovisuals, interactive screens and listening stations that explain the history of music from the Middle Ages right up to the present day, while also tracing the evolution of musical cultures around the world. The museum also explores how music has been recorded over time, displaying various forms of notation on manuscript paper next to contemporary audio recording equipment.

CATALAN MUSICIANS

Montserrat Caballé
A soprano best known for her soaring duet with Freddie Mercury, *Barcelona*, which was played at the 1992 Olympics.

Pau Casals
Known in English as Pablo Casals, he was one of the greatest cellists of the 20th century.

José Carreras
Born in Barcelona in 1946, Carreras was one of the famous "Three Tenors", alongside Plácido Domingo and Luciano Pavarotti.

The undisputed highlight of the music museum, however, is the world-class collection of classical guitars, including pieces made by Antonio de Torres, considered the world's preeminent guitar-maker. Guitar enthusiasts, take note: a visit here culminates with the chance to play some of the instruments.

Perfect for rainy days, regular concerts, including final degree performances, are often free. Musical children will love the family-friendly workshops, which cover everything from making your own ukelele to introducing the sounds of Indonesian gamelan and Korean janggu.

Every Sunday (except in August and the first half of September), visitors can join a free guided tour. The tours should be booked well in advance; see website for details. Alternatively, an audio guide can also be downloaded for free from the website.

Did You Know?

The Egyptian Museum has a substantial collection of fertility figures engaged in sexual activity.

Museu Egipci de Barcelona

G4 Carrer de València 284 Passeig de Gràcia 10am-2pm & 4-7:30pm Mon-Fri, 10am-3pm & 4-7:30pm Sat, 10am-2pm Sun museuegipci.com

This private collection of ancient Egyptian art is one of the finest in the world, with more than 1,000 artifacts dating back several millennia. The collection begins with the Egyptian pharaohs, who were worshipped as gods. One of the most popular sections features sarcophagi, which range from early, simply decorated terracotta versions to huge, elaborately painted caskets. The sarcophagi are displayed with canopic jars, used to hold the intestines of mummified bodies. These jars were often decorated with the symbols of the four sons of Horus, who were believed to protect the contents.

There is also an excellent collection of intricate jewellery, pottery, weapons and even an Egyptian bed. Note that the information available in English is limited, so it is worth downloading the museum's own app (available on the website). The museum offers an extensive range of activities, from sleepovers, where kids camp among the exhibits, to breakfast talks.

↑ Viewing an Egyptian sarcophagus at the Museu Egipci de Barcelona

Hotel Constanza

This boutique hotel has rooms in soothing Mediterranean shades, some with balconies.

H5 Calle Bruc 33 hotelconstanza.com

Cotton House Hotel

A plush 5-star hotel offering elegant white-on-white "cotton rooms", sumptuous suites filled with antiques and a rooftop plunge pool.

H5 Gran Via de les Corts Catalanes 670 hotelcottonhouse.com

A SHORT WALK
QUADRAT D'OR

Distance 1.5 km (1 mile) **Nearest metro** Passeig de Gràcia, Diagonal **Time** 25 minutes

The hundred or so city blocks centring on the Passeig de Gràcia are known as the Quadrat d'Or, "Golden Square", because they contain so many of Barcelona's best Modernista buildings *(p84)*. This was the area within the Eixample favoured by the wealthy bourgeoisie, who embraced the new artistic and architectural style with enthusiasm. Take a stroll through the area to discover beautiful private residences, as well as ornamented commercial buildings. The most remarkable block is the Illa de la Discòrdia, with houses by Modernisme's most illustrious exponents. Many interiors can be visited, revealing a feast of stained glass, ceramics and ironwork.

Looking through a stained-glass door at Casa Lleó Morera

Diagonal metro

CARRER DE PROVENÇA

The Eixample's main avenue, **Passeig de Gràcia** *is a showcase of highly original buildings and smart shops.*

CARRER DE MALLORCA

PASSEIG DE GRÀCIA

Topped by Tàpies's sculpture Cloud and Chair, *the building that houses the* **Fundació Antoni Tàpies** (p117) *was designed by Lluís Domènech i Montaner in 1879.*

CARRER DE VALÈNCIA

Casa Amatller

In the **Illa de la Discòrdia**, *three of Barcelona's most famous Modernista houses vie for attention* (p116). *All were created between 1900 and 1910.*

M

Museu del Perfum

Casa Ramon Mulleras

Casa Lleó Morera

START

Gaudí's **Casa Batlló** (p112)

Passeig de Gràcia metro

0 metres 100

0 yards 100

N

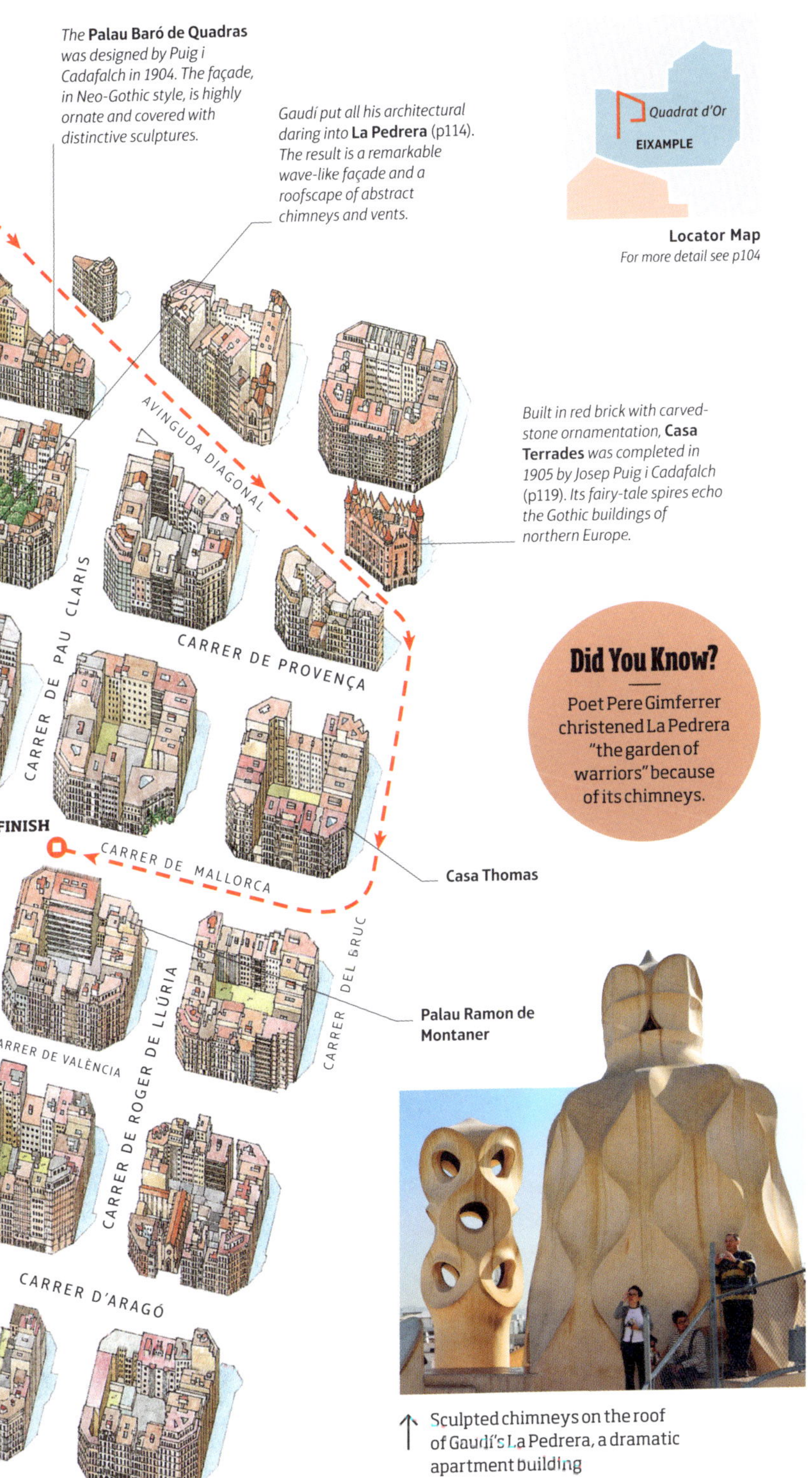

Did You Know?

Poet Pere Gimferrer christened La Pedrera "the garden of warriors" because of its chimneys.

↑ Sculpted chimneys on the roof of Gaudí's La Pedrera, a dramatic apartment building

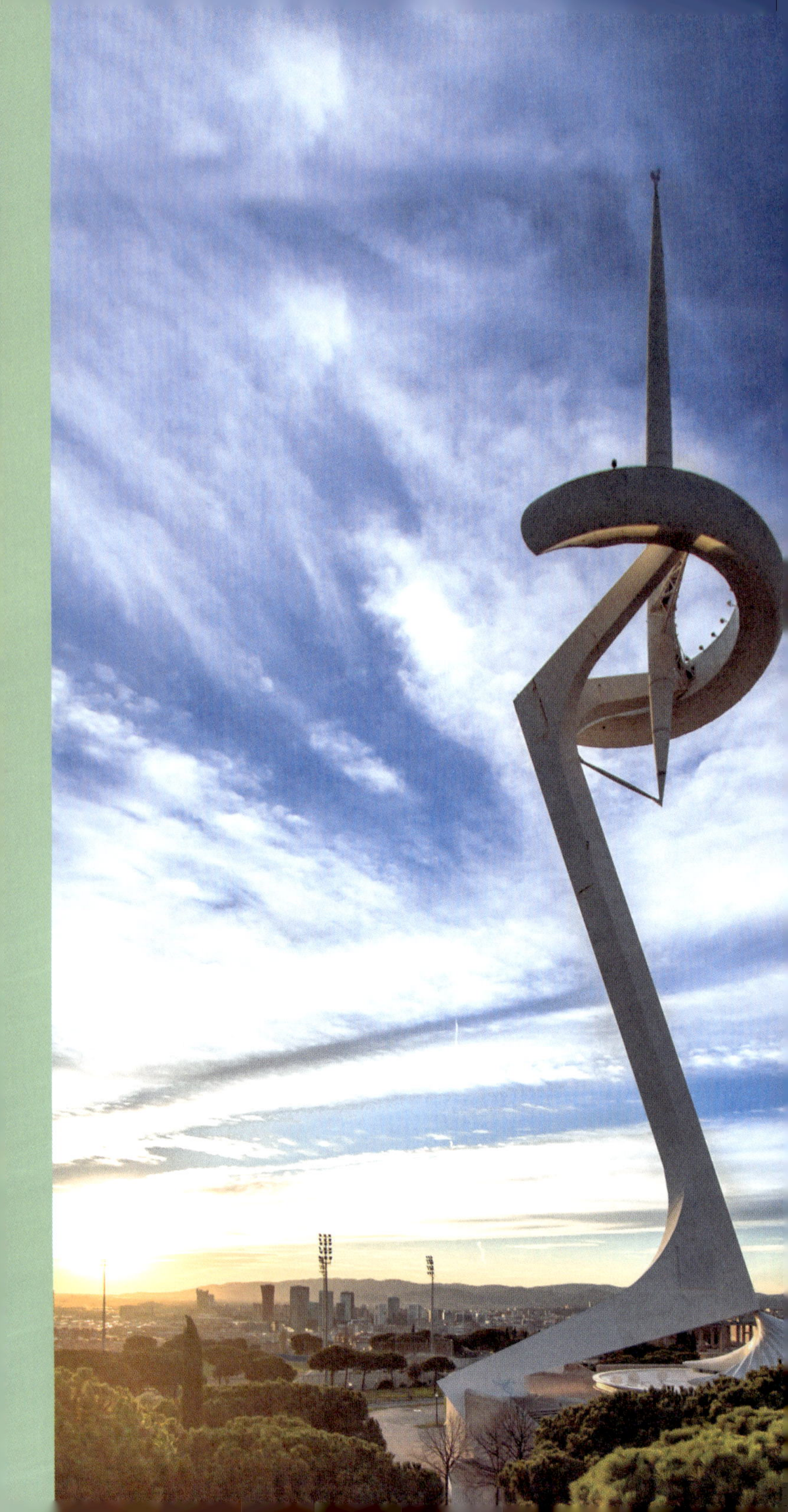

Montjuïc Communications Tower, built for the 1992 Olympics

MONTJUÏC

There was probably a Celtiberian settlement on this 185-m- (607-ft-) high hill before the Romans built a temple to Jupiter here, on what they called Mons Jovis (the Hill of Jove), which may have given Montjuïc its name. Another theory suggests that the hill was once home to a Jewish cemetery and that the name Montjuïc developed from it being called Mount of the Jews.

Naturally wooded, the slopes of Montjuïc were for years used to grow food and graze cattle to feed the Old Town. The absence of a water supply meant that there were few buildings on Montjuïc until a castle was erected on the top in 1640. This garrison famously shelled parts of Barcelona in 1842 to end an insurgency against Isabel II. The hill finally came into its own as the site of the 1929 International Exhibition. With great energy and flair, buildings were erected all over the north side, with the grand Avinguda de la Reina Maria Cristina, lined with huge exhibition halls, leading onto the base of the hill from the Plaça d'Espanya. One of these buildings was a stadium intended to host an alternative 1936 Olympics, in opposition to the Nazi-hosted competition in Berlin, but the event was cancelled on the outbreak of the Spanish Civil War. It seems fitting, then, that the last great surge of building on Montjuïc was for the 1992 Olympic Games, which left Barcelona with world-class sports facilities.

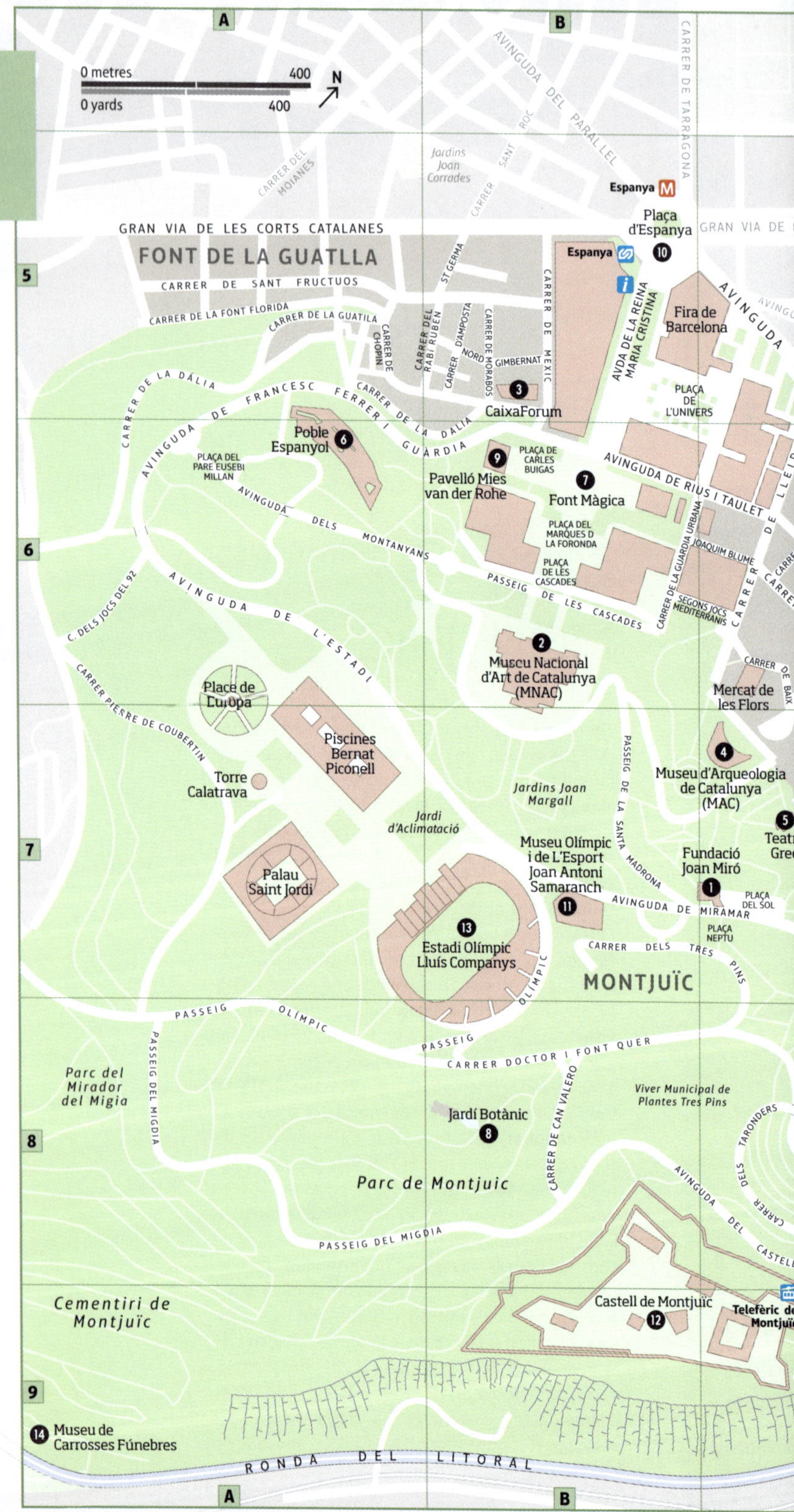
A
B
0 metres
400
0 yards
400
N
AVINGUDA DEL PARAL·LEL
CARRER DE TARRAGONA
Jardins Joan Corrades
CARRER DEL MOIANES
CARRER SANT ROC
Espanya
GRAN VIA DE LES CORTS CATALANES
Plaça d'Espanya
10
FONT DE LA GUATLLA
Espanya
5
CARRER DE SANT FRUCTUOS
CARRER DE LA FONT FLORIDA
CARRER DE LA GUATLLA
ST GERMA
CARRER DE MEXIC
AVDA DE LA REINA MARIA CRISTINA
Fira de Barcelona
AVINGUDA
CARRER DE CHOPIN
CARRER DEL RABÍ RUBEN
CARRER D'AMPOSTA
NORD
CARRER DE MORABOS
GIMBERNAT
CARRER DE LA DÀLIA
3
CaixaForum
PLAÇA DE L'UNIVERS
AVINGUDA DE FRANCESC FERRER I GUÀRDIA
CARRER DE LA DÀLIA
Poble Espanyol
6
9
PLAÇA DE CARLES BUIGAS
PLAÇA DEL PARE EUSEBI MILLAN
Pavelló Mies van der Rohe
7
Font Màgica
AVINGUDA DE RIUS I TAULET
AVINGUDA DELS MONTANYANS
PLAÇA DEL MARQUES D LA FORONDA
CARRER DE LA GUARDIA URBANA
JOAQUIM BLUME
CARRER DE LLEIDA
6
PLAÇA DE LES CASCADES
PASSEIG DE LES CASCADES
C. DELS JOCS DEL 92
AVINGUDA DE L'ESTADI
SEGONS JOCS MEDITERRANIS
2
Museu Nacional d'Art de Catalunya (MNAC)
CARRER DE BAIX
Mercat de les Flors
CARRER PIERRE DE COUBERTIN
Place de Europa
Piscines Bernat Piconell
4
Museu d'Arqueologia de Catalunya (MAC)
Torre Calatrava
Jardins Joan Margall
PASSEIG DE LA SANTA MADRONA
Jardí d'Aclimatació
5
Teatr Grec
7
Museu Olímpic i de L'Esport Joan Antoni Samaranch
Fundació Joan Miró
Palau Saint Jordi
1
11
AVINGUDA DE MIRAMAR
PLAÇA DEL SOL
PLAÇA NEPTU
13
Estadi Olímpic Lluís Companys
CARRER DELS TRES PINS
MONTJUÏC
PASSEIG OLÍMPIC
PASSEIG
CARRER DOCTOR I FONT QUER
Parc del Mirador del Migia
PASSEIG DEL MIGDIA
CARRER DE CAN VALERO
Viver Municipal de Plantes Tres Pins
Jardí Botànic
8
8
CARRER DELS TARONDERS
Parc de Montjuic
AVINGUDA DEL CASTELL
PASSEIG DEL MIGDIA
Cementiri de Montjuïc
Castell de Montjuïc
12
Telefèric de Montjuïc
9
14
Museu de Carrosses Fúnebres
RONDA DEL LITORAL
A
B

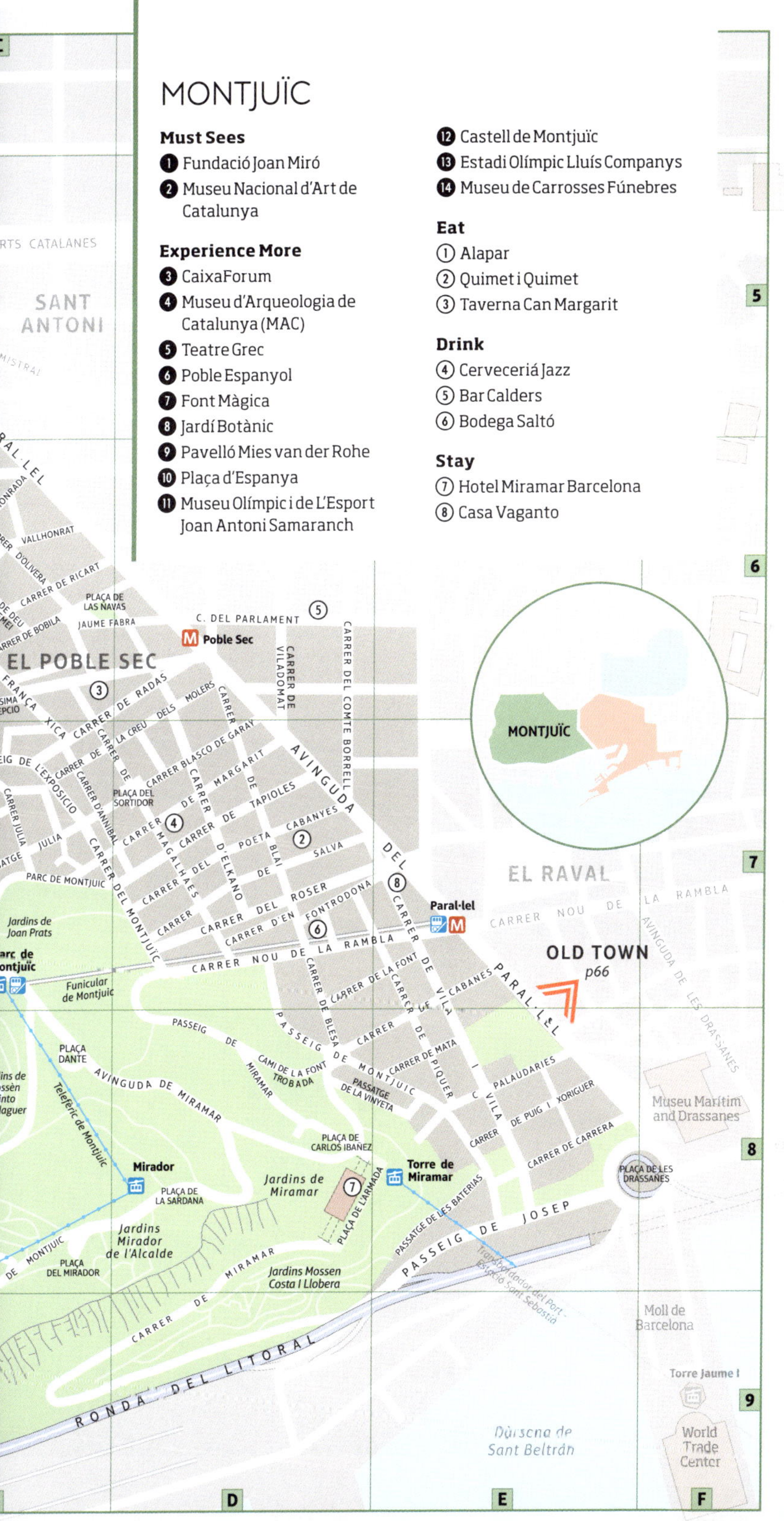
MONTJUÏC
Must Sees
1 Fundació Joan Miró
2 Museu Nacional d'Art de Catalunya
Experience More
3 CaixaForum
4 Museu d'Arqueologia de Catalunya (MAC)
5 Teatre Grec
6 Poble Espanyol
7 Font Màgica
8 Jardí Botànic
9 Pavelló Mies van der Rohe
10 Plaça d'Espanya
11 Museu Olímpic i de L'Esport Joan Antoni Samaranch
12 Castell de Montjuïc
13 Estadi Olímpic Lluís Companys
14 Museu de Carrosses Fúnebres
Eat
① Alapar
② Quimet i Quimet
③ Taverna Can Margarit
Drink
④ Cerveceriá Jazz
⑤ Bar Calders
⑥ Bodega Saltó
Stay
⑦ Hotel Miramar Barcelona
⑧ Casa Vaganto
SANT ANTONI
EL POBLE SEC
Poble Sec
Paral·lel
EL RAVAL
OLD TOWN
p66
MONTJUÏC
C. DEL PARLAMENT
CARRER DE VILADOMAT
CARRER DEL COMTE BORRELL
AVINGUDA DEL PARAL·LEL
PLAÇA DE LAS NAVAS
JAUME FABRA
PLAÇA DEL SORTIDOR
CARRER NOU DE LA RAMBLA
Funicular de Montjuïc
PLAÇA DANTE
AVINGUDA DE MIRAMAR
PASSEIG DE MONTJUÏC
Telefèric de Montjuïc
Mirador
PLAÇA DE LA SARDANA
Jardins Mirador de l'Alcalde
PLAÇA DEL MIRADOR
Jardins de Miramar
PLAÇA DE CARLOS IBAÑEZ
Torre de Miramar
Jardins Mossen Costa I Llobera
CARRER DE MIRAMAR
RONDA DEL LITORAL
PASSEIG DE JOSEP CARNER
Transbordador del Port - Estació Sant Sebastià
Museu Marítim and Drassanes
PLAÇA DE LES DRASSANES
AVINGUDA DE LES DRASSANES
Moll de Barcelona
Torre Jaume I
World Trade Center
Dàrsena de Sant Beltrán
Jardins de Joan Prats
Parc de Montjuïc
PARC DE MONTJUÏC
5
6
7
8
9
D
E
F

FUNDACIÓ JOAN MIRÓ

C7 Parc de Montjuïc 150 To Montjuïc Apr-Oct: 10am-8pm Tue-Sat, 10am-7pm Sun; Nov-Mar: 10am-7pm Tue-Sun 1, 6 & 19-25 Jan, 25 & 26 Dec fmirobcn.org

Established in June 1975 by the artist himself, the Fundació Joan Miró contains an enormous permanent collection of over 14,000 pieces, most of which were donated from Miró's private collection. The works include Miró's own as well as other pieces of modern and contemporary art.

Designed by architect Josep Lluís Sert, the stark white building that houses the foundation is a remarkable Rationalist construction arranged around courtyards and drenched with natural light that pours in through angled skylights. Guided tours of the building take place on the first Sunday of each month, in English, Spanish or Catalan.

Miró donated his own works, and some of the best pieces on display include his Barcelona Series (1939–44), a set of 50 black-and-white lithographs, and *Chapel of Sant Joan d'Horta*, painted in 1917 in the Catalan town which features prominently in Miró's early work.

The foundation also has an exquisite collection of artworks by other celebrated artists, including Alexander Calder and Lola Fernández Jiménez. When Miró first conceived of the museum, he wanted to create a space in which young artists could experiment, and the Espai 13 gallery showcases the work of emerging artists. The foundation also hosts blockbuster exhibitions, which attract such huge crowds that the queues snake down the hill.

TOP 5 UNMISSABLE WORKS

Chapel of Sant Joan d'Horta (1917)
An early landscape in vivid Fauvist colours.

Painting (The White Glove) (1925)
A poetic, abstract work influenced by the Surrealist movement.

Morning Star (1940)
Part of the celebrated Constellations series.

Poem (III) (1968)
Miró claimed to "paint colours like words that shape poems".

Tapestry of the Foundation (1979)
This tapestry of a woman dancing under the moon and stars was created for this space.

JOAN MIRÓ

Joan Miró (1893-1983) started taking art classes when he was seven years old and moved on to La Llotja's art school in 1907. From 1919, he spent much time in Paris, where he honed his own unique artistic language, displayed in remarkable paintings like *Man and Woman in Front of a Pile of Excrement* (1935) - Miró's reaction to the simmering violence that would eventually erupt in the Spanish Civil War. An admirer of Catalan art and Modernisme, Miró invented and developed a Surrealistic style, with exuberant colours and fantastical forms.

GREAT VIEW
Jardí de les Escultures

After a visit through the gallery, step into the small adjacent sculpture garden, where you'll find wonderful panoramic views of the city. It's a perfect place to rest and recalibrate.

↑ Stark white façade of the Fundació Joan Miró, designed by Josep Lluís Sert

↑ Admiring the vibrant streaks of colour in the paintings of Joan Miró

2

MUSEU NACIONAL D'ART DE CATALUNYA

B6 Parc de Montjuïc, Palau Nacional Espanya 150 May-Sep: 10am-8pm Tue-Sat, 10am-3pm Sun; Oct-Apr: 10am-6pm Tue-Sat, 10am-3pm Sun 1 Jan, 1 May, 25 Dec museunacional.cat

The grand Palau Nacional was built for the 1929 International Exhibition, but since 1934 it has housed the city's most important art collection. The artworks span 1,000 years, and include paintings, sculpture, furniture, photographs, drawings, prints and coins.

With its origins in the 19th century and the Renaixença's focus on Catalonia's artistic heritage, the museum's collection of Catalan art grew from two separate institutions: the Museu Provincial d'Antiguitats (Provincial Museum of Antiquities, established in 1880) and the Museu Municipal de Belles Arts (Municipal Museum of Fine Arts, inaugurated in 1891). These two collections were moved to the exquisite Palau Nacional between 1934 and 1942. During the rest of the 20th century the museum was expanded to include other collections, from Romanesque to modern art. Today the museum hosts regular major exhibitions – primarily showcasing the work of Catalan artists, but also that of Spanish and other European artists.

Tickets are valid for two days, so there's no need to attempt to see everything in one trip. The museum's website has a handy "create your own itinerary" function to help you make the most of your visit.

Waterfalls cascading below the must-visit Museu Nacional d'Art de Catalunya ↑

CATALONIA'S RENAIXENÇA

Just as the prosperity of the 14th century inspired Catalonia's first flowering, so the wealth from industry in the 19th century inspired the Renaixença, a renaissance of Catalan language and culture (similar to the Galician Rexurdimento). Its literary rallying points were Bonaventura Aribau's *Oda a la patria*, published in 1833, and the poems of a young monk, Jacint Verdaguer, who won prizes in the revived Jocs Florals poetry competitions. The Catalan language was finally standardized in the early 20th century.

Museum Highlights

Coins

The numismatic collection contains more than 100,000 coins, the earliest dating back to the 6th century BCE.

Romanesque Collection

▶ The museum's excellent display of Romanesque items centres on a series of magnificent 12th-century frescoes. The most remarkable are the wall paintings from Sant Climent de Taüll and La Seu d'Urgell. The displays were specially designed to recall the remote Pyrenean churches from which the frescoes came.

Gothic Collection

The superb Gothic collection includes notable works by 15th-century Catalan artists Bernat Martorell, Lluís Dalmau and Jaume Huguet. These impressive, often richly gilded works reflect Catalonia's growing wealth and power in this era.

The Cambó Bequest

▶ The Cambó Bequest, donated by the collector and politician Francesc Cambó, includes works by El Greco, Zurbarán and Velázquez. Paired with paintings on permanent loan from Madrid's Thyssen-Bornemisza collection, the bequest ensures that the museum has an impressive Renaissance and Baroque collection.

Modernisme and Noucentisme

◀ The museum's remarkable selection of 19th- and early 20th-century artworks and decorative objects include beautiful curving furniture designs by Gaudí for the Casa Batlló. Also in the collection is the famous painting by Ramon Casas of himself and Pere Romeu on a tandem, which once hung in the Els 4 Gats tavern; it's now considered a classic of poster art.

Photography Collection

The photography collection runs the gamut from early 19th-century portraits to gritty photo-journalism from the Spanish Civil War.

EXPERIENCE MORE

CaixaForum

B5 Avinguda de Francesc Ferrer i Guàrdia 6-8, Montjuïc Espanya 13, 150 10am-8pm daily 1 & 6 Jan, 25 Dec caixaforum.org

Barcelona grows ever-stronger in the field of contemporary art and this intriguing exhibition centre only enhances its reputation. The foundation's collection of 700 works by Spanish and international artists is housed in the Antiga Fàbrica Casaramona, a beautifully restored textile mill built in the early 20th century in the Modernista style.

The mill was designed by Josep Puig i Cadafalch after he had completed the Casa de les Punxes. Opened in 1911, it was intended to be a model factory – light, clean and airy – but had only a short working life before the business closed down in 1920. At this point the building became a storehouse and, after the Civil War, stables for police horses. Reclaimed as a gallery space in 2002, there are a series of galleries dedicated to temporary displays (often major international touring exhibitions), plus a permanent collection of contemporary art. A free app provides visitors with an audio guide to the items on display. Look out for family workshops, concerts, talks, film screenings and other cultural events – many of which are free. Also, don't miss the roof terrace, which offers great views of the city.

Museu d'Arqueologia de Catalunya (MAC)

C7 Passeig de Santa Madrona 39-41 Espanya, Poble Sec 9:30am-7pm Tue-Sat, 10am-2:30pm Sun & public hols 1 & 6 Jan, 25 & 26 Dec macbarcelona.cat

Housed in the 1929 Palace of Graphic Arts, this fascinating archaeology museum brims with artifacts from prehistory to the Visigothic period (415–711 CE). The mysterious *talayots* (Bronze Age megaliths) from the Balearics are described here, and there are beautiful collections of Hellenic Mallorcan jewellery and Iberian silver treasures. Among the highlights of the collection is the Dama d'Eivissa (The Lady of Ibiza), a remarkable 4th-century sculpture of an elaborately dressed goddess, and the startling 2nd-century Roman fertility symbol Priapus of Hostafrancs.

The museum has a superb collection of artifacts gathered from the Greco-Roman town of Empúries *(p186)*, once the most important Greek colony on the entire Spanish peninsula. The displays include exquisite mosaics, everyday items such as oil lamps and amphorae, and several statues, including a copy of the famous Asclepius (the original remains in situ). Finally, the collection has a hoard of ornate, gem-encrusted Visigothic jewellery, belt buckles, helmets

GREAT VIEW
Cable Car

Barcelona has many great viewpoints, but none quite as vertiginous as Montjuïc's cable car. It runs from just below the castle *(p138)* and delivers a citywide panorama as it glides above manicured gardens.

Teatre Grec, a renowned festival venue nestled amid lovely gardens

and armour. In addition to this permanent collection, there are temporary exhibits.

Written information in English can be sparse throughout the museum; instead, pick up the excellent English-language audio guide.

Teatre Grec

C7 Parc de Montjuïc Poble Sec, then 55 bus Dawn to dusk daily (only ticket holders permitted during the El Grec Festival) barcelona.cat/grec/en

This remarkable outdoor amphitheatre is hidden away amid greenery at the foot of Montjuïc.

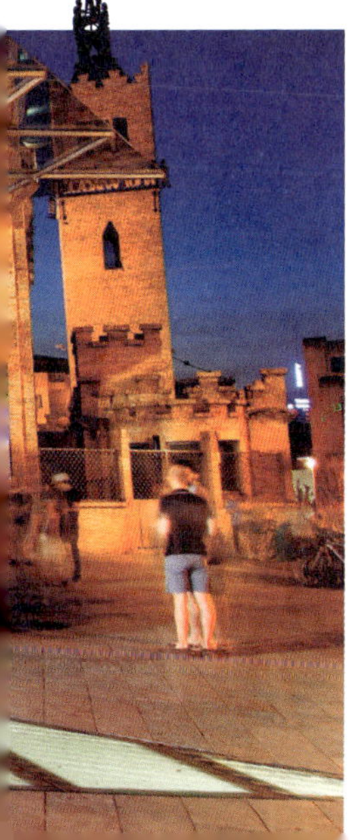

Originally a quarry, it was converted into an open-air theatre in 1929 by Catalan architects Ramon Revento and Nicolau Maria Rubió i Tudurí, when Montjuïc was remodelled as part of the International Exhibition. This is easily one of the most atmospheric venues in the city, set amid extensive gardens, with groves of orange trees, pretty pavilions and a series of terraces and viewing points that frame beautiful views of the gardens themselves and the city beyond. It is said to have been inspired by the ancient Greek theatre at Epidaurus, and it is the epicentre of Barcelona's biggest performing arts festival.

Once a year, in late June and all of July, the theatre steps up its game for the El Grec Festival. The popular arts festival has been held at the amphitheatre since 1976, when the venue was taken over by Barcelona's city council. A varied programme of events takes place and a buzzing open-air bar and restaurant pop up in the gardens during the festival.

CaixaForum, a modern art gallery, dramatically lit up at night

EAT

Alapar

Enjoy a fusion of Japanese and Mediterranean cuisine from a remarkable chef.

C6 Carrer de Lleida 5 alaparbcn.com

Quimet i Quimet

The *montaditos* (tapas mounted on bread) at this bar are among the best in the city.

D7 Carrer del Poeta Cabanyes 25 quimetiquimet.com

Taverna Can Margarit

This restaurant serves hearty Catalan cuisine, such as *pa amb tomàquet* (bread with tomato), stewed snails and wine.

C6 Carrer de la Concòrdia 21 934 41 67 23

Wandering the picturesque streets of Poble Espanyol, overlooked by balconies

STAY

Hotel Miramar Barcelona

Ask for a room with a sea view at this gorgeously swanky hotel standing in the gardens of Montjuïc.

D8 Plaça de Carlos Ibáñez 3 hotel miramarbarcelona.com

Casa Vaganto

Find great design and cosy rooms at this sanctuary in the city.

E7 Carrer d'En Fontrodona 1 vagantohotel.com

6 

Poble Espanyol

A6 Avinguda Francesc Ferrer i Guàrdia Espanya 10am–8pm Mon, 10am–midnight Tue–Sun poble-espanyol.com

The idea behind the Poble Espanyol (Spanish Village) was to illustrate and display local Spanish architectural styles and crafts. It was laid out for the 1929 International Exhibition, but has proved to be enduringly popular and now attracts well over a million visitors a year. More than 100 buildings, streets and squares from across Spain have been re-created – from whitewashed Andalusian homes to arcaded Castilian squares, Catalan villages to Basque farmhouses. Replicas of the towers in the walled city of Ávila in central Spain form the impressive main entrance. Resident artisans produce crafts, including hand-blown glass, Toledo damascene, leather goods and musical instruments. There is plenty more to entertain visitors, including restaurants, bars, a flamenco show, a museum of modern art and a programme of craft and music workshops.

7 

Font Màgica

B6 Plaça de Carles Buïgas Espanya Nov–Jan 6 & Mar: 8–9pm Thu–Sat; Apr, May & Oct: 9–10pm Thu–Sat; Jun–Sep: 9:30pm–10:30pm Wed–Sun 7 Jan–Feb

This marvel of engineering was built by Carles Buïgas (1898–1979) for the International Exhibition. The Art Deco fountain shoots kaleidoscopic jets of water to music in exuberant sound-and-light shows. Themes vary, but the show often culminates with Montserrat Caballé and Freddie Mercury's popular duet "Barcelona", performed at the 1992 Olympics. Shows may be suspended if drought restrictions are in effect.

The four columns behind the Font Màgica were originally erected by Modernista architect Josep Puig i Cadafalch at the turn of the 20th century. Designed to represent the stripes on the Catalan coat of arms, they were destroyed in 1928 as part of a ban on Catalan symbols. Now rebuilt, they are once again a potent symbol of Catalan pride.

8 

Jardí Botànic

B8 Parc de Montjuïc Espanya From 10am daily; closing hours vary, check website 1 Jan, 1 May, 24 Jun, 25 Dec museuciencies.cat/en

Set on a sloping hill in Montjuïc Park, Barcelona's botanic

1,500

The number of plant species in the Jardí Botànic.

garden offers an insight into the flora of the Mediterranean and beyond. You won't find lush tropical plants here; rather, this botanic garden is home to the types of plants that can survive Barcelona's hot, dry Mediterranean summers.

A walk around the grounds takes you through gardens reminiscent of the *matollar* scrubland that covers much of Catalonia. Native species are well represented, as well as plants from places around the world with similar climates. Try to visit in spring, when most of the garden is abloom with bright neons and muted pastels; the plants are least impressive in summer, when only those with the deepest roots can find water to flower.

9 

Pavelló Mies van der Rohe

B6 Avinguda Francesc Ferrer i Guàrdia 7 Espanya 50 Mar-Oct; 10am-8pm daily; Nov-Feb: 10am-6pm daily 1 Jan, 25 Dec miesbcn.com

The simple modern lines of the German Pavilion must have shocked visitors to the International Exhibition. The pavilion was designed by Ludwig Mies van der Rohe, director of the avant-garde Bauhaus school, and his close collaborator Lilly Reich. The pavilion was characterized by fluid, glassy spaces, in which the boundaries between inside and outside were blurred, and made use of materials like marble and onyx. This was enhanced by highly polished façades and extensive use of tinted glass. Two pools are set into the pavilion surroundings, one of which is overlooked by a bronze reproduction of the statue *Alba* (Dawn) by Georg Kolbe. Unlike other pavilions at the exhibition, this one was conceived as a place of rest and tranquillity for visitors rather than as a gallery. Nothing was displayed within its walls except the steel-and-leather Barcelona Chair. The original was made of ivory-coloured pigskin, and was designed specifically for the Spanish royal family as they made their way through the exhibition's pavilions and display spaces. The building was intended to be a temporary structure and was dismantled after the exhibition, but an exact replica was painstakingly built using the same materials in the 1980s, for the centenary of the architect and designer's birth.

PICTURE PERFECT

Dawn Chorus

The best place to get the perfect shot of *Alba* (Dawn) is to stand at the opposite end of the pool. Here, the statue is reflected not only in the water, but also in the glass façade of the pavilion to the left.

←

Stark yet soothing interior of the Pavelló Mies van der Rohe

Spanish architectural styles displayed in Poble Espanyol

10 Plaça d'Espanya

B5 Gran Via de les Corts Catalanes Espanya

At the centre of this busy junction is a fountain by Josep Maria Jujol, one of Gaudí's most faithful collaborators. The huge 1899 bullring to one side, by August Font i Carreras, features a dazzling red-brick façade. It has been converted into Las Arenas, a shopping centre with an observation deck on the roof where you can enjoy fantastic views of Montjuïc. On the Montjuïc side, the Avinguda de la Reina Maria Cristina is flanked by two campaniles modelled on the bell tower of St Mark's Basilica in Venice and built for the 1929 International Exhibition.

Museu Olímpic i de L'Esport Joan Antoni Samaranch

B7 Avinguda de l'Estadi 60 55, 150 Apr-Sep: 10am-7pm Tue-Sat, 10am-2:30pm Sun; Oct-Mar: 10am-6pm Tue-Sat, 10am-2:30pm Sun museuolimpicbcn.cat

This museum pays homage to the 1992 Olympic Games held in Barcelona. Exhibits cover the history of the modern Olympic Games and have a marvellous collection of memorabilia, including items from the personal collection of Juan Antonio Samaranch, former president of the International Olympic Committee, to whom the museum is dedicated.

Castell de Montjuïc

B9 Parc de Montjuïc Paral·lel, then funicular & cable car 150 from Plaça Espanya 10am-8pm daily (Nov-Feb: to 6pm) ajuntament.barcelona.cat/castelldemontjuic

Crowning the very summit of Montjuïc is an 18th-century castle with spectacular views over the entire city and a vast stretch of the coastline. The first fortress here was built in 1640, and became the site of numerous battles during the War of the Spanish Succession in the early 1700s. After the success of Felipe V, Montjuïc fortress was rebuilt by the Bourbon rulers in order to ensure that the local populace was kept under control. It became infamous as a prison and torture centre, a role it continued to play until after the Civil War. Notable Catalan leaders were imprisoned and executed here in the aftermath of the Spanish Civil War, including Lluís Companys.

The castle contained a military museum for several decades, but when it was formally restored to the Catalan authorities by the Spanish government in 2008, it was decided that the military museum be turned into a centre dedicated to peace. Exhibits describe the development of Montjuïc and the castle's turbulent history. There's a café with a terrace on the Pati d'Armes and, in summer, an outdoor cinema in the gardens.

HIDDEN GEM
Woodland Café

A great escape from the city in summer, La Caseta del Migdia *(lacaseta.org)* is located in the cool woods behind Castell de Montjuïc. Harbour views are a bonus.

Plaça d'Espanya and the twin campaniles of Avinguda de la Reina Maria Cristina

Estadi Olímpic Lluís Companys

B7 Passeig Olímpic 934 26 20 89 Espanya, Poble Sec 55

This stadium – the centrepiece of the so-called Anella Olímpica (Olympic Ring) of sports facilities erected for the 1992 Olympics – was originally built in 1929 for the International Exhibition. It was remodelled to host the Olímpiada Popular in 1936. This event (conceived as a protest against the Olympics being held in Berlin under Hitler) never took place due to the outbreak of the Spanish Civil War. However, the stadium got its chance to shine in the 1992 Olympics, for which it was modernized, although the original façade was preserved. It is currently used as a concert and events venue, but if you don't have tickets, you can get a glimpse of the interior from a viewing spot outside.

Next door is the modern Museu Olímpic i de l'Esport, and nearby are the steel-and-glass Palau Sant Jordi stadium, Barcelona's biggest concert venue; the Piscines Picornell, which includes a gym and indoor and outdoor swimming pools; and the diving pools used in the Olympics. These are open in summer and offer superb views over the city.

Museu de Carrosses Fúnebres

A9 Carrer de la Mare de Déu de Port 56 934 84 19 99 21 10am-2pm Sat & Sun

Within Monjuïc Cemetery is this unusual, mildly macabre museum, dedicated to the history of funeral processions. Visitors are taken downstairs to a permanent collection of funeral carriages and coaches that date back to the 18th century. Twentieth-century motor hearses are also included, with eerie mannequins in period dress keeping watch over the entire collection.

Entry is free, but the best time to visit is on the annual La Nit dels Museus festival, when you can visit after dark for added chills.

DRINK

Cervecería Jazz

One of the first bars in the city to specialize in craft beer, this joint also has excellent hamburgers - and, of course, jazz.

D7 Carrer de Margarit 43 bocadilleriajazz.com

Bar Calders

A decent selection of wine (and tapas) is available at this Sant Antoni favourite, which has tables outside on a pedestrianized street.

D6 Carrer del Parlament 25 933 29 93 49

Bodega Saltó

An eccentric little bar with barrels, papier-mâché models and mannequins on the walls. A stage sees all manner of live acts.

D7 Carrer del Blesa 36 bodegasalto.net

An ornate hearse, one of the exhibits at the Museu de Carrosses Fúnebres

A SHORT WALK MONTJUÏC

Distance 3 km (2 miles) **Nearest metro** Espanya **Time** 45 minutes

Set high on a hill, Montjuïc is a spectacular vantage point from which to view the city. On a walk through the area, you'll find a wealth of art galleries and museums, an amusement park and an open-air theatre. The most interesting buildings lie around the Palau Nacional, where Europe's greatest Romanesque art collection is housed. Montjuïc is approached from the Plaça d'Espanya between brick pillars based on the campanile of St Mark's in Venice, which give a foretaste of the eclecticism of building styles. The Poble Espanyol illustrates the traditional architecture of Spain's regions, while the Fundació Joan Miró is boldly modern.

A steel, glass, stone and onyx pavilion, **Pavelló Mies van der Rohe** *was built in the Bauhaus style as the German contribution to the 1929 International Exhibition* (p135).

Containing replicas of buildings from many regions, the **Poble Espanyol** *provides a fascinating glimpse of vernacular styles* (p134).

Displayed in the Palau Nacional, the **Museu Nacional d'Art de Catalunya (MNAC)** *includes Europe's finest collection of early medieval frescoes* (p130).

↑ Walking under an arch on a street in the Poble Espanyol

↑ People watching the dramatic Font Màgica, in front of the MNAC

Locator Map
For more detail see p126

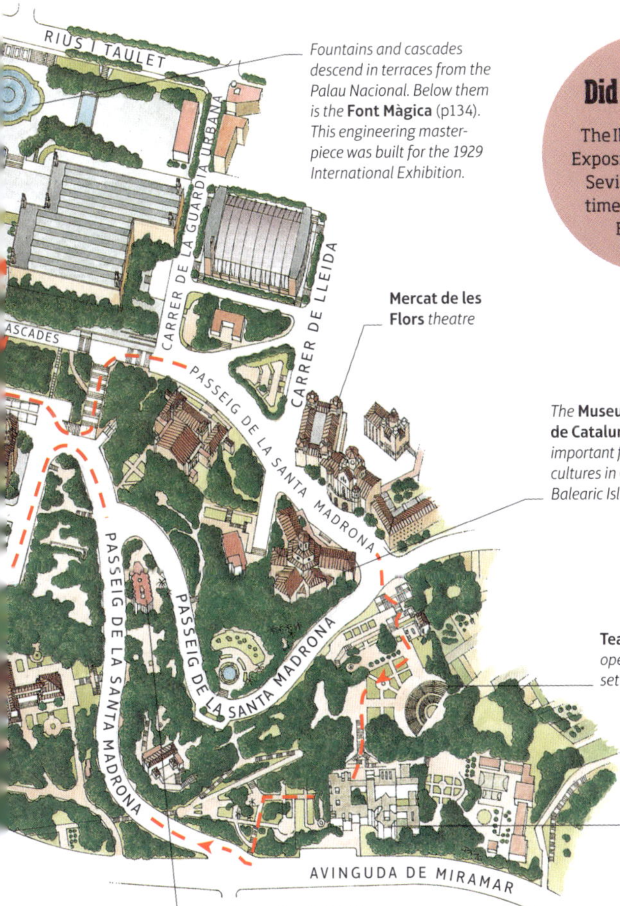

RIUS I TAULET

Fountains and cascades descend in terraces from the Palau Nacional. Below them is the **Font Màgica** (p134). *This engineering masterpiece was built for the 1929 International Exhibition.*

Did You Know?

The Ibero-American Exposition was held in Seville at the same time as Barcelona's Exhibition.

CARRER DE LA GUARDIA URBANA

CARRER DE LLEIDA

ASCADES

Mercat de les Flors *theatre*

PASSEIG DE LA SANTA MADRONA

The **Museu d'Arqueologia de Catalunya (MAC)** *displays important finds from prehistoric cultures in Catalonia and the Balearic Islands (p132).*

PASSEIG DE LA SANTA MADRONA

PASSEIG DE LA SANTA MADRONA

Teatre Grec *is an open-air theatre set among gardens.*

Miró created the **Fundació Joan Miró** *as a centre for the study of modern art (p128). In addition to Miró's works in various media, the modern building by Josep Lluís Sert is of architectural interest.*

AVINGUDA DE MIRAMAR

The **Museu Etnològic de Barcelona** *displays artifacts from Oceania, Africa, Asia and Latin America.*

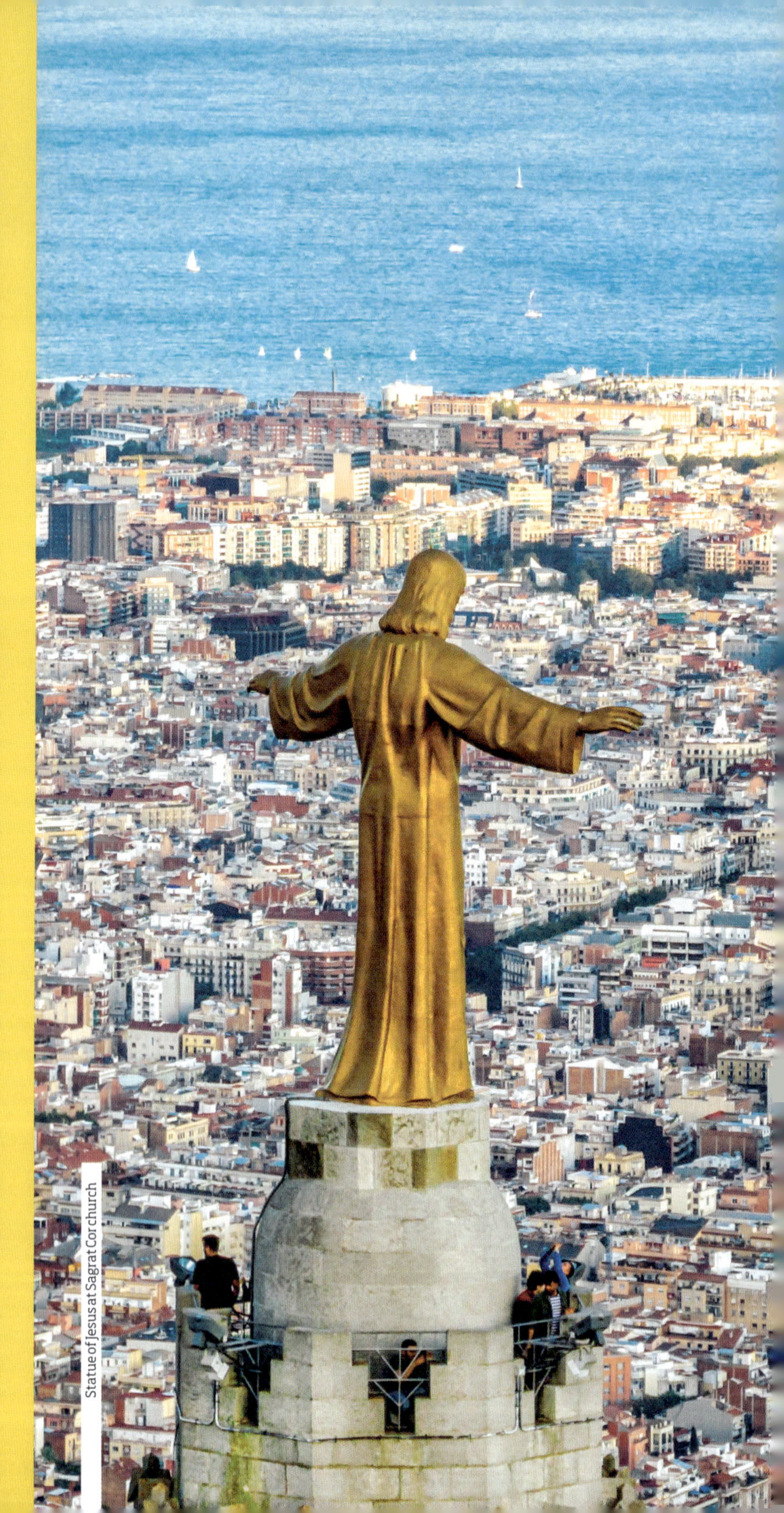
Statue of Jesus at Sagrat Cor church

BEYOND THE CENTRE

Must Sees

1. Park Güell
2. Camp Nou
3. Monestir de Pedralbes

Experience More

4. CosmoCaixa
5. Casa Vicens
6. Parc de Joan Miró
7. Tibidabo
8. Torre Bellesguard
9. Torre de Collserola
10. Parc del Laberint d'Horta
11. Museu del Disseny
12. Museu Can Framis
13. El Poblenou
14. Museu de Ciències Naturals - Museu Blau
15. Estació del Nord

A period of radical redevelopment of Barcelona's outskirts in the late 1980s and 1990s gave it a wealth of new structures, parks and squares and restored a trove of Modernista buildings. The city's main station, Sants, was rebuilt and the neighbouring Parc de l'Espanya Industrial and Parc de Joan Miró were created, containing lakes, modern sculpture and futuristic architecture. In the west of the city, where the streets start to climb steeply, the historic royal palace and monastery of Pedralbes, plus Gaudí's famous Park Güell, were restored, and the Torre de Collserola, built for the 1992 Olympics, gave *barcelonins* the chance to see it all from above.

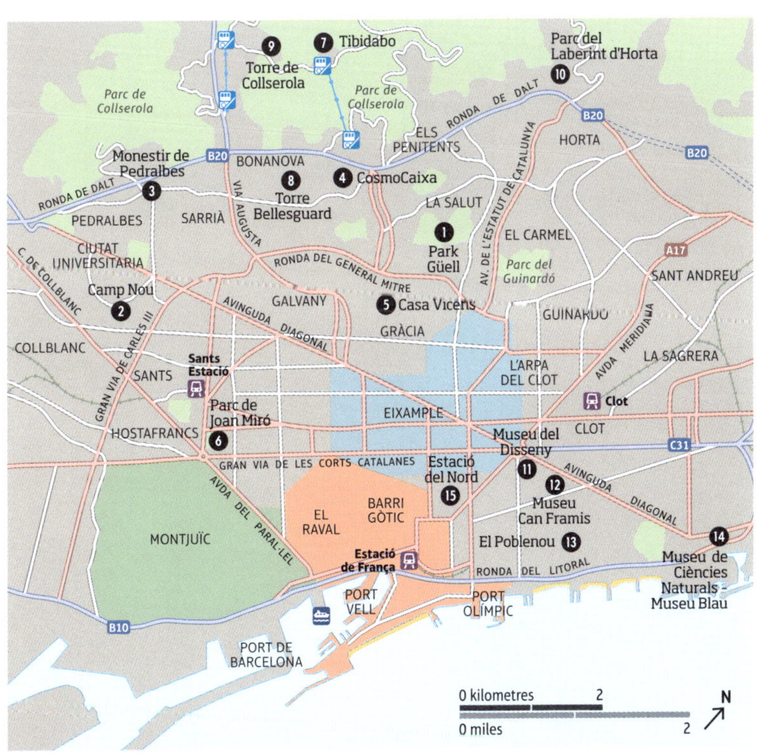

PARK GÜELL

Carrer d'Olot 7, Vallcarca Lesseps, Vallcarca 24, 32, 92, H6 Park Güell: Apr–Sep: 9:30am–7:30pm daily (Jul & Aug: from 9am); Oct–mid-Feb: 9:30am–6:30pm daily; mid-Feb–Mar: 9:30am–6pm daily (last adm: 1 hr before closing, timed tickets only); Casa Museu Gaudí: Apr–Sep: 9am–8pm daily; Oct–Mar: 10am–6pm daily Casa Museu Gaudí: 1 Jan Park Güell: parkguell.barcelona; Casa Museu Gaudí: sagradafamilia.org/casa-museu-gaudi

A UNESCO World Heritage Site, Park Güell is Antoni Gaudí's most colourful creation. Conceived as a garden city but never completed, it is now a stunning park that spills down Carmel Hill. Several of Gaudí's creations survive, including a pair of fairy-tale pavilions, a tiled salamander and the world's longest bench.

Gaudí was commissioned in the 1890s by Count Eusebi Güell to design a garden city on 20 hectares (50 acres) of his family estate, but the planned public buildings and 60 houses didn't come to fruition. What we see today was completed between 1910 and 1914, and the park opened in 1922. The Monumental Area, home to most of Gaudí's surviving works, requires a ticket, but the green expanses around the edge of this area are free to explore.

The Room of a Hundred Columns is a cavernous hall of 84 crooked pillars; it was intended as the marketplace for the estate. Above it is the Gran Plaça Circular, an open space with a snaking balcony of coloured mosaics that offers stunning views of the city.

Two pavilions at the entrance are by Gaudí, but the Casa Museu Gaudí, a gingerbread-style house where Gaudí lived from 1906 to 1926, was built by Francesc Berenguer.

PICTURE PERFECT
Double Shot

The Park Güell gives you two options for that ultimate Barcelona photograph: the mosaic-covered salamander that has become the park's emblem and the views from the Gran Plaça Circular.

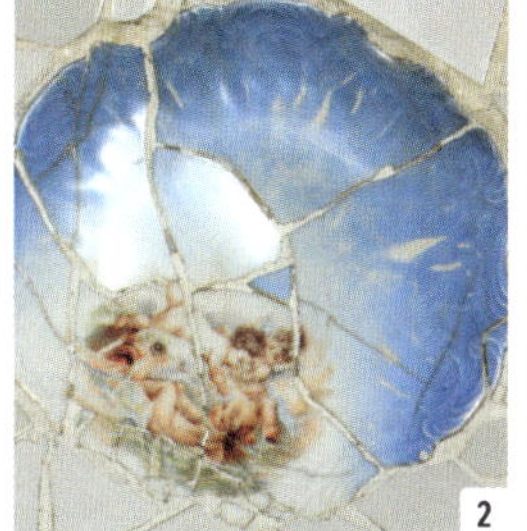

1 The two charming gatehouses have intricately tiled exteriors. Inside one is a museum with displays outlining the park's history.

2 The Casa Museu Gaudí has a beautiful garden with architectural features, such as these mosaics.

3 At the top of the stairs to the Gran Plaça Circular is Gaudí's salamander.

↑ Gran Plaça Circular, sitting on top of the Room of a Hundred Columns

99,354

The seating capacity of the stadium.

2

CAMP NOU

Carrer d'Aristides Maillol **Maria Cristina, Collblanc**
Hours vary, check website **1 Jan, 25 Dec**
fcbarcelona.cat

Camp Nou, Europe's largest football stadium, is home to the city's famous football club, Barcelona FC (known locally as Barça). Founded in 1899, it is one of the world's richest soccer clubs, and has more than 140,000 members.

Blau-grana (blue-burgundy), the colours of Barça's strip, hold an important place in the city's heart. The club's flags were used as an expression of local nationalist feelings during the Franco dictatorship, when the Catalan flag was banned.

The stadium is a magnificent, sweeping structure, built in 1957 to a design by Francesc Mitjans and Josep Soteras. An extension was added in 1982 and the entire stadium was renovated between 2023 and 2025 – it now comfortably seats around 105,000 fans.

The Barça Stadium Tour includes a visit to the club's popular museum, where Barcelona FC's many trophies are displayed. This is a glossy interactive experience, with touch-screen panels detailing the club's history and their many victories. After exploring the museum, visitors are taken on a tour of the stadium – from the changing rooms to the impossibly green pitch, the site of so many hotly contested matches.

↑ László Kubala memorial in front of the stadium

↑ Aerial view of Camp Nou, packed with fans on a match day

BARCELONA VS REAL MADRID

"Més que un club" ("More than a club") is the motto of Barcelona FC. More than anything else it has been a symbol of the struggle of Catalan nationalism against the central government in Madrid.

To fail to win La Liga is one thing; to come in behind Real Madrid is a disaster. Each season the big question is which of the two teams will win the title. In a memorable episode in 1941, Barça won 3-0 at home. At the return match in Madrid, the crowd was so hostile that the police and referee "advised" Barça to avoid any trouble. Demoralized by the intimidation, they lost 11-1.

← Walking down the colourful tunnel that takes players to the pitch

→ Admiring trophies in the Barça museum at Camp Nou

3

MONESTIR DE PEDRALBES

Baixada del Monestir 9 932 56 34 34 Reina Elisenda Apr-Sep: 10am-5pm Tue-Fri, 10am-7pm Sat, 10am-8pm Sun; Oct-Mar: 10am-2pm Tue-Fri, 10am-5pm Sat & Sun 1 Jan, 1 May, 24 Jun, 25 Dec monestirpedralbes.bcn.cat

Founded in 1326 by Elisenda de Montcada, fourth wife of Jaume II of Catalonia and Aragón, the monastery was home to the nuns of the Order of St Clare until 1983. Today, the monastery's church and cloister are considered to be an exemplar of Catalan Gothic architecture.

Approached through an ancient arch, the lovely monastery of Pedralbes retains the air of an enclosed community. This ambience is heightened by its well-preserved furnished kitchens, cells, infirmary and refectory. The nuns of the Order of St Clare moved to an adjoining property in 1983, when the monastery was opened to the public. The alabaster tomb of Elisenda de Montcada lies in the wall between church and cloister. On the church side, her effigy is dressed in royal robes; on the other, in a nun's habit.

The monastery is built around a three-storey cloister. Numerous works of art, as well as liturgical ornaments and pottery, are on display here. The Capella (chapel) de Sant Miquel has murals of the Passion and the Life of the Virgin, both painted by Ferrer Bassa in 1346. A medieval apothecary garden features medicinal herbs and other plants once used in the monastery's infirmary.

↑ Flowering plants framing the ancient walls of the well-preserved Monestir de Pedralbes

INSIDER TIP
Capella de Sant Miquel

Ferrer Bassa's murals in the quiet Capella de Sant Miquel depict the Passion and the Life of the Virgin in three pictorial strips running from left to right. On the upper level are paintings of the saints.

Admiring the Gothic monastery's carefully restored frescoes

Peaceful inner courtyard lined by the arched passages of the monastery's cloisters

Taking photos inside the Casa Vicens, designed by Gaudí

EXPERIENCE MORE

CosmoCaixa

Carrer d'Isaac Newton 26 Avinguda del Tibidabo 123, 196, H2, H4, V13, V15, V17, V19 10am-8pm daily 1 & 6 Jan, 25 Dec cosmocaixa.es

Revamped in 2004, the city's science museum is even more stimulating and interactive than its popular predecessor, which was housed in the Modernista building that still stands on site. Inside the glass-and-steel building, the museum has nine storeys, six of which are set underground, with exhibits covering the history of science, from the Big Bang to the computer age.

One of its most important pieces is a glasshouse containing a flooded forest, re-creating the environs of the Amazon. The exhibit sprawls across 1,000 sq m (10,800 sq ft) and is inhabited by fish, amphibians, insects, reptiles, birds, mammals and plant species. Elsewhere, an interactive tour through Earth's geological history explains processes such as erosion and sedimentation. Its highlight is a fascinating Geological Wall that examines various types of rock, each originating from a different geological process.

Other highlights include the Universe Room, which takes a look at the Big Bang theory; "Antarctic Base" is a re-creation of the original laboratory from the Juan Carlos I research station in Antarctica and features superb photographs of this remote region; and a 3D planetarium. There's also a number of innovative temporary exhibitions on environmental issues, and family activities.

5   

Casa Vicens

Carrer de les Carolines 20 Fontana, Lesseps 9:30am-8pm daily (Nov-Mar: to 6pm) 1 & 6 Jan, 25 Dec casavicens.org

Built in the 1880s as a summer home for the Vicens family, this magnificent building was Antoni Gaudí's first major commission and is one of the earliest buildings to be designed in the Modernista style. The captivating façade of the Casa Vicens is an explosion of colour, at once austere and flamboyant, with Neo-Mudéjar elements that hark back to Spain's Moorish architecture. The building was declared a UNESCO World Heritage Site in 2005. Inside, sgraffito floral motifs point to an obsession with nature that

The captivating façade of the Casa Vicens is an explosion of colour, at once austere and flamboyant, with Neo-Mudéjar elements that hark back to Spain's Moorish architecture.

HIDDEN GEM
Urban Jungle

Near the Parc de Joan Miró, the Parc de l'Espanya Industrial provides an interesting contrast to its neighbouring green space. Kids will love Andrés Nagel's dragon sculpture, which serves as a slide.

would become one of Gaudí's trademarks. Across the ground and first floors are perfectly preserved residential rooms, which feature original furniture designed by Gaudí and paintings by Catalan artist Francesc Torrescassana. The second floor is home to the permanent exhibition, which details the history of the house.

In typical Gaudí style, there is something of interest from top to bottom. Amble around the rooftop walkway which looks out at calming views of the Gràcia neighbourhood. Meanwhile, down in the old coal cellar you'll find an underground bookshop.

Outside, the garden is the result of a 1925 extension and today home to the pleasant Hofmann Café. Visitors can follow one of the recommended walking route maps handed out at the ticket desk, before pondering over what they have seen, while enjoying coffee and pastries at this lovely café.

A visit to Casa Vicens can easily be combined with a walk through the charming Gràcia district.

6

Parc de Joan Miró

Carrer d'Aragó 2
Tarragona 8am-9pm daily (Nov-March: to 7pm)

Barcelona's 19th-century *escorxador* (slaughterhouse) was transformed into this unusual park in the 1980s – hence its alternative name, Parc de l'Escorxador.

The park is constructed on two planes: the lower plane, fringed with shady paths and studded with palm trees, is popular with dog walkers and for football kick-abouts; the upper is paved and dominated by the park's main attraction, a magnificent 1983 sculpture by the Catalan artist Joan Miró entitled *Dona i Ocell* (Woman and Bird). Standing 22 m (72 ft) high in the middle of a pool, its surface is covered with colourful glazed tiles. The park is very popular with locals, making it a good place to get a taste of what Barcelona's like away from the main tourist hubs. Other attractions include a water feature, sports courts and play areas for children.

DRINK

Balius

This smart, atmospheric cocktail bar has a mid-century look. Music fans descend on Sunday evenings for live jazz.

Carrer de Pujades 196
baliusbar.com

Café Salambó

A split-level café with pool tables, this is a popular local haunt that does some excellent creative cocktails.

Carrer de Torrijos 51
cafesalambo.com

Elephanta

Tucked out of the way, this tiny bar serves expertly mixed cocktails, using more than 40 gins.

Carrer del Torrent d'En Vidalet 37
elephanta.cat

El Maravillas

Located not far from Camp Nou stadium, this neighbourhood bar serves excellent beers and tapas.

Plaça de la Concòrdia 15 elmaravillas.cat

Dona i Ocell, the statue by Miró himself that overlooks the Parc de Joan Miró

Visitors taking in the rainforest exhibit at CosmoCaixa

PICTURE PERFECT
Funicular del Tibidabo

Capture a cheerful shot of the funicular ascending the tracks to the top of Tibidabo. The views of the city behind make for a wonderful backdrop.

Tibidabo

Plaça del Tibidabo 3–4 Avda Tibidabo, then bus 196 & Funicular del Tibidabo; Peu del Funicular, then bus 111 & Funicular de Vallvidrera T2A from Plaça de Catalunya tibidabo.cat

The name of this high vantage point is inspired by Tibidabo's views of the city and comes from the Latin *tibi dabo* (meaning "I shall give you") – a reference to the Temptation of Christ, when Satan took him up a mountain and offered him the world spread at his feet. One of the greatest draws to the area is the hugely popular **Parc d'Atraccions** (Amusement Park), which first opened in 1908. The rides were renovated in the 1980s. While the old ones retain their charm, the newer ones have the latest innovations. Standing at 517 m (1,696 ft), their location adds to the thrill. The amusement park offers a regular programme of events throughout the year, including parades and interactive shows for children. Also in the park is the Museu d'Autòmats, displaying automated toys, jukeboxes and slot machines.

Tibidabo is crowned by the **Temple Expiatori del Sagrat Cor** (Church of the Sacred Heart). More often referred to as simply the "Temple of Tibidabo", this was built with religious zeal but little taste by Enric Sagnier between 1902 and 1911. Inside, the church is split across two floors, with the interiors a mix of Roman and Gothic style. A lift (for which there is a small fee) takes you up to the feet of an enormous figure of Christ, where you'll find an even better vantage point for exceptional views across the city.

The heights of Tibidabo can be reached by Barcelona's oldest surviving tram service, as well as via the renovated funicular. Just a short bus ride away is another viewpoint – the impressive Torre de Collserola.

Parc d'Atraccions

Plaça del Tibidabo 3
Hours vary, check website
tibidabo.cat

Temple Expiatori del Sagrat Cor

Cumbre del Tibidabo
Hours vary, check website
tibidabo.salesianos.edu

→

Looking out across the city from the Torre de Collserola's viewing platform

Torre Bellesguard

Carrer de Bellesguard 20 Avda Tibidabo 123, 196 10am-3pm Tue-Sun 1 & 6 Jan, 25 & 26 Dec bellesguardgaudi.com

Bellesguard means "beautiful spot" and this place in the Collserola hills was chosen by the medieval Catalan kings as their summer home. The castle, built in 1408, was a favourite residence of Martí the Humanist.

The surrounding district of Sant Gervasi was developed in the 19th century, after the coming of the railway. In 1900, Gaudí built the present house on the site of the castle, which had fallen into ruin. Its castellated features and the Gothic-inspired windows refer clearly to the original castle. The roof is topped by a distinctive Gaudí tower. Ceramic fish mosaics located by the main door symbolize Catalonia's past maritime power. Guided tours, running from Thursday to Sunday, can be booked ahead.

Torre de Collserola

Carretera de Vallvidrera al Tibidabo Peu del Funicular, then bus 111 & Funicular de Vallvidrera Hours vary, check website torredecollserola.com

In this city that enjoys thrills, the ultimate ride is offered by the communications tower near Tibidabo mountain. A glass-sided lift swiftly reaches the top of this 288-m- (944-ft-) high structure, standing atop a steep hill. Needle-like in form, it is a tubular steel mast on a concrete pillar, anchored by 12 huge steel cables. There are 13 levels; the top one has an observatory with a telescope and a public viewing platform with a 360-degree view of the city, the sea, and the mountain chain upon which Tibidabo sits.

Did You Know?

The Torre de Collserola was designed by English architect Norman Foster for the 1992 Olympics.

←

Multicoloured neon lights of rides in Tibidabo's popular Parc d'Atraccions

↑ Well-maintained labyrinth at the Parc del Laberint d'Horta

Parc del Laberint d'Horta

Carrer Germans Desvalls, Passeig dels Castanyers Mundet Apr-Oct: 10am-8pm daily; Nov-Mar: 10am-6pm daily guia.barcelona.cat/detall/parc-del-laberint-d-horta_92086011952.html

As you might suspect, given its name, the centrepiece of the city's oldest park, created in the 18th century for Joan Antoni Desvalls, Marquès de Llupià i d'Alfarràs, is a cypress maze.

Sloping steeply uphill, the semi-wild garden extends from the entrance just beside the marquis's palace, home to a gardening school. It is a veritable compendium of Baroque fantasies. Classical temples dedicated to Ariadne (who helped Theseus escape from the Minotaur's labyrinth) and Danae (mother of Perseus) flank the base of a monumental flight of steps that lead up to a Neo-Classical temple.

Elsewhere, there is a faux cemetery, an interpretation of a "romantic" garden and, in the woodland into which the garden eventually leads, a hermit's cave.

Museu del Disseny

Plaça de les Glòries Catalanes 37-38 Glòries 7, 92, 192, H12 9am-9pm daily (from 3:30pm Mon) 1 Jan, 1 May, 24 Jun, 25 Dec dissenyhub.barcelona

With more than 70,000 objects, the Museu del Disseny (Design Museum) is a merging of the Decorative Arts, Ceramics, Textile and Clothing Museum, and the Graphic Arts Cabinet, which were previously housed at different sites across the city. The glass-and-zinc-clad building is a design statement in its own right, and was created by architects Josep Martorell, Oriol Bohigas and David Mackay.

The combined collection pieces together a long design history. Organized on broad thematic lines, it traces the evolution of the objects that surround us in our everyday lives, from the decorative arts of past centuries (some artifacts date back to the Middle Ages) to contemporary design. The fascinating exhibits include furniture, clothing, jewellery, prints and posters, ceramics, glasswork and even exquisitely printed wallpaper. A varied programme of lectures and activities for children are held here, including textile and design workshops (ideal for young fashionistas). Tickets are valid for two days, so you

INSIDER TIP
Culture on the Cheap

To honour International Museum Day, many of the city's museums throw open their doors for free on 18 May - for many, it's the only day of the year that the fee is waived for visitors.

Modern, angular exterior of the Museu del Disseny at dusk

↑ Catalan artworks on display within the Museu Can Framis

have plenty of time to take in the entire collection. Entry is free on Sunday afternoons.

12

Museu Can Framis

Carrer de Roc Boronat 116-126, Poblenou Glòries, Poblenou 6, 7, 40, 42, 56, 141, 192, B25 11am-6pm Tue-Sat, 11am-2pm Sun Public hols fundaciovila casas.com

The Can Framis museum occupies a renovated 18th-century wool factory, which is a monument to local industry. A modern building has been attached to the factory and its striking geometric architecture is worth seeing in itself. It is managed by the Vila Casa Foundation and holds a permanent exhibition, "The Existential Labyrinth", of around 300 works, which are by a range of artists born or living in Catalonia, like Tàpies, Llimós and Cuixart. The Espai A0 gallery hosts temporary exhibitions by local artists and photographers. The museum is surrounded by a park, which makes for a pleasant stroll.

SHOP

Vinus & Brindis

The perfect place to pick up a bottle or two of excellent Catalonian wine. There's also a wide range of international wines and a counter bar.

Carrer de Calaf 46
vinusbrindis.com

Els Encants

This vast flea market in Poblenou has a rippling mirror roof that reflects the piles of clothes, furniture and bric-a-brac inside.

Avinguida Meridiana 69 encantsbcn.com

Palo Alto Market

Come to satisfy all your one-of-a-kind and epic-street-food needs. Live music and a party atmosphere make it an occasion.

Carrer dels Pellaires 30
palomarketfest.com

BARCELONA BEACHES

Sant Miquel
Overlooked by Rebecca Horn's sculpture, this is an easy-to-access beach.
Barceloneta

Barceloneta
This strand is home to "Espai de Mar", which offers a whole host of fun activities *(p92)*.
Barceloneta

Bogatell
One of the city's longest and busiest stretches of sand, this beach is popular with families.
Llacuna

Mar Bella
This is Barcelona's unofficial LGBTQ+ beach, offering bars, DJs and cocktails.
Poblenou

El Poblenou

Rambla del Poblenou
Poblenou

This former industrial district underwent rapid gentrification in the 2010s and is now home to tech hubs, trendy hotels and hip coffee shops. The area is centred on the Rambla del Poblenou, a restaurant- and bar-lined avenue that extends from Avinguda Diagonal down to the sea. Here, palm trees back a stretch of sandy beach. A walk around the quieter streets leading from the Rambla will reveal a few protected pieces of industrial architecture, legacies from the time when the city was a thriving industrial hub.

Along the parallel Carrer del Ferrocarril is the Plaça de Prim with low, whitewashed houses that are reminiscent of a small country town.

Museu de Ciències Naturals - Museu Blau

Plaça Leonardo da Vinci 4-5, Parc del Fòrum
Maresme-Fòrum H16
10am-6pm Tue-Fri (Mar-Sep: to 7pm), 1-7pm Sat, 10am-8pm Sun Mon; 1 Jan, 1 May, 24 Jun, 25 Dec
museuciencies.cat

The Natural Science Museum is a Barcelona institution. More than 100 years old, it contains 3 million specimens

One of the exhibits at *(inset)* the Natural Science Museum

in the fields of mineralogy, palaeontology, zoology and botany.

Previously located in the Old Town, it is now housed in the Parc del Fòrum in a modern, innovative building designed by architects Herzog & de Meuron, who also created the Planet Life exhibition. This vast exhibition sprawls across a third of the museum's space and is essentially a journey through the history of life and its evolution to the present day. The high-tech museum is split into three sections: "Biography of the Earth", "Earth Today" and "Islands of Science". State-of-the-art interactive and audiovisual displays take the visitor on a journey of discovery, with well-distilled explanations of the subject. There are also temporary exhibitions, a Media Library and a "Science Nest" for children up to age six at weekends, where images and sound effects re-create different natural surroundings.

Estació del Nord

Avinguda de Vilanova
Arc de Triomf

Only the 1861 façade and the grand 1915 entrance remain of this former railway station, now remodelled as a sports centre, a police headquarters, and the city's bus station.

Two elegant, blue-tiled sculptures, *Espiral arbrada* (Branched Spiral) and *Cel caigut* (Fallen Sky) by American sculptor Beverly Pepper (1992), sweep through the park opposite the station. At Avinguda de Vilanova 12 is a carefully restored Modernista building constructed as a power station in 1897 by architect Pere Falqués.

Nearby, on Carrer de Zamora, is the Teatre Nacional de Catalunya – a vast temple to culture by Barcelona architect Ricardo Bofill – and the state-of-the-art concert hall L'Auditori.

EAT

Botafumeiro

Rub shoulders with local diners over mouthwatering platters of ultra-fresh shellfish that make every meal an occasion.

Carrer Gran de Gràcia 81 **botafumeiro.es**

Cinc Sentits

This Michelin-starred restaurant has seasonal Catalan cuisine with modern twists, all made from locally sourced ingredients.

Carrer d'Entença 60
cincsentits.com

A LONG WALK POBLENOU

Distance 3.5 km (2 miles) **Nearest metro** Glòries **Time** 1 hour

The trendy district of Poblenou once had the highest concentration of smoke-belching factories in Catalonia. By the 1960s, these had gone out of business or moved to the outskirts, leaving their old buildings to decay. With the 1992 Olympics came an impetus for recovery and since then, Poblenou's warehouses have been spruced up and converted into chic studios for artists. Other industrial buildings have been replaced with global branded hotels and gleaming office spaces. Nowhere in Barcelona is change happening so quickly before your eyes.

A modern green space within the city, **Parc de les Glòries** *has playgrounds, gardens and a spacious lawn.*

A major thoroughfare, **Avinguda Diagonal** *has a wide seaward extension.*

START
PARC DE LES GLÒRIES
Glòries
Museu del Disseny
Torre Agbar
Ca l'Aranyó
AVINGUDA DIAGONAL
CARRER DE BOLIVIA
CARRER DE TÀNGER
RAMBLA DEL POBLENOU
Dr Josep Trueta
CARRER DE LA LLACUNA
El Tio Che
Casino l'Aliança de Poblenou
CARRE

It's worth visiting the **Museu del Disseny** (p156) *just to admire the curious shape of this local landmark.*

The **Torre Agbar**, *a domed cylindrical tower of 33 floors, has been described as an upended blue cigar.*

The main street of Poblenou, buzzing **Rambla del Poblenou** (p158) *leads down to the sea.*

The **memorial to Dr Josep Trueta** *honours a Poblenou-born surgeon who saved lives during the Civil War.*

El Tio Che, *a shop founded in 1912, sells ice cream and turrón (a sweet made of almonds).*

The **Casino de l'Aliança de Poblenou** *is a concert hall, not a gambling enterprise as its name suggests.*

0 metres 300
0 yards 300
N

↑ Glass-and-zinc building of the Museu del Disseny

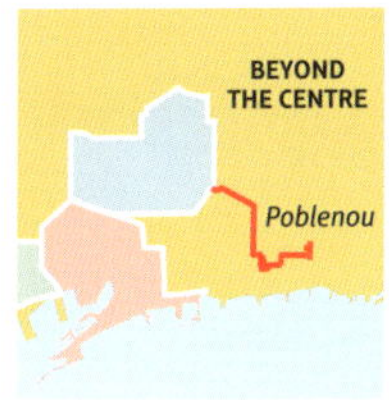

Locator Map
For more detail see p143

↑ Wandering along the Rambla del Poblenou

The **public library** *at Carrer del Joncar 35 is housed in a building that used to be a textile factory.*

Take a breather in the secret garden at the Palo Alto art complex. Nature runs riot in this haven of peace, shaded by palms and ablaze with bougainvillea and jasmine.

On a corner of Carrer de Provençals rises a graceful flat-topped **chimney**, *the highest in Barcelona.*

Pere IV
C DE PERE IV
AVINGUDA DIAGONAL
Fluvià
CAMÍ ANTIC DE VALÈNCIA
CARRER DE PALLARS
CARRER DE PUJADES
CARRER DE LLULL
CARRER DEL JONCAR
CARRER DE RAMON TURRÓ
CARRER DE BILBAO
CARRER DE LOPE DE VEGA
CARRER D'ESPRONCEDA
CARRER DE BAC
CARRER DEL FLUVIÀ
CARRER DE PROVENÇALS
CARRER DE MARIA AGUILÓ
CARRER DE LA SELVA
C DE LA SELVA
CARRER DE JOSEP PLA
Poblenou
Selva de Mar
Selva de Mar
FINISH
Chimney
Biblioteca Poblenou
Mercat del Poblenou
Palo Alto Garden
Torre de les Aigües
Parc de Diagonal Mar
TAULAT
PLAÇA DEL PRIM
PASSEIG DEL TAULAT
PASSEIG DEL TAULAT
PASSEIG DE GARCIA FÀRIA

At **Plaça del Prim**, *you'll see gnarled, leaning ombu trees and low whitewashed houses.*

The **Mercat del Poblenou** *is the district's market, where locals stock up on fresh produce.*

The round, red-brick **Torre de les Aigües** *was built to raise and store water from the nearby Besos river.*

A LONG WALK GRÀCIA

Distance 2.5 km (1.5 miles) **Nearest metro** Plaça Joan Carles I **Time** 45 minutes

When you cross the Avinguda Diagonal and plunge into the maze of streets and small squares, it is easy to think that you have left the city behind and entered a village. Since Gràcia became part of Barcelona in 1897, it has never lost its sense of identity. During the day, it feels calmly removed from the pace of modern metropolitan life. In summer and in the evening, however, crowds are drawn to its shops and nightlife.

Locator Map
For more detail see p143

Inspired by Moorish architecture, **Casa Vicens** (p150) *is an early work by Gaudí.*

Plaça de Trilla *was inaugurated under the name of Queen Amàlia.*

There is a Civil War air-raid shelter at **Plaça Diament** *– open on Sundays by appointment* (call 93 219 61 34).

Plaça Virreina *with the church of Sant Joan is one of Gràcia's most agreeable little squares.*

Plaça del Sol *is a popular nightlife hub known for its lively bars and terraces.*

Plaça Revolució de Setembre de 1868 *commemorates the coup d'état led by General Prim.*

On **Plaça de la Vila de Gràcia**, *a 33-m (108-ft) clock tower is overlooked by the sky-blue façade of local government headquarters.*

The **Casa Bonaventura Ferrer** *has stonework of swirling leaves.*

START/FINISH

From **Plaça Joan Carles I**, *the Passeig de Gràcia continues briefly as a modest avenue.*

The **Casa Fuster** *has been converted into a hotel.*

0 metres 200
0 yards 200
N

Brightly decorated Casa Vicens, designed by Antoni Gaudí

Breezy balcony and weathered façade of a house in Cadaqués

CATALONIA

It was at Empúries, on Catalonia's Costa Brava ("wild coast"), that the Romans first set foot on the land that they would name Hispania. After the fall of the Roman Empire and a period of Visigothic, then Moorish rule, the region was conquered by the Franks in the early 9th century. It later enjoyed independence as the County of Barcelona before being incorporated into the Crown of Aragón as the autonomous Principality of Catalonia. This regional autonomy survived the union of Castile and Aragón in 1492, persisting until 1714, when Felipe V centralized the Spanish government in Castile.

In the second half of the 19th century, the independence movement reemerged, but any progress towards the reestablishment of Catalan autonomy came to a brutal stop when Franco stepped into power in the 1930s.

Following Franco's death, full autonomy was restored to Catalonia and its Generalitat in 1979. Since then, the independence movement has gathered significant momentum, reaching a head in 2017 when a controversial referendum saw Catalonians vote to become an independent republic. This referendum was declared illegal by the Spanish government, and was boycotted by unionist factions; however, the Catalan push for independence continues.

VAL D'ARAN 8
BAQUEIRA-BERET 5
VIELHA 6
PARC NACIONAL D'AIGÜESTORTES 9
ANDORRA 11
PUIGCERDÀ 17
7 VALL DE BOÍ
10 LA SEU D'URGELL
SOLSONA 28
CARDONA 23
ARAGÓN
CATALONIA
LLEIDA 30
MONESTIR DE MONTSERRAT 1
MONESTIR DE POBLET 2
MONTBLANC 25
27 SANTES CREUS
26 VILAFRANCA DEL PENEDÈS
31 SITGES
4 TARRAGONA'S ROMAN RUINS
34 COSTA DAURADA
TORTOSA 33
32 DELTA DE L'EBRE
Pica d'Estats 3,115 m (10,220 ft)
Torreta de l'Orri 2,439 m (8,002 ft)
Torre de Cadí 2,567 m (8,422 ft)
Golf de Sant Jordi
Mediterranean Sea
Costa
0 kilometres 40
0 miles 40
N

CATALONIA

Must Sees

1 Monestir de Montserrat
2 Monestir de Poblet
3 Girona
4 Tarragona's Roman Ruins

Experience More

5 Baqueira-Beret
6 Vielha
7 Vall de Boí
8 Val d'Aran
9 Parc Nacional d'Aigüestortes
10 La Seu d'Urgell
11 Andorra
12 Olot
13 Sant Joan de les Abadesses
14 Ripoll
15 Cadaqués
16 Empúries
17 Puigcerdà
18 Figueres
19 Peratallada
20 Blanes
21 Tossa de Mar
22 Sant Pol de Mar
23 Cardona
24 Vic
25 Montblanc
26 Vilafranca del Penedès
27 Santes Creus
28 Solsona
29 Besalú
30 Lleida
31 Sitges
32 Delta de L'Ebre
33 Tortosa
34 Costa Daurada

1

MONESTIR DE MONTSERRAT

Parc Natural de la Muntanya de Montserrat, Barcelona
Aeri de Montserrat, then cable car; Monistrol-Enllaç, then La Cremallera rack railway From Barcelona
Basilica: 7am-8pm daily; museum: 10am-5:45pm daily (to 6:45pm Sat & Sun) montserratvisita.com

The "Serrated Mountain", its highest peak rising to 1,236 m (4,055 ft), is a magnificent setting for Catalonia's holiest place, the Monastery of Montserrat, which is surrounded by chapels and hermits' caves.

GREAT VIEW
Natural Wonder

Many locations in the Parc Natural de la Muntanya de Montserrat offer great views of Montserrat's tooth-shaped rock formations. Bird-watchers will want their binoculars at the ready as birds of prey soar above.

The monastery has a long history, and a chapel on the site was first mentioned in documents dating from the 9th century. The present-day monastery was founded in the 11th century but in 1811, when the French attacked Catalonia in the War of Independence, it was destroyed and the monks killed. Rebuilt and repopulated in 1844, it was a beacon of Catalan culture during the Franco years. Today Benedictine monks live here and the site has a hallowed atmosphere. One of the most magical experiences is listening to the Escolania boys' choir singing in the basilica. You can catch their echoing voices at 1pm Monday to Friday and at noon on Sundays (check website for additional times).

Gothic cloister

The museum has a collection of 19th- and 20th-century Catalan paintings. It also displays liturgical items from the Holy Land.

Plaça de Santa Maria's focal points are two wings of the Gothic cloister built in 1476. The modern monastery was designed by Françesc Folguera.

Inner courtyard

Monestir de Montserrat, in its dramatic setting below the mountain ↑

The mountain towering behind the Monestir de Montserrat

Awe-inspiring interior of the domed basilica

Agapit Vallmitjana sculpted Christ and the apostles on the basilica's Neo-Renaissance façade in 1900.

The Black Virgin (La Moreneta) looks down from behind the altar. Protected behind glass, her wooden orb protrudes for pilgrims to touch.

The domed basilica's interior

The rack railway (La Cremallera) follows a rail line built in 1880.

Cable car to Aeri de Montserrat station

THE VIRGIN OF MONTSERRAT

The small statue of La Moreneta (literally "the little dark one") is said to have been made by St Luke and brought here by St Peter in 50 CE. Centuries later, the statue is believed to have been hidden from the Moors in the nearby Santa Cova (Holy Cave). Carbon dating suggests, however, that the statue was carved around the 12th century. In 1881 La Moreneta became patroness of Catalonia.

Monestir de Poblet, surrounded by golden vines

2

MONESTIR DE POBLET

Off N240, 10 km (6 miles) from Montblanc, Tarragona
L'Espluga de Francolí, then taxi Tarragona
Hours vary, check website 1 & 6 Jan, 25 & 26 Dec
poblet.cat

The largest monastery in the "Cistercian triangle", the Monastery of Santa Maria de Poblet is a haven of tranquillity and a resting place of kings. At sunset, it almost seems to glow in heavenly light.

The Monestir de Poblet was the first and most important of three Cistercian monasteries that helped to consolidate power in Catalonia after it had been recaptured from the Moors by Ramon Berenguer IV. Despite this former importance, Poblet was abandoned and fell into disrepair as a result of the Ecclesiastical confiscations of 1835. Restoration began in 1930 and monks returned in 1940.

THE CISTERCIAN TRIANGLE

Built in the 12th century, the spectacular monasteries of Poblet, Vallbona de les Monges and Santes Creus are captivating examples of Gothic architecture, and each has served as the final resting place of Catalan royalty at one point or another. A scenic 100-km (60-mile) drive will take you around all three. No longer used by a religious order, Santa Creus offers visitors the best opportunity to explore a Cistercian monastery.

Timeline

1150
Santes Creus and Poblet monasteries are founded.

1156
Monastery at Vallbona de les Monges founded.

1196
▲ Alfonso II is the first king to be buried here.

1336–87
Reign of Pere the Ceremonious, who designates Poblet a royal pantheon.

1479
Juan II, last king of Aragón, buried here.

1835
Disentailment of monasteries; Poblet ravaged royal pantheon.

1940
Monks return.

1952
▼ Tombs reconstructed; royal remains returned.

The Gothic scriptorium was converted into a library in the 17th century.

Former kitchen

The perfectly square chapterhouse has tiers of benches for the monks.

Sant Esteve cloister

↑ The cloisters, with capitals carved with scrollwork

Parlour cloister

Behind the stone altar, supported by Romanesque columns, an alabaster reredos fills the apse.

New sacristy

The tombs in the pantheon of kings were begun in 1359. In 1950 the sculptures were restored by Frederic Marès.

The evocative, vaulted cloisters were built in the 12th and 13th centuries and were the centre of monastic life.

The Abbey Church, large and unadorned, with three naves, is a typical Cistercian building.

Baroque church façade

← The many rooms that make up the Monestir de Poblet

GIRONA

Girona **Rambla de la Llibertat 1; girona.cat/turisme**

This handsome town puts on its best face beside the Riu Onyar, where colourful buildings rise above the water. These were built in the 19th century to replace sections of the city wall damaged during an 1809 siege by French troops. Most of the rest of the ramparts are intact and make up the Passeig Arqueològic (Archaeological Walk), which runs around the city. Behind the houses, the Rambla de la Llibertat is lined with shops and cafés.

PICTURE PERFECT
Watercolour

When crossing the Onyar River, the Pont de les Peixateries Velles offers a chance to snap a shot of Girona's austere cathedral peeking over the colourful rooftops.

Museu d'Història dels Jueus

Carrer de la Força 8 972 21 67 61 Jul & Aug: 10am-8pm daily (to 2pm Sun); Sep-Jun: 10am-6pm daily (to 2pm Sun & Mon) 1 & 6 Jan, 25 & 26 Dec

Amid the maze of alleyways in the old town is the former Jewish quarter of El Call. One of the West's most important Jewish areas during medieval times, it is now home to the Museu d'Història dels Jueus, which gives a history of Girona's Jews, who were expelled in the late 15th century.

Cathedral

Plaça de la Catedral Hours vary, check website 1 Jan, Good Friday, 25 Dec catedraldegirona.cat

The style of Girona Cathedral's solid west face is pure Catalan Baroque; the cloister and the tower are Romanesque, but the rest of the building is Gothic. The single nave is the widest in the world. Behind the altar is a marble throne called "Charlemagne's Chair" after the Frankish king whose troops took Girona in 785 CE. The museum's most famous item is a large, well-preserved 11th- to 12th-century tapestry called *The Creation*. There are also Romanesque paintings.

Museu d'Art

Pujada de la Catedral 12 May-Sep: 10am-7pm Tue-Sat, 10am-2pm Sun; Oct-Apr: 10am-6pm Tue-Sat, 10am-2pm Sun 1 & 6 Jan, 24-26 & 31 Dec museuart.com

This former episcopal palace is one of Catalonia's best art galleries, with works ranging from the Romanesque period to the 20th century, including ecclesiastical items. Highlights are 10th-century carvings, a silver-clad altar from Sant Pere de Rodes and a 12th-century beam from Cruïlles.

Colourful apartment buildings lining the Riu Onyar in Girona

Museu d'Història de Girona

Carrer de la Força 27 May-Sep: 10:30am-6:30pm Tue-Sat, 10:30am-1:30pm Sun; Oct-Apr: 10:30am-5:30pm Tue-Sat, 10:30am-1:30pm Sun girona.cat/museuhistoria

This museum is housed in a former convent and you can still explore the cemetery.

Monestir de Sant Pere de Galligants

Carrer de Santa Llúcia 8 Jun-Sep: 10am-7pm Tue-Sat, 10am-2pm Sun; Oct-May: 10am-6pm Tue-Sat, 10am-2pm Sun macgirona.cat

This Romanesque temple provides a beautiful setting for the city's archaeological museum, with a collection spanning everything from pre-historic tools to Roman mosaics.

Basílica de Sant Feliu

Pujada de Sant Feliu 29 10am-6pm daily (from 1pm Sun) catedral degirona.cat

Begun in the 14th century, this staunch basilica was built over the tombs of St Felix and St Narcissus.

Museu del Cinema

Carrer de la Sèquia 1 Hours vary, check website museudelcinema.cat

A film buff's paradise, the Museu del Cinema offers a wide selection of exhibitions. The Tomàs Mallol Collection is particularly impressive, with around 20,000 objects that tell the history of the still image as well as motion pictures.

El Celler de Can Roca

This three-Michelin-starred restaurant serves traditional dishes with a twist.

Carrer de Can Sunyer 48 Sun & Mon, Tue lunch cellercanroca.com

Banys Àrabs

Carrer del Rei Ferran el Catòlic s/n Hours vary, check website 1 & 6 Jan, 24-26 Dec banysarabs.cat

Despite their name, the Banys Àrabs were built under King Alfons I in the late 12th century, about 300 years after the Moors had left. The most striking feature is the octagonal pool, with a domed ceiling.

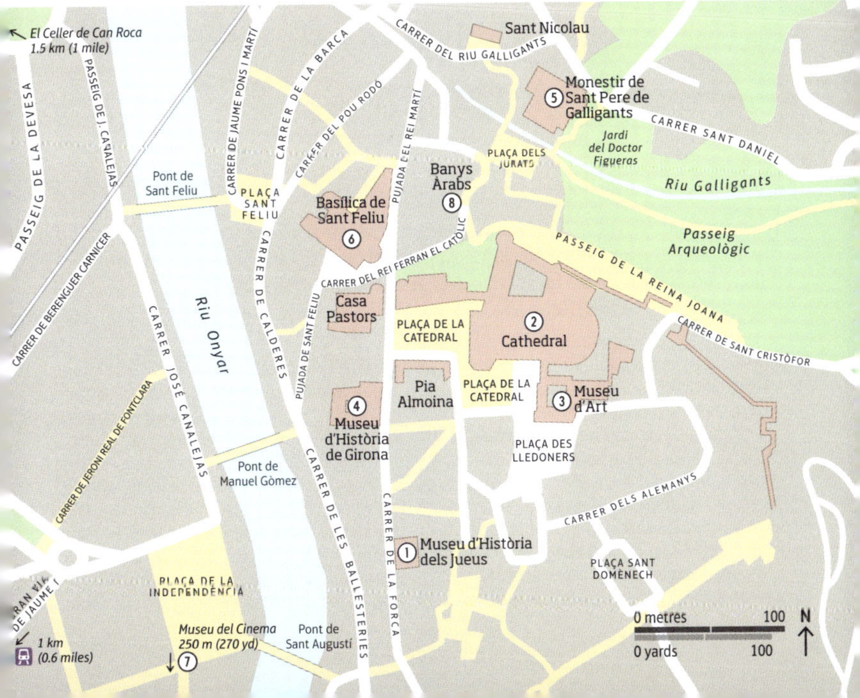

El Celler de Can Roca 1.5 km (1 mile)
Sant Nicolau
Carrer del Riu Galligants
Monestir de Sant Pere de Galligants (5)
Carrer Sant Daniel
Jardí del Doctor Figueras
Plaça dels Jurats
Riu Galligants
Passeig Arqueològic
Banys Àrabs (8)
Basílica de Sant Feliu (6)
Plaça Sant Feliu
Pont de Sant Feliu
Riu Onyar
Passeig de la Reina Joana
Carrer de Sant Cristòfor
Casa Pastors
Plaça de la Catedral
Cathedral (2)
Museu d'Art (3)
Pia Almoina
Museu d'Història de Girona (4)
Plaça dels Lledoners
Pont de Manuel Gòmez
Carrer dels Alemanys
Museu d'Història dels Jueus (1)
Plaça Sant Domènech
Plaça de la Independència
Museu del Cinema 250 m (270 yd) (7)
Pont de Sant Agustí
1 km (0.6 miles)
0 metres 100
0 yards 100
N

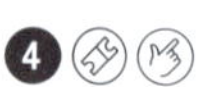

TARRAGONA'S ROMAN RUINS

Tarragona Reus Airport Carrer de los Caballeros 14; mnat.cat

Today an industrial port, Tarragona stands on the site of the oldest Roman city in Spain. The archaeological ensemble of Tarraco, as Tarragona was then called, comprises the most important Roman ruins in the Iberian Peninsula. The site was declared a UNESCO World Heritage Site in 2000.

The Romans established Tarraco as a base from which to conquer Iberia, fortifying the imperial town with thick walls and sentry towers. The town's great amphitheatre, forums and circus, as well as numerous temples, can be visited today on the Roman Route designed by the Museu Nacional Arqueològic de Tarragona, whose important collection of Roman artifacts includes bronze tools and beautiful mosaics.

A walk along the remains of the old Roman walls that line Passeig Arqueològic takes you past the Casa Canals, an 18th-century stately home built into the Roman wall. Around the corner the Fòrum Provincial now bustles with bars and restaurants. Stone steps take you up to the *recinte de culte*, an ancient site of worship.

Atop the cliffs, at the end of Rambla Nova, is the magnificent Amfiteatre Romà – and great sea views. Nearby, the Praetorium, a Roman tower, now displays excavated artifacts in rooms above the cavernous passageways of the Roman circus, where you can take a tour.

Soaring arches of the Aqüeducte de les Ferreres passing over the hiking trails of wooded "Devil Ravine"

EAT

El Llagut

This rustic tavern is known for its fresh seafood and other Catalan favourites. Sample a variety of tapas dishes or try the rice with mixed seafood.

Carrer de Natzaret 10
elllagut.com

DRINK

Barrio sur

It's all about the fabulous cocktails at this intimate bar that has occasional live music.

Carrer de les Cuirateries 12
675 66 71 46

1 Carved marble sarcophagus of Hippolytus at the Praetorium dates to the 2nd century CE.

2 Tourists explore the subterranean gallery of the ancient Roman Circus.

3 Well-preserved Amfiteatre Romà backed by turquoise seas.

1

GREAT VIEW
Aqüeducte de les Ferreres

Walk along the central ridge of this magnificent 2nd-century aqueduct that once linked ancient Tarraco with the Riu Francolí for sublime 360° views of woodland and the city. It is in Parc Ecohistòric del Pont del Diable, 4 km (2 miles) from Tarragona centre.

2

3

EXPERIENCE MORE

5

Baqueira-Beret

Lleida baqueira.es

This extensive ski resort, one of the best in all of Spain, is popular with both the public and the Spanish royal family. In the winter months, there is reliable snow cover across over 100 runs at altitudes from 1,520 m to 2,470 m (4,990 ft to 8,100 ft). The resort has a number of good beginners' slopes, although intermediate and advanced skiers will benefit most from the pistes on offer.

Baqueira and Beret were once separate mountain villages and were popular with the Romans for their fantastic thermal springs. The villages merged to form a single resort once they became popular destinations for skiing and other winter sports. These days the thermal springs are appreciated by tired skiers.

Did You Know?

With 160 km (100 miles) of slopes, Baqueira-Beret is the largest ski resort in Catalonia.

Vielha

Lleida Carrer Sarriulèra 10; 973 64 01 10

A convenient base for skiing at Baqueira-Beret, the capital of the Val d'Aran retains its medieval past. The Romanesque church of Sant Miquel has a 12th-century crucifix, the *Mig Aran Christ*, representing the Descent from the Cross. The **Musèu dera Val d'Aran** is devoted to Aranese culture.

Musèu dera Val d'Aran

Carrer Major 26 973 64 18 15 10am-1:30pm & 5-8pm Mon-Sat, 10am-1:30pm Sun Public hols; Mon; mid-Sep-mid-Jun

Vall de Boí

Lleida N230 La Pobla de Segur Pont de Suert Barruera; vallboi.cat/en

Spread across northern Catalonia is an exceptional collection of medieval buildings constructed between the 11th and 13th centuries. The Vall de Boí, located on the edge of the Parc Nacional d'Aigüestortes, has magnificent examples of this Romanesque architecture *(p178)*. Dotted throughout the valley are nine tiny villages, each built around a Catalan Romanesque church. These churches, dating from the 11th and 12th centuries, comprise the Romanesque ensemble, a World Heritage Site. The Centre del Romànic, in Boí, has maps of the Romanesque route, which takes in all nine churches, such as Sant Joan in the village of Boí itself, Sant Climent in Taüll and Santa Maria.

Between 1919 and 1923, the originals were taken for

↓ Skiers pausing at the top of a wide piste in Baqueira-Beret

Warm autumnal colours on the lush slopes of the Val d'Aran

safekeeping to the Museu Nacional d'Art de Catalunya *(p130)* in Barcelona, where their settings have been re-created. Excellent replicas now stand in their place. You can climb the towers of Sant Climent for superb views of the surrounding countryside. Other churches on the Romanesque route include those at Coll, which has fine ironwork; Erill la Val, featuring a six-storey bell tower; Barruera; and Durro, which has another massive bell tower.

At the head of the valley is the hamlet of Caldes de Boí, popular for its bubbling thermal springs and nearby ski facilities. It also makes a good base for exploring the Parc Nacional d'Aigüestortes *(p180)*, the entrance to which is only 5 km (3 miles) from here.

Val d'Aran

Lleida Vielha Carrer Sarriulèra 10, Vielha; 973 64 01 10

This valley of valleys – *aran* means valley – is a lovely 600-sq-km (230-sq-mile) haven of forests and meadows filled with flowers, surrounded by towering mountain peaks. It was formed by the Riu Garona, which rises in the area and flows out to France as the Garonne. With no proper link to the outside world until 1924, when a road was built over the Bonaigua Pass, the valley was cut off from the rest of Spain for most of the winter. Snow still blocks the narrow pass from November to April, but today access is easy through the Túnel de Vielha from El Pont de Suert.

Because it faces north, the Val d'Aran has a climate similar to that of the Atlantic coast. Many rare wild flowers and butterflies flourish in the conditions created by the shady slopes and damp breezes. The valley is also a famous habitat for many species of narcissus.

Tiny villages have grown up beside the Riu Garona, often around Romanesque churches, notably at Bossòst, Salardú, Escunhau and Arties. The valley is also ideal for outdoor sports such as skiing and walking. This area even has its own language, Aranès (Aranese in English).

BUTTERFLIES OF THE VAL D'ARAN

A huge variety of butterflies is found in the mountains and valleys of the Pyrenees. The isolated Val d'Aran is home to as many as 91 species, including rare subspecies such as the marbled white (*Melanargia galathea*) and the map butterfly (*Araschnia levana*). Lepidopterists hiking through the meadows between May and July may see black-spotted shepherd's fritillary (*Boloria pales*), boldly striped Spanish festoons (*Zerynthia rumina*), delicate clouded Apollos (*Parnassius mnemosyne*), grizzled skippers (*Pyrgus malvae*) and chequered skippers (*Carterocephalus palaemon*) fluttering between open-faced daisies and the coiling labellum of the lizard orchid.

CHEQUERED SKIPPER

CLOUDED APOLLO

GRIZZLED SKIPPER

↑ Sant Pere de Rodes, one of Catalonia's Romanesque churches

CATALONIA'S ROMANESQUE ARCHITECTURE

Romanesque was the first pan-European architectural style to emerge in Europe after the collapse of the Roman Empire. In Catalonia, the expansion of the County of Barcelona and the consolidation of Christian territories, along with the arrival of pilgrims heading to Santiago de Compostela, produced a surge in church construction. A unique local variant of the Romanesque style emerged.

Did You Know?

More than 2,000 Romanesque buildings still stand in Catalonia today.

KEY FEATURES OF CATALAN CHURCHES

Romanesque churches in Catalonia are characterized by sturdy walls, barrel-vaulted naves, rounded arches and small windows. From the 11th century, tall bell towers and square apses became features of the style. The churches were decorated with elaborately carved sculptures and dramatic wall paintings.

FRESCOES

Catalonia has an abundance of well-preserved Romanesque frescoes, which bear witness to an extraordinary period of artistic brilliance. Noted for their vivid colours and stylized forms, these powerful wall paintings tell stories that were designed to awe and educate an illiterate congregation. Today, most of the frescoes in the churches are replicas with the originals on display in museums, including the Museu d'Art Medieval *(p193)* in Vic and the Museu Nacional d'Art de Catalunya *(p130)* in Barcelona.

↑ The Baldachin of Ribes fresco, Sant Climent de Taüll, in the Museu d'Art Medieval in Vic

LOCATIONS TO VISIT

1 Monestir de Santa Maria de Ripoll

The most singular work of Romanesque art in Spain, the 12th-century portal of the monastery church of Santa María in Ripoll *(p182)* is richly covered in astonishing allegorical carvings. Known as "The Ripoll Bible", the portal shows more than 100 scenes, many of which are biblical stories. Further details include depictions of the foundation of Catalonia, showing the expulsion of the armies of al-Andalus and Catalans peacefully labouring in their promised land. The bones of the legendary founder of Catalonia, Guifré el Pilós (Wilfred the Hairy), are laid to rest in the church cloister.

2 Sant Climent de Taüll

Consecrated in 1123, this is the finest Romanesque church among the remarkable concentration in the Vall de Boí *(p176)*. It stands out for its slender seven-floor bell tower, and a mural depicting Christ in Majesty that covers the entire apse. Although a replica (the original is in Barcelona's Museu Nacional d'Art de Catalunya, *p130*), visitors can still appreciate the impact of the painting.

3 Sant Pere de Rodes

The best surviving example of the Catalan Romanesque style is Sant Pere de Rodes, a mighty former Benedictine monastery in the rugged mountains behind Cadaqués *(p186)*. Strategically located to guard over the surrounding headland and provide refuge in times of conflict, it is austere and unadorned on the exterior with intricate detailing inside. The church nave contains columns from a Roman temple, which once occupied this site.

4 Tarragona Cathedral

Set on the highest point of Tarragona, the city's cathedral was begun in 1171 and completed in 1331. While most of what visitors see today is Gothic, a handsome Romanesque portal leads into the enchanting 12th-century cloister, where the capitals are sculpted in a sublime example of the Romanesque style. Look out for the commemoration of a clever cat who fooled rats into thinking he was dead, then ate them at his "funeral".

5 Sant Pere de Besalú

Sant Pere de Besalú is the 12th-century church of an earlier Benedictine monastery. A pair of finely carved stone lions guard the window over the portal, intricately decorated with biblical scenes. The simple barrel-vaulted nave, typical of the Romanesque style, is framed by an ambulatory where a menagerie of mythical beasts and knights on horseback have been beautifully carved into the capitals.

1

2

3

4

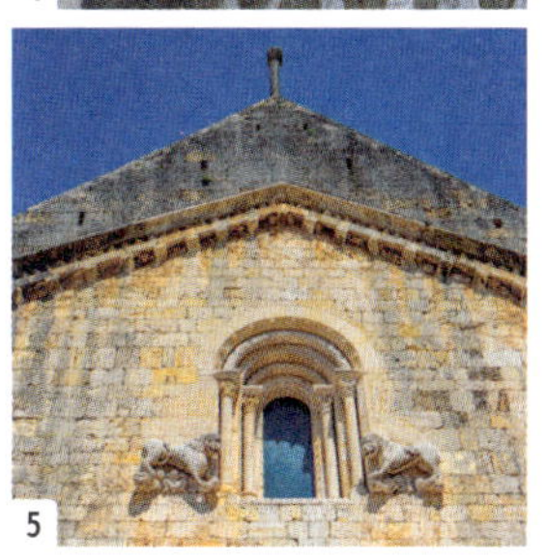

5

Lone hiker passing glassy lakes in the Parc Nacional d'Aigüestortes

Parc Nacional d'Aigüestortes

Lleida W parcs naturals.gencat.cat/en/ xarxa-de-parcs/aigues tortes/inici/index.html

The pristine mountain scenery of Catalonia's only national park is among the most spectacular that can be found in the Pyrenees.

Established in 1955, the park's full title is Parc Nacional d'Aigüestortes i Estany de Sant Maurici, named after the *estany* (lake) of Sant Maurici in the east and the Aigüestortes (literally, twisted waters) area in the west. The main village is the mountain settlement of Espot, although you can access the park from Boí in the west. Around the park are waterfalls and some 150 lakes and tarns which, in an earlier era, were scoured by glaciers to depths of up to 50 m (164 ft).

The finest scenery is around Sant Maurici lake, beneath the twin shards of the Serra dels Encantats (Mountains of the Enchanted). From here, there are many walks, while to the south is the dramatic vista of Estany Negre, the highest and deepest tarn in the park.

Early summer on the lower valley slopes is marked by rhododendrons, while in later months wild lilies bloom in the forests of fir, beech and silver birch.

The park is also home to a variety of wildlife. Chamois (also known as izards) live on the mountain screes and in the meadows, while beavers and otters can be spotted by the lakes. Golden eagles nest on mountain ledges, and grouse and capercaillie are found in the woods.

The park is popular with walkers in summer and the mountains are ideal for cross-country skiing in winter.

PICTURE PERFECT
Stunning Sant Maurici Lake

For postcard-perfect snaps, head to the lake's eastern shore. Here the turquoise waters provide a shimmering mirror for the fir-dotted hillsides rising up to join the mountains.

LES QUATRE BARRES

The four red bars on the *senyera*, the Catalan flag, represent the four provinces: Barcelona, Girona, Lleida and Tarragona. The design derives from a legend about Guifré el Pelós, Count of Barcelona, who received a call for help from Charles the Bald, King of the West Franks. Guifré turned the tide of battle, but was mortally wounded. Charles dipped his fingers in Guifré's blood and dragged them across his plain gold shield, giving him a coat of arms.

10

La Seu d'Urgell

Lleida · Carrer Major 8; turismeseu.com

This Pyrenean town became a bishopric in the 6th century. Feuds between the bishops of Urgell and the Counts of Foix over land gave rise to Andorra in the 13th century. The Romanesque cathedral has a peaceful cloister and gardens. The **Museu Diocesà** contains a 10th-century copy of St Beatus of Liébana's *Commentary on the Apocalypse.*

Museu Diocesà

 Plaça del Deganat
973 35 32 42 · Jun-Sep: 10am-1:30pm & 4-7pm Mon-Sat; Oct-May: 10am-1:30pm & 4-6pm Mon-Sat · 1 & 6 Jan, 15 Aug, 1 Sep, 25 & 26 Dec
museudiocesaurgell.org

11

Andorra

Principality of Andorra
Andorra la Vella
Plaça de la Rotonda, Andorra la Vella; visit andorra.com/en

Andorra occupies 464 sq km (179 sq miles) of the Pyrenees between France and Spain. In 1993, it became fully independent and held its first ever democratic elections. Since 1278, it had been an autonomous feudal state under the jurisdiction of the Spanish bishop of La Seu d'Urgell and the French Count of Foix (a title adopted by the president of France). These are still the ceremonial joint heads of state.

Andorra's official language is Catalan, though French and Castilian are also spoken by most residents. For many years, Andorra has been a tax-free paradise for shoppers, a fact reflected in the crowded stores of the capital, Andorra la Vella. Nearby Les Escaldes, Sant Julià de Lòria and El Pas de la Casa (the towns closest to the Spanish and French borders) have also become busy shopping centres.

Most visitors never see Andorra's rural charms, which match those of other parts of the Pyrenees. The region is excellent for walkers. One of the main routes leads to the Cercle de Pessons, a bowl of lakes in the east. In the north is the picturesque Sorteny valley, with farmhouses converted into snug restaurants.

EAT

Casa Irene

A local favourite, this restaurant gives classic dishes a modern twist.

Carrèr Major 22, Arties
hotelcasairene.com

La Granja

Enjoy tasty local meat and vegetables cooked *a la brasa* (over a wood fire) at this cosy spot.

Carrer de Santa Eulàlia 1A, Erill la Val
lagranjaderill.com

DRINK

REFU Birreria Vielha

An unpretentious gastro-brewery with great local craft beers and street-food tapas.

Carrèr Major 18A, Vielha
refubirreria.com

Simple stone cathedral in La Seu d'Urgell

12

Olot

Girona  Carrer del Francesc Fàbregas 6; turismeolot.com

This sizeable market town sits at the centre of a dramatic landscape pockmarked with extinct volcanoes. But it was an earthquake in 1474 that destroyed its medieval past.

By the late 18th century, the textile industry was booming and the wealthy bourgeoisie began to patronise the arts. The Olot school of landscape painting emerged, inspired by the natural beauty of the area and displaying an Impressionistic approach to light. You can see some of these works in the excellent **Museu Comarcal de la Garrotxa.**

Museu Comarcal de la Garrotxa

Carrer Hospici 8 10am-1pm & 3-6pm Tue-Fri, 11am-2pm & 4-7pm Sat, 11am-2pm Sun museus.olot.cat

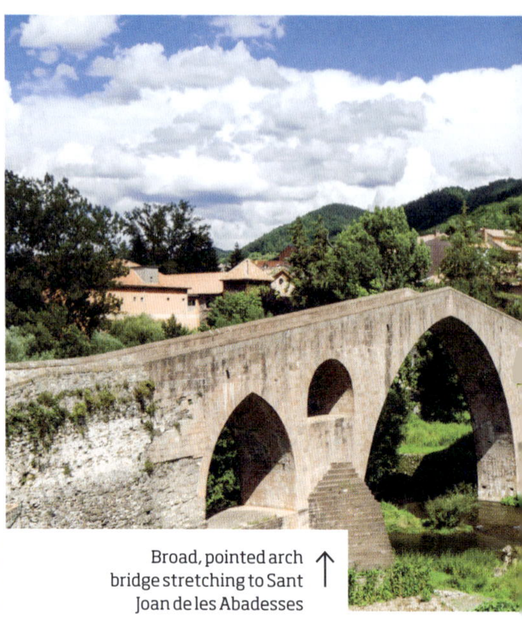

Broad, pointed arch bridge stretching to Sant Joan de les Abadesses

13 

Sant Joan de les Abadesses

Girona  Plaça de l'Abadia 9; santjoande lesabadesses.cat

A fine 12th-century Gothic bridge arches over the Riu Ter to this unassuming market town whose main attraction is its monastery.

Founded in 885, the monastery was a gift from Guifré, the first count of Barcelona, to his daughter, the first abbess. The church has little decoration except for a wooden calvary, *The Descent from the Cross* (1250). Simple, stark and powerful, it is considered a jewel of Catalan Romanesque sculpture. The museum also features beautiful Baroque and Renaissance altarpieces. To the north are the small towns of Camprodon and Beget, both worth visiting for their handsome Romanesque churches. In Camprodon, seek out its renowned *botifarra* sausage in the delis around the central square, Plaça del Carme.

Intricately carved sculpture at the door to Museu Comarcal de la Garrotxa in Olot

14

Ripoll

Girona Plaça Abat Oliba; visit.ripoll.cat

Once a tiny mountain base from which raids against the Moors were made, Ripoll is now best known for the Monestir de Santa Maria *(p179)*, founded in 879. The town is called the "cradle of Catalonia" as the monastery was the power base of Guifré el Pilós (Wilfred the Hairy), founder of the House of Barcelona. He is buried here. In the late 12th century, the west portal was decked with what are regarded as the finest Romanesque carvings in Spain. This and the cloister are the only parts of the original medieval monastery to have survived.

In the late 12th century, the west portal was decked with what are regarded as the finest Romanesque carvings in Spain.

Ripoll has always been an industrial area, and the best place to explore its dynamic heritage is at the Museu Etnogràfic de Ripoll, which takes visitors through the region's history of agriculture, nail and weaponry making, the textile industry and more. The permanent collection is exhibited across three floors, and there are also temporary exhibits throughout the year.

Every July and August, the town hosts the Ripoll International Music Festival, which provides an enjoyable programme of classical music concerts.

↑ Passing below the Romanesque portal of the Monestir de Santa Maria in Ripoll

STAY

Hotel El Ciervo
This cosy hotel in the charming Aranese capital is the perfect place to relax after a day on the slopes.

Plaça Sant Orenç 3, Vielha hotelelciervo.net

Hostal Sa Rascassa
Enjoy personalized service at this gorgeous boutique spot.

Cala d'Aiguafreda 3, Begur hostalsarascassa.com

Sant Pere del Bosc
Luxuriate in the lavish suites and spa at this bucolic Modernista villa near the sea.

Paratge de Sant Pere del Bosc, Lloret de Mar hotelsantperedelbosc.com

Mas El Mir
Relax in rustic luxury at this converted farmhouse, set just outside Ripoll.

Carretera de les Llosses s/n, Ripoll maselmir.com

Hotel Horta d'En Rahola
Enjoy the timeless setting of this 18th-century manor house within easy reach of the beach.

Carrer de Sa Tarongeta 1, Cadaqués hortacadaques.com

The marina of Cadaqués on the Costa Brava, aglow at dusk

A peaceful harbour in Cadaqués, and (*inset*) its lively beach in summer

15

Cadaqués

Girona  Carrer Cotxe 1; visitcadaques.org

This pretty resort is overlooked by the Baroque Església de Santa Maria. In the 1960s, it was dubbed the "St Tropez of Spain", due to the young crowd that sought out Salvador Dalí in nearby Port Lligat, where he lived for six months of the year in a fisher's cabin, from 1930 until his death in 1989. Today the much modified house is known as the **Casa-Museu Salvador Dalí**. Managed by the Gala-Salvador Dalí Foundation, the museum provides a unique interpretation of Dalí's life.

After the museum, head down to the picture-book waterfront, lined with cafés.

THE ART OF DALÍ

Born in Figueres in 1904, Salvador Dalí mounted his first exhibition at the age of 15. After studying at the Escuela de Bellas Artes in Madrid, and dabbling with Cubism, Futurism and Metaphysical painting, Dalí embraced Surrealism in 1929, becoming the movement's best-known painter. Never far from controversy, self-publicist Dalí became famous for his hallucinatory images, which he described as "hand-painted dream photographs". He died in Figueres in 1989.

Casa-Museu Salvador Dalí

Port Lligat Hours vary, check website (reservations required) 1 Jan, 7 Jan-early Feb, 25 Dec salvador-dali.org

16 

Empúries

Girona L'Escala Mid-Feb-May & Oct: 10am-6pm daily; Jun-Sep: 10am-8pm daily; mid-Nov-mid-Feb: 10am-5pm daily 1 & 6 Jan, 25 Dec macempuries.cat

The extensive ruins of this Greco-Roman town occupy an imposing coastal site. Three settlements were built between the 7th and 3rd centuries BCE: the old town (Palaiapolis); the new town (Neapolis); and the Roman town. The old town was founded by the Greeks in 600 BCE as a trading port. It was built on what was a small island, and is now the site of the tiny hamlet of Sant Martí de Empúries. In 550 BCE, this was replaced by a larger new town on the shore that the Greeks named Emporion, meaning "trading place". In 218 BCE, the Romans landed at Empúries and built a city next to the new town.

Under the umbrella of the Museu d'Arqueologia de Catalunya (*p132*), a packed calendar of workshops and events takes place here. Culinary workshops and historical re-enactments introduce children to Roman life. At night, Catalan rock groups and jazz nights are hosted as part of the Concerts in the Forum series.

Puigcerdà

Girona Plaça del Santa Maria; puigcerdaturisme.cat

Puig is Catalan for "hill". And despite sitting on a relatively small hill compared with the encircling mountains – which rise to 2,900 m (9,500 ft) – Puigcerdà nevertheless commands a fine view down into the beautiful Cerdanya valley, the largest in the Pyrenees. The town of Puigcerdà was founded in 1177 by Alfonso II as the capital of Cerdanya, an important agricultural region, which shares a history and culture with the French Cerdagne. The town has links with the Spanish enclave of Llívia, an attractive little town with a medieval pharmacy, which lies 6 km (4 miles) inside France.

Nearby, at the valley's edge, is the mountainous Parc Natural del Cadí-Moixeró, a stunning area laced with trails ideal for ambitious walkers.

Figueres

Girona Plaça de l'Escorxador 2; visitfigueres.cat

Figueres is the market town of the Empordà plain and is perhaps best known as the birthplace of Salvador Dalí, who in 1974 turned the town theatre into the **Teatre-Museu Dalí**. The town's biggest draw is one of the best collections of art by Dalí in the world, housed under the theatre's glass dome, as well as works by a number of other painters. The museum stands as a monument to Catalonia's most eccentric artist, who is also buried here. In the building next door is a permanent collection of flamboyant jewellery that was designed by Dalí between 1941 and 1970.

Another point on the "Dalí Triangle", **Casa-Museu Castell Gala Dalí**, 55 km (35 miles) south of Figueres, is the medieval castle Dalí bought in the 1970s. It contains some of his paintings.

Beyond Dalí, east of Figueres is the Romanesque monastery Sant Pere de Rodes. On the plane tree-shaded Rambla is the former Hotel de Paris, now home to the **Museu del Joguet** (Toy Museum). At the bottom of the Rambla is a statue of Narcís Monturiol i Estarriol who, it is believed, invented the submarine.

Teatre-Museu Dalí

Plaça Gala-Salvador Dalí 5 Hours vary, check website 1 Jan, 25 Dec salvador-dali.org

Casa-Museu Castell Gala Dalí

Carrer de Gala Dalí, Púbol (La Pera) Hours vary, check website salvador-dali.org

Museu del Joguet

Carrer de Sant Pere 1 Hours vary, check website mjc.cat

TOP 5 WORKS BY DALÍ

The Persistence of Memory, 1931

Perhaps the best known of Dalí's works, these intriguing melting clocks question the meaning of time.

Lobster Telephone, 1936

In this quintessentially Surrealist piece a lobster sits atop a rotary phone.

Metamorphosis of Narcissus, 1927

Dalí's interpretation of the Greek myth of Narcissus through an oil on canvas painting.

Swans Reflecting Elephants, 1937

A lake's unusual reflection causes a double-visual of swans and elephants, from Dalí's "Paranoiac-Critical" period.

Galatea of the Spheres, 1952

Spheres show an image of Gala, Dalí's wife and muse.

→ Quirky egg-topped exterior of the Teatre-Museu Dalí in Figueres

FLOWERS OF THE MATOLLAR

Furnishing swathes of the eastern Mediterranean coast is the distinctive Catalan *matollar* (matorral). Where once stood forests of holm oak trees, many of which were felled for timber and to provide land for grazing and cultivation, now lies this scrubland landscape blooming with vibrant plants.

Each spring, the *matollar* becomes a kaleidoscope of colourful plants, when hillsides are daubed with yellow broom and pink and white cistuses. The air is filled with the scent of aromatic herbs such as rosemary, lavender and thyme, as well as the low drone of insects as they buzz around, feeding on the abundance of nectar and pollen.

All the plants in the *matollar* have adapted to the extremes of climate. They protect themselves from losing water during the dry summer heat with thick leaves or waxy secretions, or by storing moisture in bulbs or tubers.

Several plants from the Americas also managed to colonize the bare scrubland ground. The prickly pear, thought to have been brought to Europe by Christopher Columbus, produces a delicious fruit that can be picked only with thickly gloved hands. The century plant, a native of Mexico, thrives in the *matollar's* Mediterranean climate, rapidly erupting from the earth as a splay of tough, spiny green leaves. Only as it approaches the end of its life (10 to 15 years) does it send up a tall flower shoot, after which it dies.

INSIDER TIP

Head to the Hills

Garraf Park, near Sitges, is an excellent place to observe the incredible plants and wildlife that Catalonia's *matollar* landscape has to offer, while also enjoying the sea and mountain views. The vegetation typical of the area includes wild olive, Mediterranean fan palm and evergreen oaks. You may also spot rabbits, Mediterranean tortoises and falcons.

Highlights

Jerusalem Sage

An attractive shrub of greyish-white, woolly leaves, with tall stems surrounded by showy yellow flowers. It's often grown in gardens.

Rose Garlic

This plant has round clusters of violet or pink flowers at the end of a single stalk. It survives the summer as the bulb familiar to all cooks for its strength of flavour.

Spanish Broom

A small bush with yellow flowers on slender branches. The black seed pods split when dry, scattering the seeds on the ground.

Star Clover

This is a low-growing annual whose fruit develops into a star-shaped seed head. Its flowers are often pale pink, or sometimes yellow or purple.

↑ Centaury and St John's wort in bloom in Catalonia

TOP 4 ANIMALS OF THE MATOLLAR

Ladder Snakes
Young ladder snakes are identified by a black pattern like the rungs of a ladder, but adults are marked with two simple stripes.

Scorpions
These venomous predators hide under rocks or wood by day. The scorpions in Catalonia are not deadly to humans, but their sting can pack a punch

Dartford Warbler
This skulking bird has dark plumage and a cocked tail, and sings melodiously during its mating display. Males are more vividly coloured than females.

Swallowtail Butterfly
One of the most conspicuous insects living in the *matollar*. Its pale yellow wings hemmed with black are unmistakable.

HIDDEN GEM
The Ruins of Ullastret

A short drive from Peratallada are the extensive ruins of this Iberian settlement dating back to the 6th century BCE. Discover what was once a walled hillfort with commanding views.

Peratallada

Girona Plaça del Castell 3; visit peratallada.cat

This tiny village is the most spectacular of the many that lie a short inland trip from the Costa Brava. Together with Pals and Palau-sator, it forms part of the "Golden Triangle" of medieval villages. Its name is derived from the Catalan for "carved stone", and the village does indeed appear to be cut from the hillside, with its mountaintop position offering dramatic views of the area. A labyrinth of cobbled streets winds up to the well-conserved castle and lookout tower, whose written records date from the 11th century. Peratallada's counts and kings made sure they could fend off any attackers by constructing a sturdy wall enclosing the entire village, which even today limits the nucleus from further expansion.

Blanes

Girona Plaça Catalunya; blanescostabrava.cat

The working port of Blanes has one of the longest beaches on the Costa Brava, but the highlight of the town is undoubtedly the **Jardí Botànic Marimurtra**. These gardens, designed by Karl Faust in 1928, are spectacularly sited above cliffs. Their 7,000 species of tropical and Mediterranean plants include African cacti.

Jardí Botànic Marimurtra

Passeig de Carles Faust 9 Hours vary, check website 1 & 6 Jan, 24-26 & 31 Dec marimurtra.cat

Tossa de Mar

Girona Avinguda Pelegrí 25; visittossa.com

At the end of a tortuous corniche, the Roman town of Turissa is one of the prettiest along the Costa Brava. Above the modern town is the Vila Vella (Old Town), a protected national monument. The medieval walls enclose tidy fisher's cottages, a 14th-century church and countless bars. The **Museu Municipal** in the Old Town exhibits local archaeological finds and modern art.

Museu Municipal

Plaça Pintor Roig i Soler 1 972 34 07 09 Mar, Apr & Oct: Sat & Sun; Jun-Sep: daily; Nov-Feb: Tue-Sat

EAT

La Caseta Blanes

Savour seasonal seafood and tapas right by the beach.

Passeig Pau Casals 35, Blanes lacasetablanes.cat

Compartir

Creative plates have earned this place a spot in the Michelin guide.

Riera de Sant Vicenç, Cadaqués Mon compartircadaques.com

Rafa's

Indulge in fresh-off-the-boat seafood.

Carrer de Sant Sebastià 56, Roses 972 25 40 03

Cal Sagristà

Refined traditional Catalan cuisine served under medieval arches.

Carrer Rodona 2, Peralada 972 53 83 01

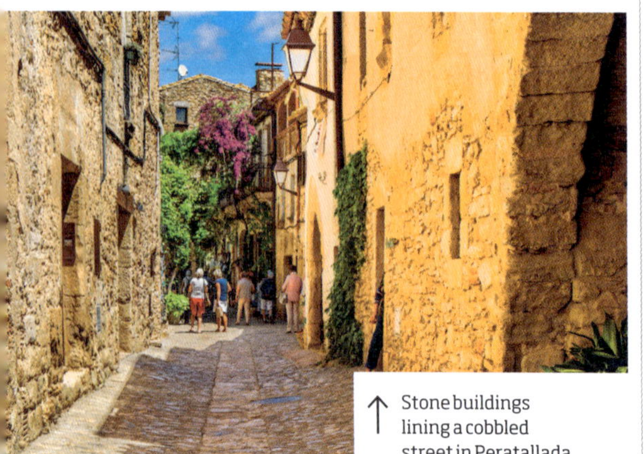

↑ Stone buildings lining a cobbled street in Peratallada

THE "WILD COAST"

A mix of rugged cliffs and sandy beaches, the Costa Brava ("wild coast") runs for some 200 km (125 miles) from Blanes northwards to the region of Empordà, on the border with France.

With its craggy shoreline, pine-backed sandy coves and crowded modern resorts, the Costa Brava is Spain's answer to the Côte d'Azur. Wine, olives and fishing were the mainstays of the area until the arrival of tourists in the 1960s. They were drawn by some of the finest Blue Flag beaches in Europe, from broad, sandy stretches to horseshoe coves. The busiest resorts are to the south. To the north are quieter fishing villages, while just inland are Roman ruins and medieval villages.

Golden sands and turquoise seas at Aiguablava beach on the Costa Brava

COASTAL RESORT TOWNS

Roses lies at the head of a sweeping bay. Its long, sandy beach has become a haven for lovers of watersports.

L'Escala, a small resort popular with Spanish tourists, has a series of fine beaches and a small port where fishing nets dry in the sun.

Llafranc, a whitewashed resort with a promenade leading to neighbouring Calella, is one of the coast's most pleasant resorts.

Lloret de Mar has more hotels than anywhere else on the coast. There are some unspoiled beaches nearby, such as Santa Cristina.

Platja d'Aro's long and sandy beach is lined with modern hotels and buzzy beach bars.

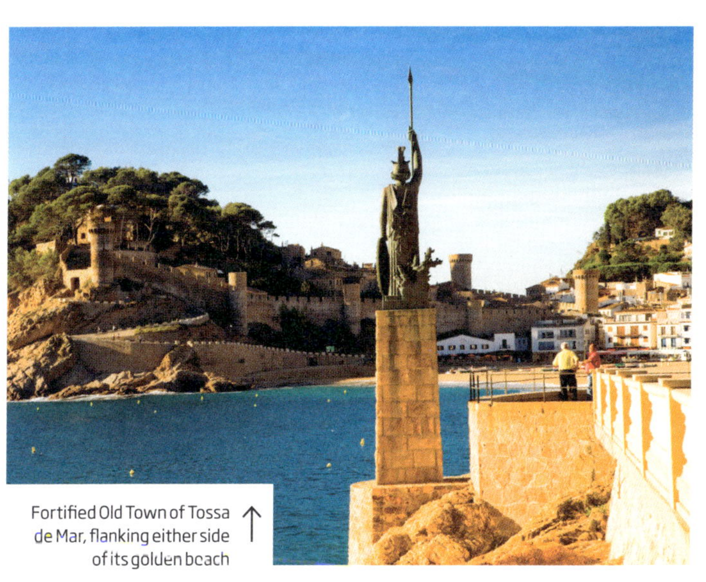

Fortified Old Town of Tossa de Mar, flanking either side of its golden beach

SHOP

Casa Riera Ordeix
Established in 1852, this time-honoured shop has been run by the same family, skillfully crafting Vic's famous cured sausages.

Carrer Manlleu 24, Vic casarieraordeix.com

Vinum Porrera
Pick from a wide-ranging selection of regional wine and craft beers. There's a small tasting room in the back to sample before you commit to buy.

Plaça de Catalunya 1, Porrera 977 82 81 18

Ceràmica Planas Marquès
Unique ceramics, often crafted from unusual materials, are on sale here. Pieces are offered at reasonable prices, and there's also a workshop attached.

Plaça de l'Ajuntament 8, Pals ceramicaplanasmarques.com

Sant Pol de Mar

R1 santpol.cat

This small seaside town is an hour's train ride along the coast from Barcelona on the R1 line; a nice excursion if you're looking to escape the hustle and bustle of the city for a day. A variety of spacious, family-friendly beaches spread out from the centre, all within easy reach of a host of bars and restaurants.

The town once convened around the **Ermita de Sant Pau**, a 10th-century monastery. The remains of this are still standing on a small hill just back from the seafront, and the building also features Romanesque additions dating from the 13th century. A visit to this monastery is worth it for the incredible views alone, but you can also take a look inside the building itself by getting in touch with the local tourist office in advance.

Elsewhere in the town, typically Catalan Modernista architecture can be seen, with the colourfully elaborate **Can Planiol** an especially eye-catching example. Designed by Ignasi Masi Morell and completed in 1910, it is closed to the public, but the captivating façade – sprinkled with ceramic flowers – makes for a great photo opportunity.

No stranger to the Catalan *festa*, the town holds regular festivals throughout the year. In spring, it plays host to Spain's oldest jazz festival, the acclaimed Festival de Jazz de Sant Pol. Towards the end of July, a weekend of celebrations dedicated to Sant Jaume sees the streets come alive with Catalan dancers and *castellers*, and the skies erupt with fireworks. Come September, head to Platja dels Pescadors just up the coast for the popular Festival d'Havaneres. This festival of sea shanties and the last catch of the season is celebrated with barbecues and towering beach bonfires.

Ermita de Sant Pau
Plaça Sant Pau 2 Hours vary, check website

Can Planiol
Carrer Abat Deas 30 To the public

Cardona

Barcelona Plaça de la Fira; cardonaturisme.cat

Situated on a hill near the meandering Riu Cardener is this small historic town, with a Gothic and Romanesque centre that dates back to the 11th century. Its crowning feature is the ancient, ruddy-stoned Castell de Cardona. In the 14th century the castle belonged to the Dukes of Cardona – the most powerful family in Spain besides the royal family itself, who, as constables of Aragón, became known as the "kings without a crown". The castle was rebuilt in the 18th century and is now a luxurious parador. Beside it

Whitewashed houses gazing out to sea in pretty Sant Pol de Mar

↑ Firing up a great hot-air balloon at Vic's Plaça Major

is an 11th-century church, the handsome Església de Sant Vicenç.

Set on a hill, the castle gives views of the town and of the Muntanya de Sal (Salt Mountain), a huge salt deposit next to the Riu Cardener that has been mined since Roman times. The Muntanya rises 120 m (394 ft) into the air, but even more of its mass is below ground. The mine stretches 2 km (1.2 miles) under the surface; visitors can delve to a depth of 86 m (282 ft) during a tour of the mine.

Vic

Barcelona
Plaça del Pes; victurisme.cat

Market days are the best time to visit this small country town. This is when the local *embotits* (sausages) for which the area is renowned are piled high in the Gothic Plaça Major, along with other produce from the surrounding plains.

In the 3rd century BCE, Vic was the capital of an ancient Iberian tribe, the Ausetans. The town was then colonized by the Romans – the remains of a Roman temple survive today. Since the 6th century, the town has been a bishop's see. In the 11th century, Abbot Oliva commissioned El Cloquer tower, around which the cathedral was built in the 18th century. The interior is covered with vast murals by Josep Maria Sert. Painted in reds and golds, they represent biblical scenes.

Adjacent to the cathedral is the **Museu d'Art Medieval**, which has one of the best Romanesque collections in Catalonia. The large display of art and relics includes simple murals and wooden carvings from rural churches. Also on display are 11th- and 12th-century frescoes.

Museu d'Art Medieval
Plaça Bisbe Oliba 3
Apr-Sep: 10am-7pm Tue-Sat, 10am-2pm Sun; Oct-Mar: 10am-1pm & 3-6pm Tue-Fri, 10am-7pm Sat, 10am-2pm Sun
1 & 6 Jan, 25 & 26 Dec
museuartmedieval.cat

THE CATALAN LANGUAGE

Catalan has recovered from the ban it suffered under Franco's dictatorship and has supplanted Castilian (Spanish) as the region's primary language. Spoken by more than 9.5 million people, it is a Romance language akin to the Provençal of France. Suppressed by Felipe V in 1717, Catalan only officially resurfaced in the 19th century, when medieval poetry contests and Catalan literature were revived.

Montblanc

Tarragona
Muralla de Santa Tecla 54; montblanc medieval.cat

Montblanc's medieval walls are arguably Catalonia's finest example of military architecture. At the Sant Jordi gate, St George allegedly slew a dragon. There is a plaque at the site and an annual festival is held every April to celebrate this mythic victory. The interesting **Museu Comarcal de la Conca de Barberà** showcases an impressive array of local crafts.

Museu Comarcal de la Conca de Barberà
Carrer de Josa 6
Hours vary, check website
mccb.cat

Vilafranca del Penedès

Barcelona
Carrer Hermenegild Clascar 2; 938 18 12 54; turisme vilafranca.com

This market town is set in the heart of Penedès, the main wine-producing region of Catalonia. The fascinating **Vinseum** (Wine Museum) documents the history of the area's wine trade and organizes tastings every fortnight. Local *bodegues* (wineries) can also be visited for wine tasting. Sant Sadurní d'Anoia, the capital of Spain's popular sparkling wine, cava *(p201)*, lies just 8 km (5 miles) to the north.

Vinseum
Plaça de Jaume I 10am-7pm Tue-Sat, 10am-2pm Sun
vinseum.cat

Santes Creus

Tarragona
Plaça Jaume el Just s/n, Monestir; larutadelcister. info

The tiny village of Santes Creus is home to the prettiest of the "Cistercian triangle" monasteries. The other two, Vallbona de les Monges and Poblet, are located nearby. The **Monestir de Santes Creus** was founded in 1150 by Ramon Berenguer IV during his reconquest of Catalonia. Its imposing façade is crowned with battlements, and the Gothic cloisters inside are decorated with figurative sculptures, a style first permitted by Jaume II, who ruled from 1291 to 1327. His tomb is in the 12th-century church, which features a rose window.

Monestir de Santes Creus
977 63 83 29
Jun-Sep: 10am-7pm Tue-Sun; Oct-May: 10am-5:30pm Tue-Sun 1 & 6 Jan, 25 & 26 Dec

DRINK

L'Àngelus Bar a Vin
Located opposite the town's cathedral is an elegant wine bar with a terrace perfect for sampling some of the local vintages.
Plaça de Santa Maria 3, Vilafranca del Penedès
938 90 64 04

L'Ombra d'un Sifó
This friendly spot decorated with LPs occasionally hosts live music performances.
Riera St 19, Sant Pol de Mar lombradunsifo. blogspot.com

Rockaway Bar
Rock paraphernalia and a wide selection of craft beers are the mainstays of this seafront bar.
Passeig del Mar 31, Tossa de Mar
rockawaybeach.cat

Sputnik Pub
Head to this quirky bar for friendly staff, great drinks - usually served with free tapas - and midnight bingo rounds.
Carrer de Sant Agusti 18b, Solsona
973 48 34 01

↓ Pink-painted 12th-century Monestir de Santes Creus

WINE CATHEDRALS

Catalonia is covered with wineries, and none are more grandiose and spectacular than those designed by Cèsar Martinell. Built with austere reverence to the region's wine heritage, they are known as *les catedrals del vi* (the wine cathedrals).

Cèsar Martinell i Brunet (1888–1973), a protégé of Catalonia's archetypal Modernista architect Antoni Gaudí, was steeped in the Modernista style, though later he moved towards the reactionary Noucentisme. Both styles are represented in his wineries, some of which can be visited today.

His work is typified by finding opulence in his immediate surroundings. He used local materials and traditional techniques to create magnificent buildings that pay homage to the fruits of Catalonia's fertile wine country.

His wine cathedrals are visually reminiscent of their religious counterparts, with arches soaring over large open naves. As well as designing the buildings' structure, he meticulously planned internal layouts, finding balance between practicality and architectural style.

Another Modernista architect, Josep Puig i Cadafalch, designed the famous Codorníu winery in Sant Sadurní d'Anoia.

NULLES (1918)

Typical Gaudían Modernista stonework is topped by magnificent pillars of red brick whose varied heights form a roof of sharp peaks and troughs. As well as the striking visual effect, this roof helps regulate the temperature of the winery. Guided group tours can be arranged when booked in advance.

FALSET (1919)

An almost fortress-like white exterior, outlined with red brick and punctuated by arched windows, leads to a large central nave and two adjacent smaller naves, separated by brick pillars and arches. Guided tours are available.

GANDESA (1919)

The naves within this wine cathedral are covered with Catalan vaults; bricks are laid upon an exposed wooden structure, which is itself supported by large brick arches. The smooth, subdued curves of the vaulting lend an unmistakably Modernista style to the unusual roof. The building was extended in 1983 by Manuel Ribas Piera, with respect to the building's original style. Leaflets are handed out for a self-guided tour.

↑ Codorníu's striking façade designed by Josep Puig i Cadafalch

→ Crypt-like cellar beneath the Codorníu winery

Atmospheric beachside town of Sitges, dotted with palm trees

Solsona

Lleida Carretera de Balsell 1, Lleida; turisme solsones.com

Three gateways and nine towers are all that remain of Solsona's fortifications. Inside is an ancient town of noble mansions. The town's cathedral houses a beautiful black stone Virgin. The **Museu Diocesà i Comarcal** contains Romanesque paintings; a wonderfully preserved ice store, the **Pou de Gel**, is also worth a visit.

Museu Diocesà i Comarcal

Plaça del Palau Episcopal 1
Hours vary, check website
1 & 6 Jan, 25 & 26 Dec
museusolsona.cat

Pou de Gel

Portal del Pont s/n
973 48 23 10 For guided tours: check website or call ahead entrade ssolsones.com

Besalú

Girona Carrer del Pont 1; besalu.cat

A magnificent medieval town with a striking approach across a fortified bridge over the Riu Fluvià, Besalú has two fine Romanesque churches: Sant Vicenç and Sant Pere. The latter is the sole remnant of a Benedictine monastery founded in 977 but pulled down in 1835.

In 1964, a *mikvah*, a Jewish ritual bath, was discovered by chance. Built in 1264, it is one of only three dating from that period to survive in Europe. To the south, the sky-blue lake of Banyoles, where the 1992 Olympic rowing contests were held, is ideal for picnics.

HIDDEN GEM

Prehistoric Cave Art

Thirty minutes south of Lleida are the Roca dels Moros *(patrimoni.gen cat.cat/en/monuments)*, home to a collection of Levantine rock art in Iberia. See a ritual dance painting daubed in vivid reds approximately 5,000 years ago.

Lleida

Lleida Carrer Major 31; turismede lleida.cat

Dominating the capital of Catalonia's only land-locked province is La Suda, a large fort taken from the Moors in 1149. Within its walls stands La Seu Vella, the old cathedral founded in 1203, with a beautiful cloister and Gothic rose window. The well-restored fort complex contains a visitor centre and panoramic viewpoints. The city's **Museu de Lleida** is also a highlight, presenting artifacts that date back to the Stone Age.

Museu de Lleida
Carrer del Sant Crist 1 Hours vary, check website Mon; 1 & 6 Jan, 25 & 26 Dec museudelleida.cat

Sitges

Barcelona Plaça Eduard Maristany 2; sitgesanytime.com

With a lively LGBTQ+ scene and 17 fabulous beaches, Sitges is famous for its nightlife. Bars and restaurants line its main boulevard, the Passeig Marítim, while Modernista architecture is scattered among the 1970s blocks. Artist Santiago Rusiñol spent time here and left some of his art and curios to the **Museu del Cau Ferrat**, at Sebastià beach, next to the 17th-century church of Sant Bartomeu i Santa Tecla.

Museu del Cau Ferrat
Carrer de Fonollar 10am–7pm Tue–Sun (Nov–Mar: to 5pm) museusdesitges.cat

Walking through the cloister of beautiful La Seu Vella in Lleida

TOP 5 NIGHT SPOTS IN SITGES

Pub Voramar
This laid-back pub looks out at the beach.
pub-voramar.com

El Piano
The lively atmosphere here is fuelled by live performances.
elpianositges.com

Hollywood Nights Sitges
Cinema-themed speak-easy with karaoke nights.
676 11 89 68

Vivero
Swanky beach club and restaurant with sea views from the terrace.
elviverositges.com

Parrots
Located on Plaça de la Indústria, it's perfect for people-watching.
parrots-sitges.com

Flamingos wading in the briny waters of the Delta de L'Ebre

Delta de L'Ebre

Tarragona Aldea Deltebre, Aldea Palau Climent, Carrer Montcada 32 3a planta, Tortosa; terresdelebre.travel

The delta of the Riu Ebre is a prosperous rice-growing region and wildlife haven. The Parc Natural del Delta de L'Ebre protects a significant water-bird habitat over 70 sq km (27 sq miles). The **Ecomuseu** has an aquarium featuring species found in the delta.

The park is celebrated for its incredible bird-watching. Head to the shores of the Punta del Fangar in the north and the Punta de la Banya in the south for the best bird spotting. Here, flamingos breed and can be glimpsed from tourist boats that leave from Riumar and Deltebre. Amposta and Sant Carles de la Ràpita, the main towns in the area, are good bases for exploring the reserve.

Nearby, up the eastern side of Sierra de Godal, a series of rock shelters house incredible 8,000-year-old cave art. Learn more at the informative **Centro de Interpretación de Arte Rupestre Abrics de la Ermita**.

Ecomuseu

Carrer Doctor Martí Buera 22, Deltebre 977 48 96 79 10am-2pm & 3-6pm Mon-Sat, 10am-2pm Sun

Centro de Interpretación de Arte Rupestre Abrics de la Ermita

Ermita de la Pietat, Carretera Ulldecona Hours vary, check website visitmuseum.gencat.cat/en

HUMAN TOWERS

The province of Tarragona is famous for its *casteller* festivals, in which *colles* (groups) of people stand on each other's shoulders in an effort to build the highest human *castell* (tower). Configurations depend on the size of the *colles* who form the base. Teams wear similar colours, and often have names denoting their home town. The small child who has to undertake the perilous climb to the top, where he or she makes the sign of the cross, is called the *anxaneta*. *Castellers* assemble in competition for Tarragona province's major festivals throughout the year. At the end of the tower-building season on St Ursula's Day (21 October), teams from all over Catalonia converge on the town square in Valls.

Tortosa

Tarragona Carrer del Castell de la Suda 5; tortosaturisme.cat

A ruined castle and medieval walls are clues to Tortosa's historical importance. Sited at the lowest crossing point on the Riu Ebre, it has been strategically significant since Iberian times. The Moors held the city from the 8th century until 1148. The old Moorish castle, known as La Suda, is all

Did You Know?

One of Spain's prime Vías Verdes - reclaimed railways for walking and cycling - runs through Tortosa.

that remains of their defences. It has now been renovated as a parador. The Moors also built a mosque in Tortosa in 914. Its foundations were used for the present cathedral, on which work began in 1347. Although it was not finished for two centuries, the style is pure Gothic and it can still be visited today in the Old Town. Next to the cathedral is the Palacio Episcopal, begun in the 14th century. Several rooms are open to the public, as is the chapel.

Tortosa was badly damaged in 1938–9 during a fierce Civil War battle, when the Riu Ebre formed the front line between the opposing forces.

Costa Daurada

Tarragona Calafell, Sant Vicenç de Calders, Salou Passeig de Torroja s/n, Tarragona; costadaurada.info

The sandy beaches of the Costa Daurada (Golden Coast) line the shores of Tarragona province. El Vendrell is one of the area's active ports. Nearby, in Sant Salvador, the **Museu Pau Casals** is dedicated to the famous cellist; Casals was born in El Vendrell in 1876, and is buried in the town cemetery.

PortAventura World, south of Tarragona, is one of Europe's largest theme parks and has such eclectically themed attractions as Polynesia and the Wild West. Ferrari Land has a miniature F1 circuit and the highest, fastest rollercoaster in Europe. Cambrils and Salou to the south are the liveliest resorts – the others are low-key family holiday spots.

Museu Pau Casals

Avinguda Palfuriana 67
Hours vary, check website
paucasals.org

PortAventura World

Avinguda del Batlle Pere Molas Km 2, Vila-seca
Hours vary, check website
portaventuraworld.com

↓ Crowds gathered at PortAventura World on the Costa Daurada

EAT

Lo Pati D'Agustí

This is a buzzy local hotspot; come for the top-notch paella and stay for the wine list that can't be beaten.

Carrer de l'Ebre 10, El Poblenou del Delta Wed restaurant lopatidagusti.com

Komokieras

With a name that translates to "come as you wish", this homely spot serves up the perfect sharing platters. Their wider menu is filled with tasty Mediterranean staples.

Carrer d'Espalter 23, Sitges komokieras.com

A DRIVING TOUR
CAVA COUNTRY

Distance 30 km (19 miles) **Stopping-off points** Masquefa, Sant Sadurní d'Anoia, Vilafranca del Penedès, Costers del Segre **Difficulty** Easy

Catalonia is the home of cava, Spain's answer to champagne and one of its most appreciated exports. Cava country is focused on the Penedès region and surrounding districts, which together make up the prestigious Penedès DO *(Denominació de Origen)*. Follow this route through terraced villages, vineyard-corduroyed countryside and craggy passes with glinting Mediterranean views. All visits require booking in advance. You can taste the cavas on each of the tours, often accompanied by tapas; grape juice is available instead for those under 18 and the designated driver.

Did You Know?

Cava was first made in the mid-19th century by Josep Raventós, head of the Codorníu winery.

↑ Catalonia's countryside, dotted with picturesque vineyards

In the town of **Vilafranca del Penedès** (p194) *find the Mascaró winery, which offers tours of its cellars.*

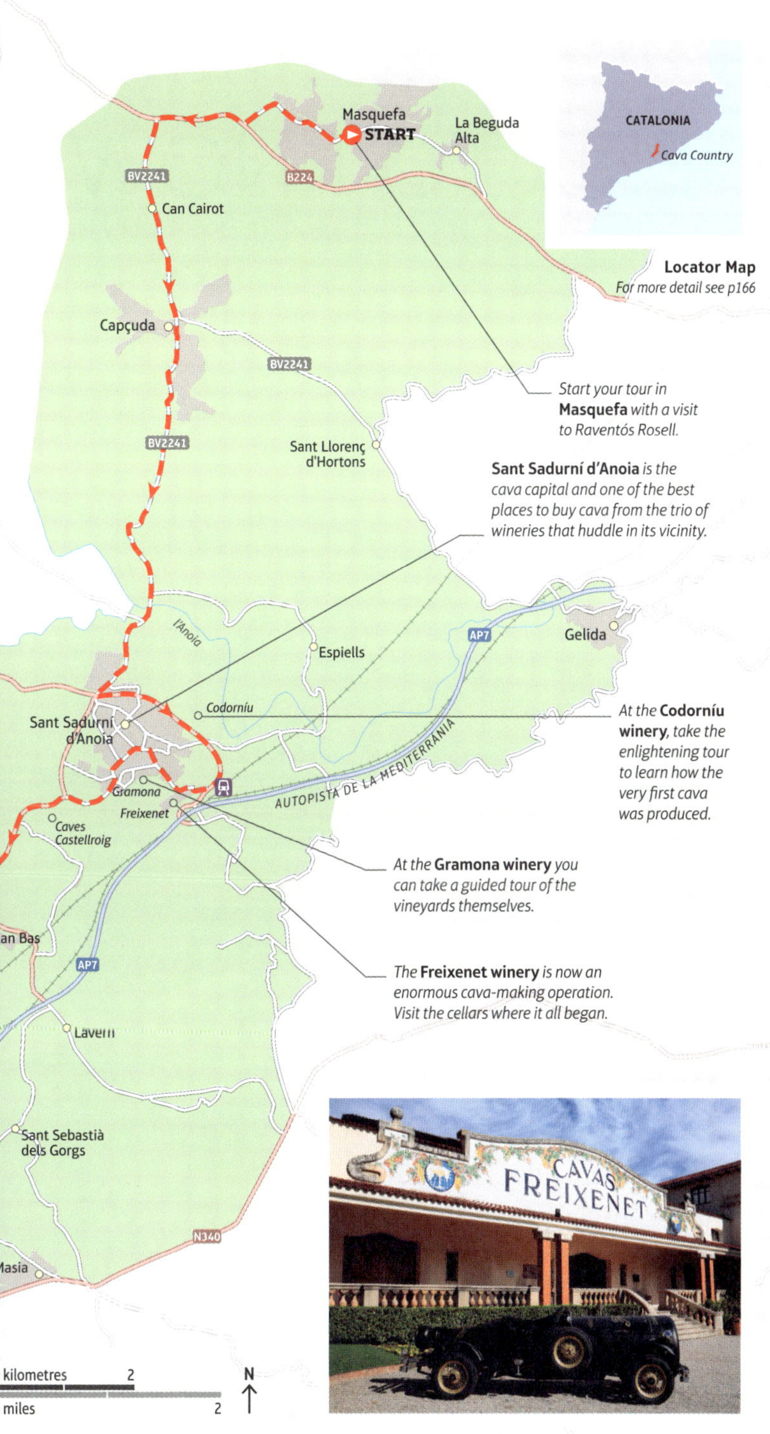

The Freixenet estate in Sant Sadurní d'Anoia, a leading cava producer

NEED TO KNOW

Lively Plaça d'Espanya, Barcelona

BUS
TAXI

BEFORE YOU GO

Things change, so plan ahead to make the most of your trip. Be prepared for all eventualities by considering the following points before you travel.

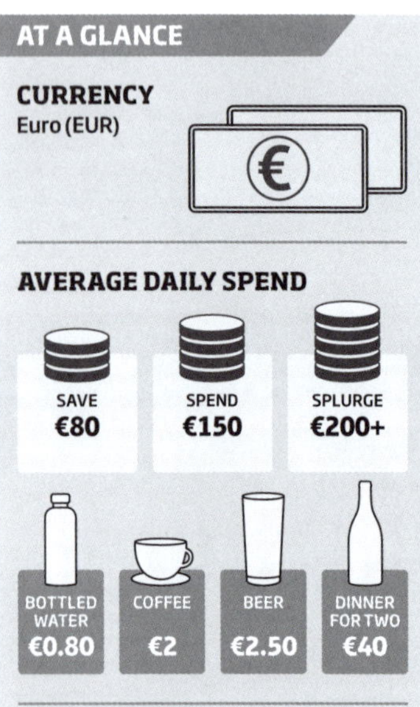

SPANISH/CATALAN PHRASES

Hello	Hola/Hola
Goodbye	Adiós/Adéu
Please	Por favor/Si us plau
Thank you	Gracias/Gràcies
Do you speak English	¿Hablas inglés?/ Parles anglès?
I don't understand	No comprendo/ No ho entenc

ELECTRICITY SUPPLY

Power sockets are type F, fitting a two-prong, round-pin plug. Standard voltage is 230 volts.

Passports and Visas

For entry requirements, including visas, consult your nearest Spanish embassy or check the **Ministerio de Asuntos Exteriores** website. Citizens of the UK, US, Canada, Australia and New Zealand do not need a visa for stays of up to three months but, since 2024, must apply in advance for the European Travel Information and Authorization System **(ETIAS)**. Visitors from other countries may also require an ETIAS, so check before travelling. EU nationals do not need a visa or an ETIAS.

ETIAS
W etiasvisa.com
Ministerio de Asuntos Exteriores
W exteriores.gob.es

Government Advice

Now more than ever, it is important to consult both your and the Spanish government's advice before travelling. The **UK Foreign, Commonwealth & Development Office**, the **US Department of State**, the **Australian Department of Foreign Affairs and Trade** and **Spain Travel Health** offer the latest information on security, health and local regulations.

Australian Department of Foreign Affairs and Trade
W smartraveller.gov.au
Spain Travel Health
W spth.gob.es
UK Foreign, Commonwealth & Development Office
W gov.uk/foreign-travel-advice
US Department of State
W travel.state.gov

Customs Information

You can find information on the laws relating to goods and currency taken in or out of Spain on **Spain Tourism** (the official tourism website).

Spain Tourism
W spain.info

Insurance

We recommend that you take out a comprehensive insurance policy covering theft, loss of belongings, medical care, cancellations and delays, and read the small print carefully. EU and UK citizens are eligible for free emergency medical care provided they have a valid European Health Insurance Card (EHIC) or a UK Global Health Insurance Card (**GHIC**).

GHIC
W ghic.org.uk

Vaccinations

No inoculations are necessary for Spain.

Booking Accommodation

Catalonia offers a range of accommodation, including government-run hotels called paradors. Try to book your accommodation well in advance if you plan to visit in July and August.

Money

Most urban establishments accept major credit, debit and prepaid currency cards. Contactless payments are common in cities, but it's a good idea to carry cash for smaller items.

Travellers with Specific Requirements

There are a number of organizations working to improve accessibility in Catalonia. The Confederación Española de Personas con Discapacidad Física y Orgánica (**COCEMFE**) and **Accessible Spain** provide useful information. Barcelona's tourism website **Visit Barcelona** has an Accessible Tourism section, listing attractions, hotels and transport with adapted facilities.

Catalonia's public transport system generally caters for all passengers, with wheelchairs, adapted toilets, and reserved car parking available at airports and stations.

Accessible Spain
W accessiblespaintravel.com
COCEMFE
W cocemfe.es
Visit Barcelona
W barcelonaturisme.com

Language

The two official languages of Catalonia are *castellano* (Castilian Spanish) and Catalan, while a third language, Aranese (a dialect of Occitan), is spoken by around 5,000 people in the northwest of the region. As a visitor, it is perfectly acceptable to speak Castilian wherever you are. English is widely spoken in the cities and other tourist spots, but not always in rural areas.

Opening Hours

Situations can change quickly and unexpectedly. Always check before visiting attractions and hospitality venues for up-to-date opening hours and booking requirements.

Lunchtime Many shops and some museums close for the siesta, between 1pm and 5pm.
Monday Many museums, public buildings and monuments are closed all day.
Sunday Churches and cathedrals are closed to tourist visits during Mass. Some public transport runs less frequently.
Public holidays Most museums, public buildings and many shops close early or for the day.

PUBLIC HOLIDAYS

1 Jan	New Year's Day
6 Jan	Epiphany/Three Kings' Day
Mar/Apr	Good Friday and Easter Monday
1 May	Labour Day
50 days after Easter	Whit Monday/Pentecost
24 Jun	St John's Day
15 Aug	The Assumption
11 Sep	Catalan National Day
12 Oct	Spain's National Day
1 Nov	All Saints' Day
6 Dec	Spanish Constitution Day
8 Dec	Feast of the Immaculate Conception
25 Dec	Christmas Day

GETTING AROUND

Whether you are visiting for a short city break or a rural country retreat, discover how best to reach your destination and travel like a pro.

AT A GLANCE

PUBLIC TRANSPORT COSTS

METRO
€2.65
Single-ride ticket

BUS
€2.65
Single-ride ticket

METRO, BUS, LOCAL TRAINS
€11.55
All-day travel ticket

The prices listed here are for travel within Zone 1.

SPEED LIMIT

MOTORWAY
120 km/h (75mph)

DUAL CARRIAGEWAYS
100 km/h (60mph)

SECONDARY ROAD
90 km/h (55mph)

URBAN AREAS
50 km/h (30mph)

Arriving by Air

Barcelona's international airport, **Josep Tarradellas Barcelona-El Prat**, is 16 km (10 miles) west of the city. European budget airlines fly to Barcelona all year round. There are regular internal flights to local airports: Lleida–Alguaire Airport, Reus Airport in Tarragona, Girona–Costa Brava Airport and Andorra–La Seu d'Urgell Airport.

For information on getting to and from Barcelona's airport, see the table opposite.

Josep Tarradellas Barcelona-El Prat
W aena.es

Train Travel

International Train Travel

International train services are operated by **Renfe**, the Spanish state-operator, and SNCF, the French operator. Buy tickets well in advance, particularly for the peak summer season.

There are several routes to Spain from France. Trains from London, Brussels, Amsterdam, Geneva, Zürich and Milan reach Barcelona via Paris, while those from Geneva and Zürich arrive in Barcelona via Nîmes or Montpellier. Direct, high-speed luxury TALGO trains, operated by Renfe, run to Barcelona from Paris, Milan, Geneva and Zürich. International trains arrive at Barcelona's Sants mainline station.

Renfe
W renfe.com

Domestic Train Travel

The state-run operator, Renfe, runs most train services, including the high-speed AVE, but other companies, including Ouigo, Avlo and Iryo, also provide services on certain lines. The fastest intercity services are the TALGO and AVE (Alta Velocidad Española), which link Madrid with Barcelona in three hours. AVE routes link Barcelona with Seville and Málaga in five and a half hours. *Largo recorrido* (long-distance) trains are cheap but so slow that you usually need to travel overnight. *Regionales y cercanías* (regional and local services) are frequent and inexpensive. There's an overnight train service offered by Trenhotel to A Coruña and Vigo, in Galicia.

GETTING TO AND FROM THE AIRPORT

Airport	Transport to Centre	Price	Journey Time
Josep Tarradellas Barcelona-El Prat	Taxi	€30-40	20 mins
(Terminals 1 & 2)	Aerobús	€7.45	35 mins
(Terminals 1 & 2)	Metro	€5.70	45 mins
(Terminal 2)	Local train	€5.05	30 mins

RAIL JOURNEY PLANNER

This map is a handy reference for travelling between Catalonia's main cities and towns by train. The journey times given below are for the fastest available service on each route.

Barcelona to Blanes	1.5 hrs	**Girona to Figueres**	30 mins
Barcelona to Monistrol de Montserrat	1 hr	**Monistrol de Montserrat to Puigcerdà**	2 hrs
Barcelona to Sitges	30 mins	**Montblanc to Lleida**	50 mins
Barcelona to Vic	1.5 hrs	**Sitges to Tarragona**	1 hr
Barcelona to Vilafranca del Penedés	1 hr	**Tarragona to Tortosa**	1.5 hrs
Blanes to Girona	40 mins	**Vilafranca del Penedès Montblanc**	30 mins

Long-Distance Bus Travel

Often the cheapest way to reach and travel around Spain is by coach. **Flixbus** runs daily services to Barcelona's Sants bus station.

Spain has no national coach company; private regional companies operate routes around the country. The largest is **Alsa**, with routes and services covering most of Spain.

Buses from towns and cities in Spain arrive at Estació del Nord and Sants. **Turisme de Catalunya** has details of companies that run day trips or longer tours around Catalonia.

Alsa
W alsa.es
Flixbus
W flixbus.es
Turisme de Catalunya
W catalunyaturisme.cat

Public Transport

Barcelona's metro, buses and Ferrocarrils de la Generalitat de Catalunya (**FGC**) suburban trains are run by Transports Metropolitans de Barcelona (**TMB**). Safety and hygiene measures, timetables, ticket information and transport maps can be obtained at metro stations and from the TMB website. For information about public transport in **Girona**, **Tarragona** and **Lleida**, check the municipal websites.

FGC
W fgc.cat
Girona
W girona.cat
Lleida
W atmlleida.cat
Tarragona
W tarragonaturisme.cat
TMB
W tmb.cat

Tickets

In Barcelona the *senzill* ticket, for a single journey, costs €2.65 and can be used on the metro, bus or FGC. A range of money-saving tickets and travel cards are available. The T-Casual ticket costs €12.55 and covers ten journeys within zone 1 on any public bus, metro or train (switching from one mode of transport to another counts as one journey if done within 75 minutes of validating your ticket). A T-Familiar ticket costs €11.05 for eight journeys, and can also be shared among several people. T-Dia and T-Mes are for unlimited daily and monthly travel respectively.

Visitors can enjoy unlimited journeys on the metro, FGC and bus with the **Hola Barcelona Travel Card**, valid for two, three, four or five days.

Hola Barcelona Travel Card
W holabarcelona.com

Metro

There are eight underground metro lines in Barcelona. The metro is usually the quickest way to get around the city, and connects with FGC lines (in Zone 1) and local Renfe services (look out for the Renfe and FGC signs at metro stations). Metro trains run from 5am to midnight from Monday to Thursday, to midnight on Sunday and weekday public holidays, from 5am to 2am on Friday and the day before a public holiday, and all night on Saturdays.

The L9 metro line connects the city with the airport, stopping at terminals 1 and 2. An airport supplement is charged on this route, and you will not be able to use the T-Casual or other standard transport passes. However, the Hola Barcelona Travel Card includes the airport supplement and is accepted on this route.

Bus and Tram

Buses are the most common mode of public transport in Catalonia, but timetables can be erratic. Many services do not run after 10pm, but there are some night buses in the cities.

In Barcelona the T-Casual and T-Familiar tickets are valid on buses and trams. The main city buses are white and red. Bus numbers beginning with H (for horizontal) run from one side of the city to another and those beginning with V (vertical) run top to bottom; D is diagonal. The Nitbus service runs nightly from around 10:30pm to 5am. Excellent bus maps are available from the main tourist office in Plaça de Catalunya.

The privately owned **Aerobús** runs between Plaça de Catalunya and Josep Tarradellas Barcelona-El Prat airport. Public transport passes are not valid on the Aerobús.

Barcelona has a limited tram service that serves the northeastern and southwestern parts of the city.

Aerobús
W aerobusbcn.com

Local Trains

Renfe's network of local trains, *cercanías* (*rodalies* in Catalan), is useful for longer distances within Barcelona, particularly between the main train stations: Sants and Estació de França. They are also handy for short hops to Sitges southwest of Barcelona or the northern coastal towns. Maps are displayed at stations, or are available on the Renfe website. Trains run from 5:30am to 11:30pm daily, but hours vary from line to line. FGC trains run services to Tibidabo, Pedralbes and the Collserola neighbourhoods.

Taxis

Barcelona's taxis are yellow and black, displaying a green light when free. All taxis are metered and show an initial starting charge of around €2.75. Surcharges usually apply for going to and from the airport, the port and major train stations. Taxis can be hailed in the street, or pre-orderd via apps such as **Free Now** and **Radio Taxis**. **Taxi Amic** has cars adapted for wheelchair users – note that these need to be booked a day ahead.

Free Now
W free-now.com

Radio Taxis
W radiotaxibarcelona.info

Taxi Amic
W taxiamic.cat

Driving

If you drive to Spain in your own car, you must carry the vehicle's registration document, a valid insurance certificate, a passport or a national identity card and your driving licence at all times. You must also display a sticker on the back of the car showing its country of registration.

Spain has two types of motorway: *autopistas*, (toll roads) and *autovías* (toll-free roads). You can establish whether a motorway is toll-free by the letters that prefix the number of the road: A = free motorway; AP = toll motorway.

Carreteras nacionales, Spain's main roads, have black-and-white signs and are designated by the letter N (Nacional) plus a number. *Carreteras comarcales*, secondary roads, have a number preceded by the letter C.

Parking in Barcelona can be difficult. The city has a pay-and-display system from 9am to 2pm and 4pm to 8pm Monday to Friday and all day on Saturday. You can park in blue zones for about € 2.50–3.75 per hour. Tickets are valid for two hours but can be renewed. Green zones are reserved for residents (resident permits must be displayed), except under certain conditions. At underground car parks, *lliure* means there is space, *complet* means full. Most car parks are attended, but in automatic ones, you pay before returning to your car. Do not park where the pavement edge is yellow or where there is a private exit *(gual)*. Blue-and-red signs saying "1–15" or "16–30" mean that you cannot park in the areas indicated on those dates of the month.

Driving to Barcelona

Many people drive to Catalonia via France. The most direct routes across the Pyrenees are the motorways through Hendaye in the west and La Jonquera in the east. Port Bou is on a coastal route, while other routes snake over the top, entering Catalonia via the Val d'Aran, Andorra and Puigcerdà in the Cerdanya. From the UK, car ferries run from Plymouth to Santander and from Portsmouth to Santander and Bilbao

Car Rental

The most popular car rental companies are **Avis**, **Europcar** and **Hertz.** All have offices at airports, major train stations and in the larger cities.

Avis
W avis.com

Europcar
W europcar.com

Hertz
W hertz-europe.com

Rules of the Road

Most traffic regulations and warnings to motorists are represented on signs by easily recognized symbols. To turn left at a busy junction or across oncoming traffic, you may have to turn right first and cross a main road, often by way of traffic lights, a bridge or underpass. If you are accidentally going in the wrong direction on a motorway or a main road with a solid white line, turn round at a sign for a *cambio de sentido*. At crossings, give way to the right unless a sign indicates otherwise.

Cycling

Barcelona is reasonably flat and has a growing network of clearly marked bike lanes, making cycling an easy and enjoyable way to explore. There are many bike rental companies, such as **Bike Rental Barcelona**, **Green Bikes** and **Mattia 46**. Orange bike stands, which are part of the **Bicing** government-run bike-sharing initiative, are dotted all around the city, but this scheme is currently open only to residents. **Steel Donkeys** offers cycling tours for a maximum of eight people, with fun and flexible itineraries giving local insights into the city.

Outside Barcelona, there are plenty of cycling routes through the Catalonia countryside, many of them incorporating the Carrilet (part of the Green Routes – or Vías Verdes), a disused railway that has been paved over.

Bicing
W bicing.barcelona

Bike Rental Barcelona
W bikerentalbarcelona.com

Green Bikes
W greenbikesbarcelona.com

Mattia 46
W mattia46.com

Steel Donkeys
W steeldonkeybiketours.com

Walking

Catalonia is full of coastal paths and mountain trails, making for great hiking opportunities. Barcelona and other towns and cities are easy to explore on foot and this is also one of the best ways to soak up their charm and atmosphere.

PRACTICAL INFORMATION

A little local know-how goes a long way in Barcelona. Here you will find all the essential advice and information you will need during your stay.

AT A GLANCE

EMERGENCY NUMBERS

EMERGENCY OPERATOR

112

TIME ZONE

CET/CEST: Central European Summer time (CEST) runs from the last Sunday in March to the last Sunday in October.

TAP WATER

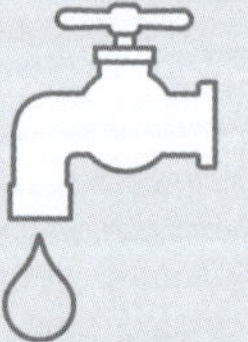

Tap water in Spain is safe to drink unless stated otherwise.

WEBSITES AND APPS

Visit Barcelona
The city's website for tourists *(barcelonaturisme.com)*

Catalunya Turisme
Catalonia's official tourism website *(catalunyaturisme.cat)*

Moovit
A route-planning app that includes public transport *(moovitapp.com)*

Wi-Fi Map
Find free Wi-Fi hotspots near you *(wifimap.io)*

Personal Security

Barcelona is generally a safe city, although petty crimes such as pickpocketing and bag-snatching remain problematic. Consider leaving your valuables, including passport, in a hotel safety deposit box when out and about. Take particular care at markets, tourist sights and stations, and wear bags across your body, not on your shoulder. Be especially careful of pickpockets when getting on or off a crowded train or metro. Contact your embassy if you have your passport stolen, or in the event of a serious crime or accident.

Barcelona is a diverse, multicultural city and as a rule, Catalans are accepting of all people regardless of their race, gender or sexuality. Homosexuality has been legal in Spain since 1979 and Spain was the third country in the world to legalize same-sex marriage, in 2005. In 2006, the Spanish government also recognized the right to legally change your gender. Barcelona has a flourishing LGBTQ+ scene centred on "Gaixample" (an area of L'Eixample) but the coastal town of Sitges is Catalonia's LGBTQ+ capital. **Gay Sitges** lists the top events, bars, beaches and hotels in town.

Gay Sitges
W gaysitgesguide.com

Health

Spain has a world-class healthcare system. Emergency medical care in Spain is free for all UK, EU and Australian citizens. If you have an EHIC or GHIC *(p205)*, be sure to present it as soon as possible. You may have to pay after treatment and reclaim the money later. For other visitors, payment of medical expenses is the patient's responsibility. It is therefore important to arrange comprehensive medical insurance before travelling.

Seek medicinal supplies and advice for minor ailments from a pharmacy *(farmacia)*, identifiable by a green or red cross. Each pharmacy displays a card in the window showing the address of the nearest all-night pharmacy and can also give details of the nearest doctor.

Smoking, Alcohol and Drugs

Smoking is banned in enclosed public spaces and on Barcelona's beaches and is a fineable offence. As of 2025, smoking is also prohibited on the terraces of bars and restaurants.

Catalonia, like the rest of Spain, has a relaxed attitude towards alcohol consumption, but it is frowned upon to be openly drunk.

Most recreational drugs are illegal, and possession of even a very small quantity can lead to an extremely hefty fine. Amounts that suggest an intent to supply drugs to other people can lead to custodial sentences. Cannabis clubs can supply the drug to members, but it remains illegal to smoke it in public spaces.

ID

By law you must carry identification with you at all times in Catalonia. A photocopy of your passport should suffice.

Responsible Tourism

The climate crisis is having a big impact on Barcelona and Catalonia, with more frequent droughts and heatwaves. Fountains, whether for drinking water or decorative (including the Font Màgica), may be turned off. Do your bit by taking quick showers and reusing towels if staying in a hotel. Catalonia is also at risk of wildfires so be careful when disposing of cigarette butts and glass bottles; starting a fire, even if accidental, is a criminal offence.

Local Customs

Regional pride is strong throughout Spain. Be wary of referring to Catalans as "Spanish", as this can sometimes cause offence.

A famous tradition is the siesta, which sees many shops closing between about 1pm and 5pm. This is not always observed by large stores.

Visiting Churches and Cathedrals

Most churches and cathedrals will not permit tourist visits during Sunday Mass. Generally, entrance to churches is free; however, a fee may apply to enter special areas, like cloisters.

Out of respect, ensure that you are dressed modestly when visiting religious buildings, with knees and shoulders covered.

Mobile Phones and Wi-Fi

Free Wi-Fi is reasonably common, particularly in libraries, large public spaces, restaurants and bars. Some places, such as airports and hotels, may charge for using their Wi-Fi. Barcelona City Council provides free Wi-Fi throughout much of the city centre and in metro stations and buses, but bandwidth is somewhat limited. Visitors on EU tariffs can use the 4G or 5G mobile network without being affected by roaming charges.

Post

Correos is Spain's postal service. Stamps can be purchased from a post office, a *papelería* (stationery shop) or an *estanco* (tobacconist). Parcels must be weighed and stamped at Correos offices.

Letters sent from a post office usually arrive more quickly than if posted in a *buzón* (postbox). In cities, postboxes are yellow pillar boxes; elsewhere they are wall-mounted postboxes.

Correos
W correos.es

Taxes and Refunds

IVA (VAT) is normally 21 per cent, but with lower rates for certain goods and services, such as restaurants and hotels. Under certain conditions, non-EU citizens can claim a rebate of these taxes. Retailers give you a form to fill out, which you then present to a customs officer with your receipts as you leave Spain. Some shops offer DIVA (digital stamping technology), which can be validated at self-service machines in the airport.

Discount Cards

Barcelona offers the **Barcelona Card**, a visitor's pass that includes entry to the city's top museums and unlimited free travel on public transport, plus discounts at participating restaurants, shops and on tours. It can also help you skip queues and is valid for three (€57), four (€67) or five (€79) consecutive days.

Barcelona Card
W barcelonacard.org

INDEX

Page numbers in **bold** refer to main entries

B

C

D

Q

R

S

CATALAN PHRASE BOOK

IN EMERGENCY

Help!	**Auxili!**	*ow-**gzee**-lee*
Stop!	**Pareu!**	***pah**-reh-oo*
Call a doctor!	**Telefoneu un metge!**	***teh**-leh-fon-**eh**-oo oon **meh**-djuh*
Call an ambulance!	**Telefoneu una ambulància!**	***teh**-leh-fon-**eh**-oo oo-nah ahm-boo-**lahn**-see-ah*
Call the police!	**Telefoneu la policia!**	***teh**-leh-fon-**eh**-oo lah poh-lee-**see**-ah*
Call the fire brigade!	**Telefoneu els bombers!**	***teh**-leh-fon-**eh**-oo uhlz boom-**behs***
Where is the nearest telephone?	**On és el telèfon més proper?**	***on**-ehs uhl tuh-leh-**fon mehs** proo-**peh***
Where is the nearest hospital?	**On és l'hospital més proper?**	***on**-ehs looss-pee-**tahl mehs** proo-**peh***

COMMUNICATION ESSENTIALS

Yes	**Si**	*see*
No	**No**	*noh*
Please	**Si us plau**	***sees plah**-oo*
Thank you	**Gràcies**	***grah**-see-uhs*
Excuse me	**Perdoni**	*puhr-**thoh**-nee*
Hello	**Hola**	***oh**-lah*
Goodbye	**Adéu**	*ah-they-**oo***
Good night	**Bona nit**	***bo**-nah **neet***
Morning	**El matí**	*uhl muh-**tee***
Afternoon	**La tarda**	*lah **tahr**-thuh*
Evening	**El vespre**	*uhl **vehs**-pruh*
Yesterday	**Ahir**	*ah-**ee***
Today	**Avui**	*uh-voo-**ee***
Tomorrow	**Demà**	*duh-**mah***
Here	**Aquí**	*uh-**kee***
There	**Allà**	*uh-**lyah***
What?	**Què?**	***keh***
When?	**Quan?**	***kwahn***
Why?	**Per què?**	*puhr **keh***
Where?	**On?**	***ohn***

USEFUL PHRASES

How are you?	**Com està?**	***kom** uhs-**tah***
Very well, thank you.	**Molt bé, gràcies.**	*mol **beh** **grah**-see-uhs*
Pleased to meet you.	**Molt de gust.**	*mol duh **goost***
See you soon.	**Fins aviat.**	*feenz uhv-**yat***
That's fine.	**Està bé.**	*uhs-**tah beh***
Where is/are ...?	**On és/són?**	***ohn ehs/sohn***
How far is it to ...?	**Quants metres/ kilòmetres hi ha d'aquí a ...?**	***kwahnz meh**-truhs/ kee-**loh**-muh-truhs **yah** dah-**kee** uh*
Which way to ...?	**Per on es va a ...?**	*puhr **on** uhs **bah** ah*
Do you speak English?	**Parles anglès?**	***par**-luhs **an**-**glehs***
I don't understand.	**No l'entenc.**	*noh luhn-**teng***
Could you speak more slowly, please?	**Pot parlar més a poc a poc, si us plau?**	***pot** par-**lah mehs pok** uh **pok** **sees plah**-oo*
I'm sorry.	**Ho sento.**	*oo **sehn**-too*

USEFUL WORDS

big	**gran**	***gran***
small	**petit**	*puh-**teet***
hot	**calent**	*kah-**len***
cold	**fred**	***fred***
good	**bo**	***boh***
bad	**dolent**	*doo-**len***
enough	**bastant**	*bahs-**tan***
well	**bé**	***beh***
open	**obert**	*oo-**behr***
closed	**tancat**	*tan-**kat***
left	**esquerra**	*uhs-**kehr**-ruh*
right	**dreta**	***dreh**-tuh*
straight on	**recte**	***rehk**-tuh*
near	**a prop**	*uh **prop***
far	**lluny**	***lyoon**yuh*
up/over	**a dalt**	*uh **dahl***
down/under	**a baix**	*uh **bah**-eeshh*
early	**aviat**	*uhv-**yat***
late	**tard**	***tahrt***
entrance	**entrada**	*uhn-**trah**-thuh*
exit	**sortida**	***soor**-tee-thuh*
toilet	**lavabos/ serveis**	*luh-**vah**-boos sehr-**beh**-ees*
more	**més**	***mess***
less	**menys**	***men**yees*

SHOPPING

How much does this cost?	**Quant costa això?**	***kwahn kost** ehs-**shoh***
I would like ...	**M'agradaria ...**	*muh-grad-uh-**ree**-ah*
Do you have...?	**Tenen?**	***tehn**-un*
I'm just looking, thank you.	**Només estic mirant, gràcies.**	***noo**-mess ehs-**teek** mee-**rahn grah**-see-uhs*
Do you take credit cards?	**Accepten targes de crèdit?**	*ak-**sehp**-tuhn tahr-**zhuhs** duh **kreh**-deet*
What time do you open?	**A quina hora obren?**	*ah **keen**-uh oh-ruh **oh**-bruhn*
What time do you close?	**A quina hora tanquen?**	*ah **keen**-uh oh-ruh **tan**-kuhn*
This one.	**Aquest**	*ah-**ket***
That one.	**Aquell**	*ah-**kehl***
expensive	**car**	***kahr***
cheap	**bé de preu/ barat**	***beh** thuh **preh**-oo/ bah-**rat***
size (clothes)	**talla/mida**	***tah**-lyah/**mee**-thuh*
size (shoes)	**número**	***noo**-mehr-oo*
white	**blanc**	***blang***
black	**negre**	***neh**-gruh*
red	**vermell**	*vuhr-**mel***
yellow	**groc**	***grok***
green	**verd**	***behrt***
blue	**blau**	***blah**-oo*
antiques shop	**antiquari/botiga d'antiguitats**	*an-tee-**kwah**-ree/ boo-**tee**-gah/dan-**tee**-ghee-**tats***
bakery	**el forn**	*uhl **forn***
bank	**el banc**	*uhl **bang***
bookshop	**la llibreria**	*lah lyee-bruh-**ree**-ah*
butcher's	**la carnisseria**	*lah kahr-nee-suh-**ree**-uh*
pastry shop	**la pastisseria**	*lah pahs-tee-suh-**ree**-uh*
chemist's	**la farmàcia**	*lah fuhr-**mah**-see-ah*
fishmonger's	**la peixateria**	*lah peh-shuh-tuh-**ree**-uh*
greengrocer's	**la fruiteria**	*lah froo-ee-tuh-**ree**-uh*
grocer's	**la botiga de queviures**	*lah boo-**tee**-guh duh keh-vee-**oo**-ruhs*
hairdresser's	**la perruqueria**	*lah peh-roo-kuh-**ree**-uh*
market	**el mercat**	*uhl muhr-**kat***
newsagent's	**el quiosc de premsa**	*uhl kee-**ohsk** duh **prem**-suh*
post office	**l'oficina de correus**	*loo-fee-**see**-nuh duh koo-**reh**-oos*
shoe shop	**la sabateria**	*lah sah-bah-tuh-**ree**-uh*
supermarket	**el supermercat**	*uhl soo-puhr-muhr-**kat***
tobacconist's	**l'estanc**	*luhs-**tang***
travel agency	**l'agència de viatges**	*la-**jen**-see-uh duh vee-**ad**-juhs*

SIGHTSEEING

art gallery	**la galeria d' art**	*lah gah-luh **ree**-yuh **dart***
cathedral	**la catedral**	*lah kuh-tuh-**thrahl***
church	**l'església la basílica**	*luhz-**gleh**-zee-uh lah buh-**zee**-lee-kuh*
garden	**el jardí**	*uhl zhahr-**dee***
library	**la biblioteca**	*lah bee-blee-oo-**teh**-kuh*
museum	**el museu**	*uhl moo-**seh**-oo*
tourist information office	**l'oficina de turisme**	*loo-fee-**see**-nuh thuh too-**reez**-muh*
town hall	**l'ajuntament**	*luh-djoon-tuh-**men***
closed for holiday	**tancat per vacances**	*tan-**kat** puh bah-**kan**-suhs*
bus station	**l'estació d'autobusos**	*luhs-tah-see-**oh** dow-toh-**boo**-zoos*
railway station	**l'estació de tren**	*luhs-tah-see-**oh** thuh **tren***

STAYING IN A HOTEL

Do you have a vacant room?	¿Tenen una habitació lliure?	teh-nuhn oo-nuh ah-bee-tuh-see-oh lyuh-ruh
double room with double bed	habitació doble amb llit de matrimoni	ah-bee-tuh-see-oh doh-bluh am lyeet duh mah-tree-moh-nee
twin room	habitació amb dos llits/ amb llits individuals	ah-bee-tuh-see-oh am dohs lyeets/ am lyeets in-thee-vee-thoo-ahls
single room	habitació individual	ah-bee-tuh-see-oh een-dee-vee-thoo-ahl
room with a bath	habitació amb bany	ah-bee-tuh-see-oh am bah-nyuh
shower	dutxa	doo-chuh
porter	el grum	uhl groom
key	la clau	lah klah-oo
I have a reservation.	Tinc una habitació reservada.	ting oo-nuh ah-bee-tuh-see-oh reh-sehr-vah-thah

EATING OUT

Have you got a table for...	Tenen taula per...?	teh-nuhn tow-luh puhr
I would like to reserve a table.	Voldria reservar una taula.	vool-dree-uh reh-sehr-vahr oo-nuh tow-luh
The bill, please.	El compte, si us plau.	uhl kohm-tuh sees plah-oo
I am a vegetarian.	Sóc vegetarià.	sok buh-zhuh-tuh-ree-ah
waitress	cambrera	kam-breh-ruh
waiter	cambrer	kam-breh
menu	la carta	lah kahr-tuh
fixed-price menu	menú del migdia	muh-noo thuhl midge dee-uh
wine list	la carta de vins	lah kahr-tuh thuh veens
glass of water	un got d'aigua	oon got dah-ee-gwah
glass of wine	una copa de vi	oo-nuh ko-pah thuh vee
bottle	una ampolla	oo-nuh am-pol-yuh
knife	un ganivet	oon gun-ee-veht
fork	una forquilla	oo-nuh foor-keel-yuh
spoon	una cullera	oo-nuh kool-yeh-ruh
breakfast	l'esmorzar	les-moor-sah
lunch	el dinar	uhl dee-nah
dinner	el sopar	uhl soo-pah
main course	el primer plat	uhl pree-meh plat
starters	els entrants	uhlz ehn-tranz
dish of the day	el plat del dia	uhl plat duhl dee-uh
coffee	el cafè	uhl kah-feh
rare	poc fet	pok fet
medium	al punt	ahl poon
well done	molt fet	mol fet

MENU DECODER

l'aigua mineral	lah-ee-gwuh mee-nuh-rahl	mineral water
sense gas/ amb gas	sen-zuh gas/ am gas	still/ sparkling
al forn	ahl forn	baked
l'all	lahlyuh	garlic
l'arròs	lahr-roz	rice
les botifarres	lahs boo-tee-fah-rahs	sausages
la carn	lah karn	meat
la ceba	lah seh-buh	onion
la cervesa	lah-sehr-ve-sah	beer
l'embotit	lum-boo-teet	cold meat
el filet	uhl fee-let	sirloin
el formatge	uhl for-mah-djuh	cheese
fregit	freh-zheet	fried
la fruita	lah froo-ee-tah	fruit
els fruits secs	uhlz froo-eets seks	nuts
les gambes	lahs gam-bus	prawns
el gelat	uhl djuh-lat	ice cream
la llagosta	lah lyah-gos-tah	lobster
la llet	lah lyet	milk
la llimona	lah lyee-moh-nah	lemon
la llimonada	lah lyee-moh-nah-thuh	lemonade
la mantega	lah mahn-teh-gah	butter
el marisc	uhl muh-reesk	seafood
la menestra	lah muh-nehs-truh	vegetable stew
l'oli	loll-ee	oil
les olives	luhs oo-lee-vuhs	olives
l'ou	loh-oo	egg
el pa	uhl pah	bread
el pastís	uhl pahs-tees	pie/cake
les patates	lahs pah-tah-tuhs	potatoes
el pebre	uhl peh-bruh	pepper
el peix	uhl pehsh	fish
el pernil salat serrà	uhl puhr-neel suh-lat sehr-rah	cured ham
el plàtan	uhl plah-tun	banana
el pollastre	uhl poo-lyah-struh	chicken
la poma	la poh-mah	apple
el porc	uhl pohr	pork
les postres	lahs pohs-truhs	dessert
rostit	rohs-teet	roast
la sal	lah sahl	salt
la salsa	lah sahl-suh	sauce
les salsitxes	lahs sahl-see-chuhs	sausages
sec	sehk	dry
la sopa	lah soh-puh	soup
el sucre	uhl-soo-kruh	sugar
la taronja	lah tuh-rohn-djuh	orange
el te	uhl teh	tea
les torrades	lahs too-rah-thuhs	toast
la vedella	lah veh-theh-lyuh	beef
el vi blanc	uhl bee blang	white wine
el vi negre	uhl bee neh-gruh	red wine
el vi rosat	uhl bee roo-zaht	rosé wine
el vinagre	uhl bee-nah-gruh	vinegar
el xai/el be	uhl shahee/uhl beh	lamb
el xerès	uhl shuh-rehs	sherry
la xocolata	lah shoo-koo-lah-tuh	chocolate
el xoriç	uhl shoo-rees	red sausage

NUMBERS

0	zero	seh-roo
1	un (masc)/una (fem)	oon/oon-uh
2	dos (masc)/dues (fem)	dohs/doo-uhs
3	tres	trehs
4	quatre	kwa-truh
5	cinc	seeng
6	sis	sees
7	set	set
8	vuit	voo-eet
9	nou	noh-oo
10	deu	deh-oo
11	onze	on-zuh
12	doce	doh-dzuh
13	tretze	treh-dzuh
14	catorze	kah-tohr-dzuh
15	quinze	keen-zuh
16	setze	set-zuh
17	disset	dee-set
18	divuit	dee-voo-eet
19	dinou	dee-noh-oo
20	vint	been
21	vint-i-un	been-tee-oon
22	vint-i-dos	been-tee-dohs
30	trenta	tren-tah
31	trenta-un	tren-tah oon
40	quaranta	kwuh-ran-tuh
50	cinquanta	seen-kwahn-tah
60	seixanta	seh-ee-shan-tah
70	setanta	seh-tan-tah
80	vuitanta	voo-ee-tan-tah
90	noranta	noh-ran-tah
100	cent	sen
101	cent un	sent oon
102	cent dos	sen dohs
200	dos-cents (masc) dues-centes (fem)	dohs-sens doo-uhs sen-tuhs
300	tres-cents	trehs-senz
400	quatre-cents	kwah-truh-senz
500	cinc-cents	seeng-senz
600	sis-cents	sees-senz
700	set-cents	set-senz
800	vuit-cents	voo-eet-senz
900	nou-cents	noh-oo-cenz
1,000	mil	meel
1,001	mil un	meel oon

TIME

one minute	un minut	oon mee-noot
one hour	una hora	oo-nuh oh-ruh
half an hour	mitja hora	mee-juh oh-ruh
Monday	dilluns	dee-lyoonz
Tuesday	dimarts	dee-marts
Wednesday	dimecres	dee-meh-kruhs
Thursday	dijous	dee-zhoh-oos
Friday	divendres	dee-ven-druhs
Saturday	dissabte	dee-sab-tuh
Sunday	diumenge	dee-oo-men-juh

ACKNOWLEDGMENTS

This edition updated by
Contributor James Taylor
Senior Editor Dipika Dasgupta
Senior Art Editor Vinita Venugopal
Project Editor Anuroop Sanwalia
Editors Eleanora Reeves, Manjari Thakur
Assistant Editor Avaantika Vivek
Assistant Art Editor Bineet Kaur
Assistant Picture Research Administrator Manpreet Kaur
Rights & Permissions Specialist Vagisha Pushp
Deputy Manager, Picture Research Virien Chopra
Publishing Assistant Simona Velikova
Jacket Designer Cristina Antequera
Senior Cartographer Mohammed Hassan
Cartography Manager Suresh Kumar
Pre-Production Coordinator Tanveer Zaidi
Production Controller Kariss Ainsworth
Deputy Managing Editor Dharini Ganesh
Managing Editor Beverly Smart
Managing Art Editor Gemma Doyle
Senior Managing Art Editor Priyanka Thakur
Editorial Director Hollie Teague
Art Director Maxine Pedliham
Publishing Director Georgina Dee

DK would like to thank the following for their contribution to the previous edition: Mary-Ann Gallagher, Debra Wolter, Helen Peters, Sally Davies, Ben Ffrancon Davies, Roger Williams, Mary Jane Aladren, Pepita Arias, Emma Dent Coad, Rebecca Doulton, Josefina Fernandez, Duncan Rhodes, Nick Rider, David Stone, Judy Thomson, Clara Villanueva, Suzanne Wales, Helen Bird.

The publisher would like to thank the following for their kind permission to reproduce their photographs:

Key: a-above; b-below/bottom; c-centre; f-far; l-left; r-right; t-top

123RF.com: Andrey Bayda 62cla; Alena Birukova 26tl; Mauro Celio 72cr; Iakov Filimonov 115crb; Olena Kachmar 144-5b; Pabkov 182-3t; Alena Redchenko 10ca; Marco Rubino 17t, 102-3; Zhanna Tretiakova 147br.

Adobe Stock: Sebastian 190

Alamy Stock Photo: AA World Travel Library 195clb; age fotostock 37crb, / Alfred Abad 197bl, / Gonzalo Azumendi 176b, / J. Ll. Banús 82tl, / Marco Brivio 116-7t, / Rafael Campillo 148bl, / Angelo Cavalli 140-1t, / Christian Goupi 27tl, / Javier Larrea 131cb, 131crb, 152-3, 175crb, / Pixtal 24crb, / Jordi Sans 132-3b, / Fco. Javier Sobrino 195tr, / Eduard Solé 148cr, / Marc Soler 96cl; ALLTRAVEL / Peter Mross 191cl, 201br; Art Collection 3 70bc; Aitor Rodero Aznarez 77cb; Album 70br; Bailey-Cooper Photography 84clb; John Baran 191tr, 191cra,191b; Juan Bautista 133tr, 192bl; Biosphoto / Antoni Agelet 188-9b; Sergi Boixader 107clb; Jordi Boixareu 13br, 56cr; Classic Image 179tr, Xavier Calvet Camats 193t; Jordi Camí 156t, 195br; Chronicle 60-1t; Classic Image 183bl; Chris Craggs 41cl; Michele D'Ottavio 11t; Ian Dagnall 71tr; domonabikeSpain 37cl; Rosmi Duaso 30-1b, 195cra; Endless Travel 169cr; Christophe Faugere 196-7t; Iakov Filimonov 181bl; Aaron Fink 71cra; Peter Forsberg 91tr; Peter Forsberg / Europe 146br; Fototext 157tr; GL Archive 62cr; Granger Historical Picture Archive / NYC © Successió Miró / ADAGP, Paris and DACS, London 2019 129tl; hemis.fr / Lionel Montico 93br, / Ludovic Maisant 122cl; / René Mattes 75crb,/ Fundacio Joan Miro © Successió Miró / ADAGP, Paris and DACS, London 2019 128-9b; Heritage Image Partnership Ltd / Mithra / Index 47cl, 178br, 179br; imageBROKER / Christian Hütter 189ftr, / Daniel Schoenen / *Barcelona Pavilion* architect Ludwig Mies van der Rohe © DACS 2019 135b, / Fabian von Poser 191cr; INTERFOTO / *portrait of Pablo Picasso* © Succession Picasso / DACS, London 2019 79clb; Invictus SARL / Citrus Stock 117bl; Image Professionals GmbH / Elan Fleisher 49t; Pawel Kazmierczak 52tl; Andrey Khrobostov 106fcrb; Brian Kinney 36-7t; Jason Knott 200clb; Engin Korkmaz 97tr; Lanmas 59crb, 61tr, 61cla, 61br, 62clb; Chris Lawrence 101tr; Paul Lindsay 10clb; Lobro 84crb; Look / Andreas Strauss 20bl, 123br, / Juergen Richter 28-9t; Lophius 198tl; Luis Pina Photography 138-9t; Stefano Politi Markovina 41tr, 75clb, 76-7t, 77br, 113tr, 158cr; Bob Masters 89br, 155tr; Matt May 30tl; Hercules Milas 42br, 55cla; Hugh Mitton 40-1t; J.Enrique Molina 131cra; Graham Mulrooney 140bl; Nathaniel Noir 78-79; North Wind Picture Archives 58t; Matthias Oesterle 48-9b, 55crb; Photo12 / Ann Ronan Picture Library 63clb; John Penney 38-39b; PhotoBliss 58cb; The Picture Art Collection 61cb; Pictureproject 114-5t; Prisma Archivo 59tl, 59tr, 59cla, 60tl, 60bc, 61tl, 106cb, 131tl, 171cra, 193br; Luca Quadrio 146-7t, 186t; Campillo Rafael 20crb, 56cl; Robertharding / Neale Clark 109tc; Pere Sanz 194b; Howard Sayer 24cr; Camila Se 109cra; Paul Shaddick 191br; M.Sobreira 11br, 53tr; Marc Soler 28bl, 88tl; Marek Stepan 10-1b, 157b; StockFood GmbH / Inga Wandinger 195crb; Stockimo / Robis 31tr; travelstock44.de / Juergen Held 151bl; Lucas Vallecillos 22t, 34-5t, 57cl, 74clb, 74b, 75bc, 90-1b, 96t, 121bl, 158-9b, 182bl, 186cra; Jorge Tutor 179cr; VSL / McPHOTO / blickwinkel 8cla; Ken Welsh 99tl; Andrew Wilson 161tr; Jan Wlodarczyk 71tc, 85clb, 98bl; World History Archive 171tl; World History Archive / AG 106clb; Gregory Wrona 41crb, 81crb; Chun Ju Wu 111b; Xavier Fores - Joana Roncero 81b; ZUMA Press; Inc. 147tr / SOPA Images / Ramon Costa 57clb.

AWL Images: Hemis 82-3b; Tom Mackie 187br; Stefano Politi Markovina 42tr; Travel Pix Collection 113tl.

Bridgeman Images: Museu Picasso, Barcelona / *Las Meninas* (3rd October 1957) by Pablo Picasso © Succession Picasso / DACS, London 2019 79bl.

El Brogit – elbrogit.com: 39br.

Used with permission of Casa Batlló (casabatllo.es): 37, 84, 112-3 all.

Centre de Cultura Contemporània de Barcelona – CCCB: Miquel Tavern 34bl.
Collage Art & Cocktails Social Club: 49br.

Compartir: Francesc Guillamet 12clb, 31cl.

Depositphotos Inc: Alexsalcedo 12t; boule1301 32tl; kovgabor79 43br; Sanguer 46-7b.

Dorling Kindersley: Max Alexander 169br.

Dreamstime.com: Claudiu Alexandru 112bl; Steve Allen 171cr; Aprescindere 29bl; Sergio Torres Baus 100bl; Daniel Sanchez Blasco 27cla; Blitzkoenig 18tl, 124-5; Artur Bogacki 47tr; Boule13 154-5b; Brasilnut 52-3b; Citalliance 33t; Massimiliano Clari 97bl; Juan Bautista Cofreces 54-5t; Cristian64 177br; Danflcreativo 76bl; Dinogeromella 26tr, 63crb; Ego450 145ca; Dudlajzov 179br; Elxeneize 94-5; Maria Luisa Lopez Estivill 40-1b; Iakov Filimonov 33clb, 56cra, 139bl; Veronika Galkina 174-5t; Gelia 191crb; Gerold Grotelueschen 44tr; Henrikhl 177bl; Juan Polo Ignacio 44bl; Ivana Jankovic 189tr; Jarcosa 56crb; Jcoronasanmartin 51cla; Veniamin Kraskov 145cla; Sebastian Kummer 175br; Bogdan Lazar 80t; Mapics 20t; Marcopachiega 57crb; Marcorubino 8-9b, 47br, 110t, 134tl; Carlos Soler Martinez 178t; Alberto Masnovo 129cra; Mavrinvlad 22br; Jelena Maximova 22cl; Juan Moyano 31br, 43tr; Roland Nagy 85tr; Natursports 13cr, 51br; Olgacov 172t; Clement Mantion Pierre Olivier 35b; Photoprofi30 27tr; Radub85 64-5; Robert309 163; Mauro Rodrigues 189tc; Dmitry Rukhlenko 202-03; Tiberiu Sahlean 177bc; Schlenger86 43cla; Olena Serditova 118-9b; Jacek Sopotnicki 88-9t; Tanaonte 54-5b; Tomas1111 2-3, 6-7; 46tr; 85br; Toniflap 20cr; Pavlo Vakhrushev 110c; Alvaro German Vilela 53cl; Vitalyedush 113cra; Xantana 11cr; Tetiana Zbrodko 169t; Мария Канатова 4.

Elsa Y Fred: 26cla.

© Escudería Targa Iberia. 50-1t.

© FC BARCELONA: 147clb.

Feel by Doing: 39tr.

Getty Images: AFP 106cr, / Lluis Gene 150t, / Josep Lago 56clb; AWL Images / Stefano Politi Markovina 86-7b; Miquel Benitez 119tr; Bettmann 62-3t; Corbis Historical / Adoc-Photos 60crb; Corbis News / Matthias Oesterle 56cla; Cover / Sigfrid Casals 35cla; Manuel Medir 120t, 120cla; NurPhoto 63tr; David Ramos 57cr; Redferns / Jordi Vidal 57tl; Roger Viollet Collection 62br; Universal Images Group / Andia 87t; Joan Valls / Urbanandsport / Nur Photo 107cb.

Harlem Jazz Club: Daniela Giannangeli 49cl.

Getty Images / iStock: alxpin 107t; anouchka 72bc; CactuSoup 177t; dem10 136-7; DigitalVision Vectors / Nastasic 58crb; E+ / Aluxum 50b, / Juergen Sack 184-85, / Orbon Alija 62tl; Eloi_Omella 13t, 18bl, 24t, 45b, 143, 145t; Ershov_Maks 115clb; ferrantraite 72-3; fotoVoyager 92-3t, 160bl; HaizhanZheng 8clb; JordiDelgado 57tr; Lokibaho 189tl; Nigel Marsh 175bc; Nikada 12-3b, 109tr; Pabkov 19b, 164-5; Portokalis 115br; Starcevic 130-1b; stefanopolitimarkovina 16c, 66-7; Ihor Tailwind 36-6b; xavierarnau 179cra.

Kayaking Costa Brava: Roger Rovira Rius 53br.

Life Drawing Barcelona – lifedrawingbarcelona.com: 29cl.

Mary Evans Picture Library: 70clb.

Paradiso: 22clb.

Parador de Tortosa – Paradores de Turismo de España, SME, SA: 24br.

Parc Astronomic de Montsec: 45cl.

Museu Picasso: 32br.

Picfair.com: Iakov 149.

PortAventura World: 33br.

Rasoterra: 38tl.

Robert Harding Picture Library: Richard Martin 170t; Lucas Vallecillos 180-1t.

Shutterstock.com: Evgeny Kuzhilev 198-9b.

SuperStock: Universal Images 59bl.
Tablao Flamenco Cordobes: Ines Rubio 48tl.

Unsplash: Peter Feghali / @peterf 111tc; Federico Giampieri / @federicogiampieri 8cl.

Yes Future Positive Supermarket: 39cl.

Front Flap
Alamy Stock Photo: Juan Bautista cra; Stefano Politi Markovina t, bl; **Depositphotos Inc:** Alexsalcedo br; **Dreamstime.com:** Juan Moyano cla; **Getty Images / iStock:** Eloi_Omella c.

Sheet Map Cover
4Corners: Sladja Kisic

Cover
Front and Spine: **4Corners:** Sladja Kisic
Back: **4Corners:** Sladja Kisic b; **Alamy Stock Photo:** Gerold Grotelueschen c; Jason Knott tr; **Dreamstime.com:** Jacek Sopotnicki cl

Illustrators: Stephen Conlin, Isidoro González-Adalid Cabezas (Acanto Arquitectura y Urbanismo S.L.), Claire Littlejohn, Maltings Partnership, John Woodcock.

First edition 1999

Published in Great Britain by Dorling Kindersley Limited, 20 Vauxhall Bridge Road, London SW1V 2SA

The authorised representative in the EEA is Dorling Kindersley Verlag GmbH. Arnulfstr. 124, 80636 Munich, Germany

Published in the United States by DK Publishing, 1745 Broadway, 20th Floor, New York, NY 10019, USA

25 26 27 28 10 9 8 7 6 5 4 3 2 1

A CIP catalogue record for this book is available from the British Library.

A catalogue record for this book is available from the Library of Congress.

ISSN: 1542 1554
ISBN: 978 0 2417 8403 7

Printed and bound in China.

dk.com

MIX
Paper | Supporting responsible forestry
FSC™ C018179

This book was made with Forest Stewardship Council™ certified paper – one small step in DK's commitment to a sustainable future.

Learn more at **dk.com/uk/information/sustainability**

A NOTE FROM DK

The rate at which the world is changing is constantly keeping the DK travel team on our toes. While we've worked hard to ensure that this edition of Barcelona and Catalonia is accurate and up-to-date, we know that opening hours alter, standards shift, prices fluctuate, places close and new ones pop up in their stead. So, if you notice we've got something wrong or left something out, we want to hear about it. Please get in touch at travelguides@dk.com